D0786825

Lincoln's Dilemma

A NATION DIVIDED: STUDIES IN THE CIVIL WAR ERA
Orville Vernon Burton and Elizabeth R. Varon, Editors

Lincoln's Dilemma

Blair, Sumner, *and the* Republican Struggle *over* Racism and Equality *in the* Civil War Era

Paul D. Escott

University of Virginia Press   *Charlottesville and London*

University of Virginia Press
© 2014 by the Rector and Visitors of the University of Virginia
All rights reserved
Printed in the United States of America on acid-free paper

First published 2014

1 3 5 7 9 8 6 4 2

LIBRARY OF CONGRESS CATALOGING-IN-PUBLICATION DATA
Lincoln's dilemma : Blair, Sumner, and the Republican struggle over racism and equality in
the Civil War era / Paul D. Escott.
      pages   cm.—(A nation divided: studies in the Civil War era)
Includes bibliographical references and index.
ISBN 978-0-8139-3619-2 (cloth : alk. paper) — ISBN 978-0-8139-3620-8 (e-book)
1. Lincoln, Abraham, 1809–1865—Views on slavery. 2. United States—History—Civil War,
1861–1865—African Americans. 3. United States—Race relations—History—19th century.
4. Slavery—United States—History—19th century. 5. Racism—United States—History—
19th century. 6. United States—Politics and government—1861–1865. I. Title.
E457.2.E729 2014
973.7092—dc23

2013047221

Para Candelas
ahora y siempre

Contents

Preface

THIS IS A BOOK about America's problem of slavery and racism and the president who confronted it. By the middle of the nineteenth century the United States somehow had to come to terms with slavery, race, and the contradiction between its founding values and human bondage. Abraham Lincoln was at the center of the nation's struggle. His political career turned on issues of slavery and racism. He felt the moral challenge of bondage and discrimination. He rose to power by opposing slavery's extension and found himself embroiled in a hugely destructive war. His entire era was a violent one in which divisions over race and equality proved even deeper than those over slavery.

The focus of this book is naturally on Lincoln—his personal life, his beliefs, his politics, and his policies. But no leader can be understood apart from his time and his surroundings. The social context in which Abraham Lincoln worked helped to define him. To understand that context, a secondary focus will trace the careers of two contemporaries—Charles Sumner and Montgomery Blair. They merit recurring notice for three reasons: they were personally close to Lincoln; they were powerful members of his party; and on the crucial issue of race they held sharply differing views of vital importance to policy. Their differences on race reflected both the spectrum of opinion and the basic disagreements within the Republican Party.

Another vital part of the context of Civil War America was the fact of violence, violence fed by conflict over slavery and by racial hate. An ugly racism soiled politics and public discourse, and the possibility of an explosion of racist violence hung like a specter over society. Repeated, intensifying acts of violence preceded a war that ushered in mass killing, atrocities against black Union soldiers, and anti-Negro riots in the North. This element of context appears both in key events and through the career of John Wilkes Booth. An extremist like Booth marked one of the boundaries of racial thought, and the distance between Booth, Blair, and Sumner captured the full range of white society's attitudes. These stretched from a defense of slavery and white supremacy that could turn violent at any moment, through an antislavery that was also antiblack, to a belief in the ideal of equality.

Abraham Lincoln and his Republican allies were part of a slowly awakening reformist impulse in Northern society. Lincoln was bonded to Charles Sumner and Montgomery Blair through ties of party, interest, and friendship. Starting from different backgrounds before the war, they became united in the conviction that slavery must not be allowed to expand. In some way, gradually or rapidly, it should be eliminated from American life. But they did not all oppose racism. Nor did they or their party move, united, toward equality. The events of war convinced them to attack slavery, but they disagreed sharply on what should come afterward. While they urged different types of racial change, confronting racism proved exceedingly difficult, and there the divisions among them ran deep.

Charles Sumner argued insistently for equal rights after slavery, but his was a minority view. Montgomery Blair and the other members of his powerful and influential family consistently demanded separation of the races— removal of black people from a free nation. Lincoln fell between Sumner and the Blairs. His natural affinity was for the attitudes of the Blairs, and for a long time his policies and their ideas were virtually identical. The close connection between Lincoln's policies and the Blairs' beliefs is often forgotten today, despite the fact that it marked the center of gravity of white racial opinions and preferences. But war unleashes change. With the transforming events of war, Lincoln eventually moved part of the way toward Sumner. He struggled with deeply rooted racial attitudes, while trying to defeat the rebellion and preserve the Union.

At the opposite end of the spectrum, many whites stood with John Wilkes Booth. The belief that African Americans were inferior and that the United States must remain a white man's country was widely shared. Many Northern voters, like Booth, despised everything the three Republicans did, and racist attitudes drove much of politics in the North. Stephen Douglas was only one candidate for office who played on economic and cultural insecurities or sought advantage from the assumption of white privilege. Editors, politicians, and virtually the entire Democratic Party exploited a prejudice that was deeply rooted and always potentially violent.

Booth was unusual in the active support he gave to the Confederacy, but he was all too emblematic of the racism that infected the North. His seething resentment at any sign of racial change or progress was mirrored in murderous riots and individual acts of rage. Such hatred caused social and political violence throughout the era, and through Booth, this long-standing racism eventually claimed the life of Abraham Lincoln.

The events of war destroyed slavery, but they barely softened racism. Through a violent era and four years of unparalleled military bloodletting, American society emerged only partially transformed. The Union was victorious and slavery was ended. But along with national progress came societal failure: the challenge of equality defeated white Americans in the Civil War era. That remained a task for later generations, even to the present. The events surrounding the Civil War reveal how formidable the barriers to equality were.

Lincoln's Dilemma

Introduction

TWO SPEECHES

REJOICING AT LAST! Washington was alight with celebration. A "general illumination" turned dark streets bright and gave the capital a festive air. Candles burned in every window, gaslights flared, and fireworks lit up the sky. "City Hall sat dressed in gas jets, with as many as sixty candles apiece in some of its windows; while from the square, the radiating streets seemed to stretch in unbroken vistas of flame."[1] Victory had finally banished the pall of death and defeat. After four discouraging, painful years, April 1865 brought success as one historic victory followed another.

The rebel capital, Richmond, fell on April 3, and "the city [Washington] has been in an uproar through the day. Most of the clerks," wrote Secretary of the Navy Gideon Welles, "left the Department, and there were immense gatherings in the streets. Joy and gladness lightened every countenance . . . it seemed as if the entire population, the male portion of it, was abroad. . . . Flags were flying from every house and store."

Exactly one week later, on April 10, a salute of guns at dawn signaled the surrender of Lee's army. "[T]he nation seems delirious with joy. Guns are firing, bells ringing, flags flying, men laughing, children cheering; all, all are jubilant." After calling on the president, who had just returned from the Virginia front, Secretary Welles wrote that Abraham Lincoln was "looking well and feeling well."[2]

The illumination on April 13 celebrated Lee's surrender of his Army of Northern Virginia. April 14 would mark the anniversary of the fall of Fort Sumter, where the war had begun in Charleston harbor. Francis Preston Blair, the grand old man of Washington politics, came into the district from his fabled home in Silver Spring, Maryland. A founder of the Republican Party and a friend and adviser to everyone important, Blair wanted to "witness the celebration of the end of the war." He stayed that night across from the White House, at the home of his son Montgomery, until recently the postmaster general in Lincoln's cabinet. The Blairs "went to bed while the city was at its gayest and brightest and woke to find it the gloomiest and saddest city imaginable."[3] Lincoln had been assassinated.

Two speeches had everything to do with the sudden descent from joyous victory to shock and gloom. Three days before, on April 11, Abraham Lincoln had spoken to "a multitude" of happy serenaders who had gathered outside at the White House. Excited over Lee's surrender and the war's end, they came to cheer the president and hear his thoughts about better days ahead. At least, the great majority of serenaders were in a celebratory mood. Among them was a young actor whose talents Abraham Lincoln admired. John Wilkes Booth, described in playbills as "A STAR OF THE FIRST MAGNITUDE!—THE YOUNGEST TRAGEDIAN IN THE WORLD!" had already gained considerable fame in the theater. Praised by critics, he had earned as much as $20,000 a year in the early years of the war.[4] But Booth loved the Confederacy and had been aiding the rebellion. Until recently he had been planning to kidnap the president. He listened intently as Lincoln spoke.

When the young actor heard Lincoln mention, cautiously, a personal preference that some black men might vote, he felt nothing but rage. Turning to two of his fellow conspirators, Booth spat out the words, "That means nigger citizenship. Now, by God! I'll put him through. That is the last speech he will ever make."[5] On the night of the fourteenth, while a weary president sought relaxation at Ford's Theatre, Booth fired a bullet into Abraham Lincoln's brain.

Booth shared the beliefs of a different speech, one that Lincoln himself may have thought about as he addressed the question of race that night in 1865. Four years earlier, in March of 1861, Alexander Stephens—once Lincoln's colleague in Congress but lately vice president of the newly formed Confederate States of America—had spoken to a cheering crowd in Savannah, Georgia. The Confederate Constitution, Stephens boasted, marked a great advance in governance. It "has put at rest, *forever,* all the agitating questions relating to our peculiar institution—African slavery as it exists among us—the proper *status* of the negro in our form of civilization." Thomas Jefferson and the Founding Fathers, said Stephens, had been wrong to regard slavery as a "violation of the laws of nature." The Declaration of Independence was a lie. The self-evident truth to rebelling Confederates was that "the negro is not equal to the

Frankly, unapologetically, **Alexander Stephens** proclaimed that the seceded South aimed to create an aristocratic republic based on slavery and racial domination.

white man . . . slavery—subordination to the superior race—is his natural and normal condition." Racial domination conformed to "the ordinance of the Creator" and was the "corner-stone" of the Confederacy. Proudly Stephens asserted that "our new government, is the first, in the history of the world, based upon this great physical, philosophical, and moral truth."[6]

STEPHENS WAS ONE of many leaders to make the South's position clear. For him slavery was the foundation not only of his personal fortune but also of the South's social system and way of life. Enslavement of black people and domination by whites defined the South. It supported the ruling class and gave status to poorer men who owned no slaves. Christian ministers defended it as ordained by God, and no one was allowed to question it.

But racism was not simply a Southern problem. White supremacy and racist beliefs drove the feelings of many Northerners as well. With casual virulence it defined the norm for white Americans. Most Northerners shared Stephens's contempt for African Americans, if not his enthusiasm for slavery. The national sickness of racism sanctioned injustice and cruelty in both sections.

Even more dangerously, it fed attitudes of hatred and violence. It encouraged discontented individuals to discharge their anger on black men and women and to strike out in defense of white supremacy.

The powerful emotions surrounding "the proper *status* of the negro" were well known to Abraham Lincoln. In past political campaigns he had often defended himself against racist attacks. His party, he explained, looked "upon the institution of slavery *as a wrong*" while his opponents did not. But he had denied that "the real issue" was any desire on his part to introduce "a perfect social and political equality between the white and black races."[7]

What, then, could Abraham Lincoln say to guide the North's racial future? Four years of war had crippled and undermined the institution of slavery. What did that mean for race relations and the position of African Americans in society?

On April 11, in his last address to the serenaders, the president spent little time rejoicing. First he expressed gratitude to "H[im], from Whom all blessings flow" and to "Gen. Grant, his skillful officers, and brave men" to whom "the honor . . . all belongs." Then Lincoln turned his thoughts to the future. Hoping for "a righteous and speedy peace," he focused on "reconstruction" which now "is pressed much more closely upon our attention."

It was a matter, he admitted, "fraught with great difficulty." The Constitution was silent on this great challenge. How should the nation be reassembled from "disorganized and discordant elements"? Lincoln acknowledged an additional problem: the fact that "we, the loyal people, differ among ourselves as to the mode, manner, and means."[8] Differences based on race divided not just Republicans and Democrats—they also split the ranks of Republicans.

Two great questions loomed over all thinking about Reconstruction. How should loyal governments be reestablished in the rebellious Southern states? And what would be the status of African Americans?

The Constitution—a document designed for permanence—provided little guidance on the first question. It said nothing about which branch of government should oversee Reconstruction. It was equally silent as to how the rebellious states could regain their rights or what roles should be permitted to leaders of the rebellion.

As for African Americans, slavery was not yet dead, though the events of war had gravely wounded the institution. After Lincoln had proclaimed emancipation as a war measure, almost 500,000 Southern slaves made themselves free in fact, by leaving their masters and entering Union lines. Of them,

147,000 men had taken up arms and fought for the Union army. Just two months before, in February, Congress had proposed an amendment to the Constitution to prohibit slavery throughout the United States, in the South as well as the loyal border states.

On the issues of Reconstruction Lincoln had been at odds with his own party for more than nine months. He had collided with Republican lawmakers over which branch of government should direct the process and what rules should be followed. His views on the future of African Americans, whatever he said, were sure to be even more controversial.

Racism flourished even in the Republican Party, and leading figures, from Massachusetts senator Charles Sumner to former postmaster general Montgomery Blair, disagreed profoundly on the place black people should hold in society. Northern Democrats, meanwhile, opposed all racial progress. Defeated Southern whites were likely to be hostile to change. Thus, for the nation, the status of black people complicated the already thorny issue of how to reassemble a divided nation.

Turning first to the question of how to reconstruct the Union, Lincoln defended his "ten percent plan." As president he had invited rebelling states to organize loyal governments with only 10 percent of a state's 1860 voters. Congress had more-rigorous ideas. But Lincoln argued that the occupied portions of Louisiana had organized a new government, with emancipation and without apprenticeship for former slaves. Yes, he admitted, it would be "more satisfactory to all" if "the new Louisiana government" rested on "fifty, thirty, or even twenty thousand [voters], instead of only about twelve thousand." Some also objected that "the elective franchise is not given to the colored man." But *"sustaining"* that new government, he insisted, would be better than *"discarding"* it. If Louisiana's government was merely "the egg" rather than "the fowl, we shall sooner have the fowl by hatching the egg than by smashing it." While counseling flexibility, the president stood behind his approach. He urged admission of his 10 percent government.[9]

What role for the former slaves? Here Lincoln took advanced and conservative positions at the same time. For the first time Lincoln publicly stated a personal preference that some black men might be allowed to vote. "I would myself prefer," he said, that the right to vote "were now conferred on the very intelligent, and on those who serve our cause as soldiers." These words would delight Charles Sumner, but to others they were outrageous. Only a few New England states allowed blacks to vote. The Democratic Party constantly warned that King Abraham the Tyrant planned to degrade the white race. Lincoln's words on black voting were also anathema to Montgomery Blair and many conservative Republicans.

On the other hand, when Lincoln moved on to discuss the proposed Thirteenth Amendment ending slavery, his statements would have comforted Blair and alarmed Sumner. Since the Emancipation Proclamation was a war measure, its postwar status was unclear. In addition, it did not affect slaves in the loyal states, and thus a constitutional amendment was needed to put the end of slavery beyond question. But the Constitution required that three-quarters of the states ratify any proposed amendment. That meant that ten states could block emancipation. Eleven states had actively supported the Confederacy, and Kentucky, New Jersey, and Delaware were so firmly in the Democratic Party's camp that they were unlikely to vote yes.[10]

Facing these facts, Charles Sumner had been arguing in the Senate that only the loyal, Northern states should vote on the Thirteenth Amendment. It made no sense, he reasoned, to let disloyal rebels, who had broken the Union, dictate key terms of its Reconstruction. While refraining from a firm commitment "against this," Lincoln made his disagreement with Sumner plain. "Such a ratification," argued the president, "would be questionable, and sure to be persistently questioned." On the other hand, "a ratification by three fourths of all the States would be unquestioned and unquestionable."

To suggest that some black men should vote challenged society's racism and offended many. Yet Lincoln's position on ratification of the Thirteenth Amendment was controversial in the other direction; it revealed his desire to engage and conciliate the South through a respect for states' rights. This alarmed Republicans who doubted the loyalty of defeated Confederates or their readiness to accept emancipation.

Lincoln could find no easy consensus or escape controversy where race was concerned. Neither could his party. More than secession or slavery's power in politics, what Alexander Stephens called "the proper *status* of the negro" was the war's fundamental issue.

1

Prejudice and Human Sympathy

Conflict over slavery and "the proper *status* of the negro" caused the disruption of the Union. In the prewar decade, events related to race had unsettled the prejudice that dominated the nation. Many Northerners in the 1850s developed more sympathy for the slave without discarding their prejudice against black people.

Everywhere in the United States the deck was stacked against African Americans. Racism was part of life—the social norm in a white man's country. Prejudice was in the air that people breathed. Few questioned it, and those few who did were ostracized. But an evolution was taking place in the North. Sympathy for human suffering was beginning to crack the monolith of racism, causing people to question slavery if not inequality.

In the South humanitarian impulses could merely chip away at a mountain of racial hostility. Slavery and racism became more entrenched with each passing year. Public criticism or even questioning of slavery had been banished since the 1830s. Violence or prison silenced the rare minister who spoke against human bondage.[1] Not only was slavery defended as God's plan and a "positive good," but it also was seen as the basis of white equality and democracy. Writers and physicians multiplied supposedly scientific theories about black inferiority.

In the North free black Americans faced a profoundly discouraging reality. Politicians in the Democratic Party regularly denied that an African American could be a citizen. Ninety-three percent of Northern blacks lived where they were denied the right to vote in 1840. Only Massachusetts, Vermont, New Hampshire, and Maine allowed black suffrage under the same rules that applied to whites; in New York a few black men voted who met certain property and residence requirements. Twenty years later there had been little progress. Rhode Island had joined the short list of states that allowed equal suffrage. But by then the percentage of black Northerners who could vote had shrunk to only 6 percent.[2]

Prejudice seemed strongest at freedom's frontier—in the western states that were being added to the Union. In Oregon black people could not own real estate, make contracts, or bring lawsuits. Illinois, Ohio, Indiana, Iowa, and California prohibited black testimony in any case in which a white man was a party—thus giving license to any white man to commit a criminal act against a black person, so long as there was no white witness. Few African Americans ever served on an antebellum jury.[3]

New states and territories in the West—Ohio, Indiana, Illinois, Michigan, Iowa, and Oregon—legally barred African Americans or demanded the posting of an expensive bond to guarantee good behavior. The percentage of voters in Illinois, Indiana, Oregon, and Kansas who supported measures to prohibit the entry of free black people reached almost 80 percent. And the western states were not alone. "Nearly every northern state considered, and many adopted, measures to prohibit or restrict the further immigration of Negroes." Though not always strictly enforced, these laws discouraged black in-migration and aided harassment of black people.[4]

Cradle-to-grave discrimination was the rule throughout the free states. African Americans had their "place" in the North as much as in the South, and that place was everywhere an inferior one. Black people were sent to the "Jim Crow" section in railway cars, stagecoaches, buses, and steamboats. They had to sit in separate sections in theaters, lecture halls, and churches. If they were able to attend school, it was a segregated school. Most restaurants, hotels, and resorts were closed to them. Their jobs were the most undesirable and most poorly paid. Segregation followed them into prisons, hospitals, and even cemeteries. The specter of racial prejudice "haunts its victim wherever he goes," even into "the graveyards."[5]

Such realities drove black leaders almost to despair. James McCune Smith, a physician and reformer from New York City, lamented that whites were "ignorant of our capacity" and "laughed at us in our wretchedness." He asked, "What press has not ridiculed and condemned us?" Samuel Ringgold Ward, who escaped from slavery and then fled from the United States, said that "'American' and 'Negro-hater' were nearly 'synonymous terms.'"[6]

Those who tried to change this situation paid a severe price. Riots and mob violence had greeted the abolitionist campaigns of the 1830s, and the public applauded. The leaders of anti-abolition mobs were usually respectable men, upstanding pillars of their local communities. The murder of an abolitionist editor, Elijah Lovejoy, in Illinois underscored the extent of anger over threats to white supremacy. Even on the eve of the Civil War, hostility toward the abolitionists remained strong, and many saw criticism of slavery as an attack on the Constitution. To disturb the racial status quo was, as Southern leaders contended, to endanger the Union. Slavery was protected, and racism was patriotic.[7]

But politics repeatedly raised a troubling question: what was slavery's role in the nation's future? The war with Mexico had added vast new territory to the national domain. With every discussion of settling or organizing that territory, new controversies arose. Increasingly, Northerners worried about the influence Southern leaders had over national politics. Slavery certainly was legal and protected where it existed. But should it expand? How would its expansion affect non-slaveholders and Northerners? Could Congress limit slavery's growth?

Arguments about the law and the Constitution could become theoretical, but human dramas had the power to grip people's emotions and multiply the efforts of the abolitionists. A best-selling novel and a new federal law captured the emotions of many Northerners in the 1850s. They set in motion a slow but widespread emotional awakening. The novel was Harriet Beecher Stowe's *Uncle Tom's Cabin.* It made ordinary people understand a mother's pain when slave children were torn from their parents. The law was the fugitive slave law, a key part of the Compromise of 1850. It put the anguish of losing one's freedom before the eyes of a previously indifferent public. Together, Stowe's book and growing conflicts over fugitive slaves deepened Northerners' awareness of the emotional cruelty that was inseparable from slavery.

Harriet Beecher Stowe began publishing *Uncle Tom's Cabin* in 1851. It first appeared chapter by chapter in the *National Era,* an abolitionist newspaper. This serialized version of her story immediately struck a chord. Hearing about its popularity, a publisher contacted Stowe and convinced her to let him print it in book form. *Uncle Tom's Cabin* appeared between covers in March of 1852 and sold a remarkable 300,000 copies in the first year—"an unprecedented number for any book, except the Bible, in so short a period of time." By mid-1853 sales were over a million. Bargain-priced editions extended the novel's reach, and numerous theatrical groups adapted the novel for the stage. Countless people saw *Uncle Tom's Cabin* performed as a stage play or read other novels imitating it.[8]

The scenes that most affected readers and audiences described human suffering that anyone could understand—parents protecting their children, mothers devastated by the sale of a child, slaves at the mercy of a cruel master. The highlight of most stage productions was the flight of Eliza, a slave mother. Learning that her little boy was going to be sold away from her, Eliza fled from Kentucky toward the free state of Ohio. Closely pursued by slave catchers and vicious dogs, she took an enormous chance. To cross the partially frozen Ohio River, she jumped from one block of ice to another, holding little Harry in her arms. A mother would do anything to protect her child as Eliza did; another slave in the novel, who had been separated from her child, wasted away from sorrow.

After Eliza reached Ohio, she remained in danger. Her encounter with a white family underscored the sacredness of family ties—vital to whites as well as blacks. In that chapter a state legislator in Ohio returned to his home after helping to pass a law to capture runaway slaves. He and his wife were still grieving over the death of their young son. Suddenly Eliza appeared on their doorstep with little Harry. When the senator's wife saw Eliza, her heart immediately went out to her. "[T]he law . . . don't forbid us to shelter these poor creatures a night, does it?" she asked her husband. Dutifully, the legislator affirmed that "that would be aiding and abetting." But soon he relented, moved like his wife by Eliza's love for her child and by his own love for the boy he had lost. Thus a lawmaker aided and abetted Eliza's escape, contrary to law, because his heart compelled him. And his wife's question remained in the mind of the reader: do "you think such a law as that is right and Christian?"[9]

Uncle Tom, the central figure of Stowe's novel, was far from the spineless, submissive character that his name later came to represent. In what was a very religious nation, Stowe made Tom a man of religious courage and commitment. Otherworldly in his priorities, Tom dedicated his life to preparing for eternity. Rather than fighting against the injustices of slavery, he worked constantly to treat all those around him with love. Tom helped many, white as well as black, and in the novel he ultimately died a martyr's death by refusing to betray two slaves who had escaped. As his vicious owner, Simon Legree, beat him to death, Tom pleaded for Legree's soul. Before dying he converted two slaves to Christianity.[10] Tom's Christianity and Eliza's devotion to her child showed Northerners that African Americans were human, even admirable at times, and could feel as they did.

Still, few considered that blacks might deserve equal treatment. Sympathy could remain in the realm of thought; prejudice affected daily realities and action. But outrage over the fugitive slave law convinced a small but growing number that no free person should lose his freedom. Especially troubling was the role of the federal government. How could the government of a nation dedicated to liberty be the agent of enslavement? A series of well-publicized events caused many Northerners to ask this question.

The small body of abolitionists assailed the fugitive slave law soon after its passage in 1850. Several provisions of the legislation were questionable. If a slave ran away and escaped to freedom, his owner could go before a U.S. magistrate and file a description of his escaped "property." Then, when the owner or his detectives located a runaway, that description would serve as sufficient evidence to identify the fugitive. A U.S. magistrate in the free states had to decide whether the living, breathing person, arrested and standing before him, matched the descriptive words on a page. The magistrate's decision could send a free person into bondage. But no contrary evidence could be presented; no challenge to the supposed facts was allowed; no jury trial was to take place. In addition, the magistrate was paid more for his work when he condemned a man to bondage than when he preserved his freedom. The reason for this, ostensibly, was that the former required more paperwork. Yet this strange feature made the law suspect and more objectionable.

Almost immediately several cases attracted great public attention. In October 1850 hundreds of blacks gathered and threatened to free a slave captured in Detroit. In Boston early in 1851 Frederick Jenkins, whose slave name had been Shadrack, was taken into custody. Shadrack had escaped from slavery in Virginia and found work in a Boston restaurant. During a break in the legal proceedings for his return to slavery, a mob (consisting mostly of African Americans) burst into the courtroom and carried Jenkins away. Before federal agents could seize him again, he made his escape to Canada. Later that year a slave owner tried to claim a fugitive in Lancaster County, Pennsylvania, where many Quakers lived. African Americans and others assembled to resist the sending of a human being into slavery. A gunfight occurred, the fugitive was rescued, and the slave owner and three black people died. These events sparked widespread publicity, and the United States charged forty-five people with treason—unsuccessfully. In Syracuse, New York, abolitionists twice rescued William Henry, whose slave name was Jerry. William Henry made it to safety in Canada, but twenty-six people were indicted for riot and one was convicted. These well-publicized events aroused concerns, and "each year thereafter until the Civil War, Syracuse commemorated the Jerry rescue on its anniversary date."[11]

These cases were the first cracks in the wall of racial indifference, but after

1854 Northern opposition to the fugitive slave law increased exponentially. A major catalyst was the Anthony Burns case in Boston. Anthony Burns had escaped from slavery in Virginia by stowing away on a ship. Once in Boston he found a job and made a new life for himself. Then an understandable human error put him in jeopardy. He wrote a letter intended for an enslaved member of his family, but the letter was intercepted, and his former owner learned where to find him. Federal marshals arrested Burns and put him under guard in Boston's federal courthouse. Alarmed abolitionists organized meetings in protest, and a mob tried to rescue Burns by breaking into the courthouse. Their attack failed, and one guard was killed.

At this point the actions of the federal government took center stage. President Franklin Pierce moved decisively to enforce the fugitive slave law. "Incur any expense to insure the execution of the law," he telegraphed to local officials. The government sent marines, cavalry, and artillery to Boston and alerted ships in the harbor. The legal proceedings against Anthony Burns moved inexorably forward. At one point his former owner was ready to sell his human property to abolitionists, but the U.S. attorney blocked the sale. The federal government seemed absolutely determined to return this man to bondage. And it succeeded. Facing huge public protest, the army sent in troops from Rhode Island and New Hampshire. One thousand five hundred militia also were ordered to help maintain order. All business came to a stop in the heart of Boston as troops marched Burns to the harbor. "Most offices were draped in mourning, a coffin covered with black cloth hung suspended across State Street," and American flags "union down and edged in black" hung from windows. As spectators cried "Shame! Shame!" Burns "held his head up, and marched like a man" toward bondage.[12]

The government had succeeded in ending a man's freedom and returning him into slavery. To execute the law in this one case, it had spent more than $2 million in today's currency. Anthony Burns suffered, while many felt that a government dedicated to liberty had betrayed its values and paid far too high a price to appease slaveholders. One conservative-minded Bostonian wrote, "When it was all over, and I was left alone in my office, I put my face in my hands and wept. I could do nothing less." Amos A. Lawrence, a textile manufacturer, summed up the impact on public opinion in Boston. "We went to bed one night old fashioned, conservative, Compromise Union Whigs & waked up stark mad Abolitionists."[13]

Though less intense, the reaction was similar throughout the North. Resistance to the law by antislavery people grew. After the Anthony Burns case not a single runaway slave was returned to bondage from New England. More slaves were rescued successfully, and new cases in Wisconsin and Ohio attracted enormous publicity. In all, federal courts remanded 191 fugitives in the 1850s. This represented more than 82 percent of all the legal cases initiated. But public opinion had turned against the government's efforts. In almost half the cases, federal marshals had to become involved in transporting someone into bondage. Increasingly, citizens were troubled by the return of fugitive slaves and criticized the federal authorities who did their duty as slave catchers. Northern states passed personal liberty laws to try to give some protections, such as trial by jury, to fugitives. And far more slaves escaped than were captured. An estimated eight thousand to fifteen thousand slaves "stole themselves" during the prewar decade.[14]

White Northerners, in general, were still mired in racial prejudice. They did not want to associate with African Americans. They did not want them to have equal rights or greater opportunities. But a feeling was growing in the Northern public that slaves were people and that slavery was wrong and un-American.

2

Founding the Republican Party

THE POLITICAL PARTY that grew from these concerns over slavery was the Republican Party. In turn, it nourished and carried forward the public's antislavery feelings. But the party was an amalgam of strangely different elements. It contained men from different political backgrounds, and it combined antislavery convictions and antiblack prejudices.

"He was more nearly the founder of the Republican Party than any other one man." So declared Alexander K. McClure, the well-connected Pennsylvania journalist and politician, in regard to Francis Preston Blair. This grand old man of Washington politics, father of Postmaster General Montgomery Blair and Congressman and General Frank Blair, had far-reaching influence. With his sons, he played a key role in the Lincoln White House. Lincoln's Illinois friend and bodyguard, Ward Lamon, said, "Between Francis P. Blair and Mr. Lincoln there existed from the first to last a confidential relationship as close as that maintained by Mr. Lincoln with any other man. To Mr. Blair he almost habitually revealed himself upon delicate and grave subjects more freely than to any other." When facing "an important but difficult plan, he was almost certain . . . to try it by the touchstone of Mr. Blair's fertile and acute mind."[1]

Both Lincoln and Blair came originally from Kentucky. That common bond gave them a feeling of kinship toward each other and toward Southerners. But their party backgrounds were different, mirroring the diversity in the newly formed Republican organization. Lincoln had followed and admired the great Whig leader Henry Clay. Francis Preston Blair, older by eighteen years, had been devoted to Old Hickory, the Democratic president Andrew Jackson, and his political ideology.

Blair first made his name and career supporting Jackson in the nation's capital. As a close friend of the president, he laid the basis for his fortune by

Francis Preston Blair Sr., from his time as an intimate of Andrew Jackson until the end of the Civil War, was one of the most influential figures in Washington politics.

publishing a pro-administration newspaper, the *Globe*. Blair shared Jackson's hostility to the Bank of the United States and to any aristocratic concentration of power. While favoring states' rights and a limited central government, he also agreed passionately with Old Hickory that the Union must be defended against Southern threats. Soon Blair launched another business, publishing the debates of Congress in the *Congressional Globe*. By the time he turned the *Congressional Globe* over to others, he had amassed great wealth and influence.[2]

Blair "retired" to a beautiful home and country retreat in nearby Maryland. Charmed by a spring whose waters carried shiny flecks of mica, Blair bought up the surrounding land. There he built an elegant home, created a small artificial lake, and decorated his grounds with statuary and honeysuckle. "Silver Spring" welcomed a wide range of prominent visitors from the nation's capital. In this way Blair's homestead supported and magnified the remarkable talent he possessed for forging friendships with political leaders. Charles Sumner and President Lincoln were among the many who enjoyed the beauty and restfulness of Blair's creation.[3]

Politically, however, Francis Preston Blair never retired. Through the 1840s he stayed in close contact with leaders of the Northern Democracy, many of whose members were growing impatient with Southern demands and Southern control, all focused on the extension of slavery. That feeling burst into the open in 1846. A Pennsylvania Democrat, David Wilmot, broke with his party's president, James K. Polk, to offer his famous proviso. The Wilmot Proviso bluntly declared that slavery should not be allowed into any lands gained through the war with Mexico. Leaders of the slaveholding South repeatedly blocked the proviso in the U.S. Senate, but the legislatures of fourteen Northern states endorsed it. The Blairs were part of this growing movement toward "free soil."

In 1848 Blair threw his support to the new Free Soil Party. Though he owned slaves, he believed, like the Founding Fathers, that slavery was a social and political evil that should someday end. "Bold, defiant, adroit, and vitriolic," Blair argued that slavery must not expand. The Free Soil Party could further that mission. To former president Martin Van Buren, who agreed to be the new party's candidate, Blair wrote, "To my mind, this appears the greatest act of your life." The new party won 10 percent of the vote, and Blair pressed Northern antislavery Democrats to become more aggressive.[4]

In the 1850s battles over the admission of California to the Union, a stronger fugitive slave law, and the Kansas-Nebraska Act further inflamed controversy. By the beginning of 1856 a variety of Northern antislavery forces were ready to unite in a new party. The newly minted Republican Party had its founding convention in Pittsburg. There delegates chose Francis Preston Blair as permanent president of the proceedings. They also named him to the convention's Committee on Resolutions and Address and placed him on the National Executive Committee.

The senior Blair published a letter identifying the Republicans with Andrew Jackson's love of the Union. He also blasted the "sinister designs of the nullifiers of the South" and laid out a history of efforts by the slave interests to gain "extended dominion." For the party's candidate he favored John C. Frémont, a celebrated former army officer who had explored the West with Kit Carson. Thanks to Blair's influential support, Frémont won the nomination. The older man's insight that the Pathfinder could win Northern and western votes proved correct. The new Republican Party won one-third of the popular vote in 1856.

Blair's sons also pioneered as free-soilers and Republicans. During the

1850s Montgomery and Frank added energy and substance to the cause of antislavery and to the new party. Both men had moved to Missouri, where they became active in politics. They relied on the law, which they had studied at Transylvania University, as the basis of their professional careers. Montgomery became a judge in St. Louis and served as U.S. district attorney for four years. In 1850 he joined others in Missouri who condemned slavery's influence on whites. To allow slavery to expand would be "neither honest nor democratic," he said. The South's so-called peculiar institution retards "growth and prosperity . . . impairs enterprise . . . paralyzes the industry of a people and impedes the diffusion of knowledge." Other evils of slavery were its encouragement of "aristocratic tendencies and the degradation which it attaches to labor." As for the territories, they must be held "in trust for unborn millions" as a free-soil legacy. These views were common currency to all in the Blair family.[5] Though they held slaves, they were critical of the institution, adamant against its expansion, and enthusiastic about colonization of blacks abroad. Defenders of the Union and foes of Southern domination, they also revered states' rights and a limited federal government.

About this time Montgomery resigned his position as judge in order to earn more money. He declined a seat on the Missouri Supreme Court for the same reason. It was a sound financial decision. He developed a busy and "lucrative" practice before he answered his father's invitation to come to Washington in 1853. Installed in the family's mansion (later known as Blair House) across the street from the White House, Montgomery developed an extensive practice before the Supreme Court. By 1856 he was preparing briefs and arguments in Dred Scott's suit for liberty. He took this case, which would prove so important to the Republican Party, without a fee. Such service to antislavery won the respect of Abraham Lincoln.[6]

Frank, or Francis Preston Blair Jr., was the younger brother. A superior orator, the family hoped that Frank might become president someday. After practicing law in St. Louis, he fought in the war with Mexico and then became attorney general of the New Mexico Territory. Returning to Missouri, he won election to the state House of Representatives as a Free-Soiler in 1852. By 1856 he was running successfully for Congress as a Republican—the first Republican elected from a slave state. Energetic and determined, he used his powers as a public speaker to aid Frémont and many Republican candidates.

One of those recruits to the new party was Abraham Lincoln, in nearby Illinois. Frank Blair and Lincoln coordinated their thoughts on party strategy, and in the fall of 1856 they arranged to have a St. Louis newspaper, the *Missouri Democrat,* become a Republican paper. With its large circulation in southern Illinois, the paper could aid both the party and Lincoln's political aspirations. Before taking his seat in Congress in 1857, Frank went to Illinois to confer with Lincoln. One result of their meeting was favorable coverage by the pro-Blair paper of the Lincoln-Douglas debates.[7] Such cooperation would grow and deepen.

ABRAHAM LINCOLN's prominence in the Republican Party came a bit later than the Blairs'. Lincoln had been a Whig, not a Democrat. Following Henry Clay's example, he was more interested in promoting commerce and banking than in Andrew Jackson's opposition to concentrated wealth and power. As a state legislator, first elected in 1834, his most notable achievement—moving the state capital to Springfield—came through support for a wildly ambitious plan for internal improvements. Funded by bonds, this plan was so unrealistic that within a few years Illinois owed eight times as much in annual interest as it received in revenue. Payments had to be suspended, the state's credit was damaged, and the final payments were not made until 1880.[8]

As a young politician, Lincoln engaged in the race-baiting and racist rhetoric that was common among Illinois politicians. While his party's newspaper, the *Sangamo Journal,* accused a Democratic presidential nominee of "love for free negroes," the young Lincoln charged that his "very trail might be followed by scattered bunches of *Nigger wool.*" His skills as a storyteller also drew on a deep repertoire of racist jokes; moral growth and a greater human sympathy were not evident before the mid-1850s. But Lincoln did signal an early disapproval of slavery, in principle. With only one other state legislator, he issued a protest in 1837 that "slavery is founded on both injustice and bad policy." To balance this position their statement added that "the promulgation of abolition doctrines tends rather to increase than to abate its evils."[9]

Elected to Congress in 1846 for a single term, Lincoln was a loyal and partisan Whig. His "spot" resolutions attacked Democratic president Polk by demanding to know whether Polk had provoked war with Mexico by sending troops to a spot in Mexican territory. But Lincoln's education in antislavery ideas also made some progress. He introduced a bill to abolish slavery in the District of Columbia. This proposal involved gradual, compensated emancipation that would not take place without the approval of the district's residents. Nor would slaves outside Washington be able to gain their liberty by fleeing into the district. Freed slave children would have to serve an apprenticeship before they reached adulthood. As a campaigner for Republican candidates, Lincoln met men like New York's William Seward and Hannibal Hamlin of Maine who were more outspoken against slavery than he. The influential editor of the *New York Tribune,* Horace Greeley, categorized Congressman Lincoln as "one of the very mildest type of Wilmot Proviso Whigs from the free States."[10]

What galvanized Lincoln as an antislavery leader, and turned him toward the Republican Party, was the Kansas-Nebraska Act of 1854. After several years outside politics, practicing law, he now emerged as an eloquent opponent of the expansion of slavery. Illinois's senator Stephen Douglas had bowed to Southern demands in order to pass this law. It repealed that portion of the Missouri Compromise that prohibited slavery north of 36 degrees, 30 minutes. Throughout the North the Kansas-Nebraska Act alarmed and outraged both black and white citizens. A regional conference of the African Methodist Episcopal Church denounced the act as "wicked and cruel." An eloquent congressional protest, dubbed "The Appeal of the Independent Democrats," condemned the opening to slavery of land that had been dedicated to freedom. When Douglas returned to Illinois to defend his law, he ruefully noted that he could have made the trip at night by the light of his burning effigies. His chief critic in Illinois was Abraham Lincoln.[11]

Speaking in Peoria, Lincoln attacked slavery in the abstract and for the effect its extension would have on white people. He showed that slavery clashed with the nation's ideals while he carefully and adroitly avoided a defense of racial equality.

Lincoln began with Thomas Jefferson. The author of the Declaration of Independence had originated "the policy of prohibiting slavery in new territory." In 1784 Jefferson drafted an ordinance banning slavery in western lands claimed by the original states.[12] This wise policy, unfortunately, had now been abandoned. The new law concealed a "covert *real* zeal for the spread of slavery," and that "I can not but hate," said Lincoln. He hated it because of "the monstrous injustice of slavery itself" and because it robbed "our republican example of its just influence in the world." Extending slavery made hypocrites of liberty-loving Americans. It forced them into "open war with the very fundamental principles of civil liberty."[13]

Lincoln's words about African Americans were carefully crafted. Their presence in the nation was a problem. His "first impulse" would be to free them and "send them to Liberia," but that could not be done quickly. He doubted that freeing them to be "underlings" improved their condition. However, it was impossible to "free them, and make them socially and politically our equals. My own feelings will not admit of this," nor would the feelings of "the great mass of white people." Still, when Lincoln turned to Douglas's theory of self-government in the territories, he indirectly argued for the slave's humanity. Whether "the doctrine of self-government is right

> depends upon whether the negro is *not* or *is* a man. If he is *not* a man, why in that case, he who *is* a man may, as a matter of self-government, do just as he pleases with him. But if the negro *is* a man, is it not to that extent, a total destruction of self-government, to say that he too shall not govern *himself*? When the white man governs himself that is self-government; but when he governs himself, and also governs *another* man, that is *more* than self-government—that is despotism. If the negro is a *man,* why then my ancient faith teaches me that "all men are created equal;" and that there can be no moral right in connection with one man's making a slave of another.

Quoting the Declaration of Independence, Lincoln then made a careful choice of emphasis. After repeating familiar words about the "self-evident" truths that "all men are created equal" and have "certain inalienable rights," Lincoln placed his stress on the next sentence about governments. To secure their rights, men created governments "DERIVING THEIR JUST POWERS FROM THE CONSENT OF THE GOVERNED." Instead of equality, which most whites rejected, he focused on the principle of consent.

Continuing an efficient dissection of Douglas's policy, Lincoln specifically defended the self-interests of white people. "The whole nation," he insisted, "is interested that the best use shall be made of these territories. We want them for the homes of free white people." Allowing slavery into Kansas and Nebraska would ruin those territories for white men seeking opportunity. "Poor white people" remove themselves "FROM" slave states. "The nation needs these territories" as "places for poor people to go to and better their condition."

It was bad enough, Lincoln added, that under the Constitution slave states gained extra representation—"five slaves are counted as being equal to three whites." Thus South Carolina, with half the white population of Maine, enjoyed the same number of representatives in Congress. Every voter in a slave state "has more legal power" than a voter in a free state. This provision was part of the original Constitution and had to be accepted, Lincoln said, but he "respectfully" objected to allowing "the same degrading terms" to apply to new states.

The Peoria speech was so potent on various levels that it identified Lincoln as a coming figure in the free-soil movement. With politics in flux, he initially hesitated, watching the Whig Party disintegrate while the anti-immigrant American Party flashed briefly into prominence. But by 1856 Lincoln had declared himself a Republican. His gift for incisive but careful arguments soon made him the leading Republican in Illinois and a man to watch beyond his state.

A VERY DIFFERENT MAN from far-off Massachusetts had aided Lincoln's emergence in 1854. Charles Sumner helped stir the outrage over Kansas-Nebraska. He was one of three politicians who created the "Appeal of the Independent Democrats." After Joshua Giddings and Salmon Chase drafted this manifesto, Sumner polished the prose that awakened the North. It was difficult to imagine a Republican further removed from Lincoln in personality and background.

Born into a respectable but second-rank Boston family, Charles Sumner soon established himself in the intellectual and cultural elite of New England. Whereas Lincoln was a self-taught frontiersman, Sumner graduated from Harvard College and Harvard Law School. He then became a protégé of Judge William Story. After publishing learned articles and teaching occasionally at Harvard, Sumner interrupted his growing legal practice to go to Europe. In a year and a half of travel, he managed to meet leading figures in all the major European nations and later entertained them when they visited the United States. Ignoring the moneymaking aspects of law, Sumner turned his energies increasingly to various reforms.[14]

Whereas Lincoln was humble and down-to-earth, a storyteller with the common touch, Sumner was formal and serious, incurably pedantic, and totally lacking in a sense of humor. Terrified of women as a young man, he made influential male friends such as Henry Wadsworth Longfellow. His connection with Samuel Gridley Howe soon led Sumner into reform. As he boldly criticized society, Sumner offended conservative elements of Boston's elite. Taking up the cause of prison reform, he used intemperate language against his foes. This won respect from the more advanced reformers but cost Sumner the backing of respectable Boston Brahmins. Seeing himself as a badly treated but virtuous individual, he became more extreme and more convinced that he was right.[15]

Opposition to the war with Mexico moved Sumner into the antislavery politics of the Conscience Whigs. Soon he participated prominently in the formation of the Free-Soil Party. With "one of the most effective speeches" of a lifetime of speech making, Sumner helped launch Massachusetts's free-soil coalition. Ostracized by most of the elite, Sumner presented himself as the idealist in politics and ran unsuccessfully for Congress.[16] At the same time, a pure self-image did not prevent the ambitious Sumner from flirting with antislavery Democrats.

In support of equality, in 1849 he challenged segregation in Boston's public schools. Attacking "discrimination on account of race or color," he argued that the Massachusetts Constitution established "Equality before the Law." Segregation was "in the nature of *Caste.*" It imposed a "stigma" felt by black children and separated them from the "healthful, animating influences" of study with their "white brethren." Massachusetts's common schools should further "the Christian character of this community." Instead, segregation was "a monster" and constituted "Slavery, in one of its enormities." Though Sumner lost his case, the direction of public sentiment in Massachusetts was on his side. Only six years later the legislature outlawed segregation in public schools.[17]

The Compromise of 1850 roiled Massachusetts politics. Daniel Webster shocked many when he supported the Compromise measures, including its fugitive slave law, and then resigned his Senate seat to become secretary of state. As parties splintered, Charles Sumner promoted cooperation between Free-Soilers and other opponents of the Compromise. Consistently he denounced the soon-to-be-hated fugitive slave law. Its provisions seemed to encourage federal magistrates to return individuals to slavery without a trial or sufficient evidence. Sumner always called this law a "bill," saying that it was unconstitutional. Soon a strange coalition of anti-Compromise politicians won the state elections, and after months of balloting, the legislature sent Sumner to the U.S. Senate over the aristocratic Whig candidate, Robert Winthrop.[18]

There he began a career marked not by legislative success but by periodic, principled speeches. These were lengthy, formal, pedantic addresses—oral performances filled with literary and historical allusions and occasionally abusive language. For each speech Sumner dressed elegantly and spoke from memory for hours. Often visitors packed the Senate galleries to hear his orations. His reputation as a symbol of Massachusetts's idealism and morality, plus the timely recurrence of national crises, kept him in the Senate for decades.

In August 1852 the new senator staked out his free-soil position in an address titled "Freedom National; Slavery Sectional." Declaring that he was no politician, no party loyalist, but "a friend of Human Rights," Sumner attacked the fugitive slave law and slavery's influence. After citing "the injunctions of Christianity," he reviewed history to show that slavery in the United States was "in every respect *sectional,* and in no respect *national.*" The Founders fought for human rights, condemned slavery, and viewed slaves as persons. Both the Declaration of Independence and the Northwest Ordinance proved that the federal government "was Anti-slavery in character." At its founding slavery existed nowhere "on the *national* territory." Though some original states held slaves, the federal government was "a Government of limited powers" with "no power to make a slave or support a system of Slavery."[19]

In an era when the federal government was far smaller than it is today, states' rights was a principle accepted, in large measure, by all. It also was less than a principle—a tool that proved useful for supporters or opponents of slavery. To halt slavery's growing influence, Sumner emphasized that "the States are the peculiar guardians of *personal* liberty." Congress had no power to legislate for slavery's "abolition in the States or its support anywhere." States' rights thus protected "Freedom in the Free States." No law could take away "Trial by Jury in a question of Personal Liberty." The fugitive slave law was a "usurpation by Congress of powers not granted by the Constitution, and an infraction of rights secured to the States." Lacking "that essential support in the Public Conscience of the States," it became a "dead letter." Approvingly Sumner quoted the man who sat next to him: Senator Andrew Butler of South Carolina. Butler had declared that a law that has to be enforced at the point of a bayonet "was no law." Sumner agreed and praised the older man as someone who, had he "been a citizen of New England, would have been a scholar." At this early date Butler was one of a number of Southerners with whom Sumner was "on excellent terms."[20]

His antislavery stand won Sumner some important friends in the nation's capital. Francis Preston Blair and other prominent Washingtonians invited him to dinner. But the new senator soon faced criticism in Massachusetts. None of the elements of the unwieldy coalition that had elected him trusted him fully. Abolitionists always wanted him to be more energetic and outspoken—they felt he wasn't doing enough. Former Democrats distrusted him because he had been a Whig. Then, in 1854, debate on the Kansas-Nebraska bill altered Sumner's fortunes. It revived his popularity in Massachusetts and severed his previously friendly relations with Southern legislators.

Sumner fought Douglas's bill both in a formal address and in spontaneous debate. His "Landmark of Freedom" speech identified the Missouri Compromise as a sacred "compact" between the sections. The Founding Fathers had been antislavery. They had opposed its spread and expected the institution to die out. Their guiding principle was *"its prohibition in all the national domain."* Following that principle, the Missouri Compromise had outlawed slavery in most of the Louisiana Purchase, north of 36 degrees 30 minutes. Northerners had not wanted slavery to spread at all, but in the Missouri Compromise they bowed to the South, which was the "conquering party." Southern lawmakers were parties to the Compromise and shared in its "solemn obligations." Now, thirty-four years later, the South had no right to rescind the agreement and open Kansas and Nebraska to human bondage. All depended on preserving the "compact," for *"nothing can be settled which is not right."* North Carolina's senator George Badger called this speech a "masterpiece" of oratory, even though it was "on the wrong side."[21]

Sumner's speech enraged Stephen Douglas and Southern senators. The Appeal of the Independent Democrats and the arrest in Boston of fugitive slave Anthony Burns inflamed emotions further. Southern senators called Sumner a "fanatic," a "serpent," and a "filthy reptile." Sumner retaliated in kind. He said that his critics' "plantation manners" were on display—they imagined they were not in the Senate chamber but on "a plantation well stocked with slaves, over which the lash of the overseer had full sway." When Senator Butler challenged him to say whether he and Massachusetts would return a fugitive slave, Sumner replied, "Does the honorable Senator ask me if I would personally join in sending a fellow-man into bondage? 'Is thy servant a dog, that he should do this thing?'"[22]

Thereafter Southerners cut Sumner socially and tried to ignore him in debates. But his importance as an antislavery leader grew. Late in 1855 Sumner met with Salmon Chase, Nathanial Banks, soon to be Speaker of the House, and Francis Preston Blair. Together they considered steps to achieve "an organization of the Anti-Nebraska forces for the presidential election." Sumner also talked with John C. Frémont, who was being mentioned as a possible nominee of the new party. When the Republicans had their first meeting in

Pittsburgh in February 1856, Sumner enthusiastically endorsed its declaration of principles.[23] Along with the Blairs and Lincoln, Sumner had done his part to build a Republican Party.

But to African Americans this party seemed to offer little. "Free soilism," said Frederick Douglass, was "lame, halt, and blind" because it would not demand the "overthrow" of slavery. "Limiting it, circumscribing it" was inadequate. Black Americans wanted and deserved "practical recognition of our Equality." "That," said Douglass, "is what we are contending for."[24]

Unending conflict over Kansas and slavery would soon aid the new party. Its stature in national politics would increase, and its ability to influence events would grow. The members of the Republican Party stood united on one great question: they were against the extension of slavery. But race and the status of African Americans remained divisive questions for Republicans and for the nation.

3

Attitudes toward Slavery and Race

THOMAS JEFFERSON embodied the problem. In the Declaration of Independence his stirring words captured the nation's ideals of freedom and human equality. In other writings he expressed a deep social pessimism and racist views.

Jefferson was convinced that slavery had to end, but he could not imagine a democracy embracing black and white. "Nothing is more certainly written in the book of fate than that these people are to be free." The former president wrote this in 1821. But then he added: "Nor is it less certain that the two races, equally free, cannot live in the same government."[1]

Years before, in his *Notes on the State of Virginia,* Jefferson had deplored the "unremitting despotism" and "degrading submissions" involved in slavery. "The whole commerce between master and slave," he said, "is a perpetual exercise of the most boisterous passions." In the face of "daily exercised tyranny ... the man must be a prodigy who can retain his manners and morals un-depraved by such circumstances. . . . Indeed I tremble for my country when I reflect that God is just; that his justice cannot sleep forever." Yet in these same *Notes* Jefferson the slave master wrote that blacks "secrete less by the kidnies, and more by the glands of the skin, which gives them a very strong and disagreeable odour." Compared to whites, they were "in reason much inferior." The color of their skin gives an "eternal monotony" to their faces. He even wrote that the "Oranootan" uniformly preferred "black women over those of his own species." It seemed that Jefferson had far more than a "suspicion" that "blacks are inferior to the whites in the endowments both of body and mind."[2]

Since Jefferson's day, the clash of conflicting attitudes had become more extreme. Slavery's advocates abandoned the apologetic defenses of the past.

Where the founders once had called the existence of slavery a "necessary evil," now Southern leaders pronounced it a desirable virtue. At the same time, criticism of slavery became more pointed and insistent.

South Carolina's John C. Calhoun declared in 1837 that slavery "is, instead of an evil, a good—a positive good." Not only were slaves treated better than "the laborer" in other societies, but Southern slavery was also "the most solid and durable foundation on which to rear free and stable political institutions." Human bondage was "indispensable to the peace and happiness" of black and white Southerners, said Calhoun. "[T]o destroy it would be to destroy us as a people." Southern pastors and editors explained that "the Bible teaches clearly and conclusively that the holding of slaves is right." God "permitted, recognized, and commanded" slavery. Southern writers argued that masters were the "parent or guardian" of the "inferior" Negro. "Our Southern slavery," said George Fitzhugh, "has become a benign and protective institution, and our negroes are confessedly better off than any free laboring population in the world." Politicians like South Carolina's James Henry Hammond gloried in the economic power of the slaveholding cotton South. "Cotton is King," declared Hammond, who charged that the North had a "hireling class" that was "essentially slaves. The difference between us is, that our slaves are hired for life and well compensated. . . . Yours are . . . not cared for."[3]

Massachusetts's William Lloyd Garrison exemplified the new boldness and determination of slavery's critics. Garrison founded his newspaper, the *Liberator,* in 1831. Believing in the Declaration of Independence, Garrison declared that he would "strenuously contend for the immediate enfranchisement of our slave population." Rejecting gradual emancipation, he warned, "I will be as harsh as truth, and as uncompromising as justice. . . . I will not equivocate—I will not excuse—I will not retreat a single inch—AND I WILL BE HEARD." Using the new steam printing press, Garrison and abolitionists blanketed communities with petitions, protests, and broadsides. They insisted that slavery was a "sin" and that "the slaves ought instantly to be set free." Even more radical was their demand that freed slaves enjoy all the rights of American citizens. "[A]ll persons of color who possess the qualifications which are demanded of others, ought to be admitted forthwith to the same privileges, and the exercise of the same prerogatives, as others. . . . [T]he paths of preferment, of wealth, and of intelligence, should be opened as widely to them as to persons of a white complexion." Compensated emancipation, they charged, was wrong. If anyone was to be compensated, it should be the slaves.[4]

From the start, the abolitionists' campaigns inflamed controversy. Although most Northerners detested their cause, they gained some followers in the 1830s. Petitions poured into Congress. Alarmed Southern lawmakers quickly put a stop to agitation they viewed as dangerous. They passed a "Gag Rule," and for six years consigned all abolition petitions to silent oblivion. But the tactic backfired, causing many non-abolitionists to resent this infringement of the right of free speech and petition. Then the war with Mexico and disputes over the future of the territories made slavery a dominant issue. Although abolitionists remained a small minority, many Northerners began to see the slavery interest—or the Slave Power, as abolitionists called it—as a threat to them. Antislavery thus became a movement far wider and more diverse than abolitionism; it included and motivated many racists. Attitudes toward slavery and race covered a wide spectrum in society, including among Republicans.

JOHN WILKES BOOTH stood at one end of the spectrum—an example of the dangerous, combustible material that threatened society. His was the racist, pro-Southern, anti-immigrant extreme, with emotions tending toward violence. Born into a distinguished theatrical family, Booth spent his early years in rural, slaveholding Maryland. There he developed a love of the South, its slaveholding society, and its social pretensions. Ever ambitious, he viewed himself as one of the aristocrats in a society where different types of people occupied markedly different places. Slaves were despised, immigrants were little better, and laborers needed to be kept at a social distance. The ideas of honor and chivalry of the Southern aristocrat attracted Booth powerfully, even as a teenager. His sister acknowledged that he had the attitudes of the "southern American."[5]

The Booth family owned some slaves, or "darkies" as his sister put it. She described them in stereotypical racist terms, saying that once, when a magistrate came to their house, they reacted with "idiocy and terror." Her brother John Wilkes enjoyed being their condescending superior. One day, when he rode up to the house on his horse, some of the slaves greeted him with a cheery "How'd, Mars' Johnnie." Booth dismounted and reached into his saddlebag. Taking from it a packet of candies, he threw the package far beyond where he stood. Then he called to the slaves, "After it Nigs! Don't let the dogs get it."[6] It amused him to make social inferiors of a subject race scamper at his command.

Booth was only seventeen in 1855 when the anti-immigrant American Party briefly surged to prominence. He fervently embraced its attitudes of hostile superiority, despite the fact that his was an immigrant family. Junius Brutus Booth, his father and a renowned Shakespearean actor, had come to the United States in 1821. Arriving from Britain with his mistress, Junius soon achieved success in the theater. But it was not until 1851 that he obtained a divorce and regularized his marriage. These facts may have encouraged John Wilkes, born illegitimate, to aspire not just to respectability but to aristocratic hauteur. He passionately insisted on his superiority to black people, immigrants, and social inferiors. Enthusiastic about measures to restrict immigrants and deny them citizenship for many years, he threw himself into American Party politics. Frequently he attended party meetings that lasted until dawn.[7]

Before John Wilkes Booth attained any fame as an actor, he displayed an imperious streak toward others. A tenant farmer working on the family's land encountered the young man's aristocratic ire. A dispute had arisen between the farmer and Booth's mother. She felt that the tenant had been working the family's horses and slaves too hard. He denied the charge in terms she felt were rude. As soon as he heard of it, John Wilkes, who was then only sixteen, went to the tenant's home and confronted him. "I'll whip you like the scoundrel you are," he shouted. Then he beat the tenant over the head and shoulders with a stick and insisted that the man apologize to the ladies of the Booth family. Afterward he boasted to a friend about the assault. Laborers, too, were to be taught their place. Though the family occasionally hired men to work on the property, John Wilkes refused to eat at a table with them. He would not associate with those he deemed his inferiors.[8]

At age seventeen, he began to appear, occasionally, on the stage, in Baltimore and Philadelphia. After gaining some experience, he moved in 1858 to Richmond, Virginia, where he became part of the Richmond Theatre. Living in Virginia, the oldest Southern state, delighted him and confirmed his passion to be "of the South," as he put it. His sister recalled a dream that he had shared with her at the family home one night. "He could never hope to be as great as father, he never wanted to try to rival Edwin [his older brother], but he wanted to be loved of the Southern people above all things. He would work to make himself essentially a Southern actor." Gaining confidence and skill, Booth had success in Richmond, where audiences embraced him "as one of their own." As the sectional crisis increased, he felt an ever deeper loyalty to the South. He burned with a desire to defend the region and its enslavement of black Americans.[9]

MONTGOMERY BLAIR, along with his father and brother Frank, was a very different kind of racist. Strange as the combination may seem today, the Blairs were sincerely antislavery racists. They also were strongly states' rights Unionists. Their political and social beliefs—which were constant and unchanging—came from an earlier time in U.S. history, when such combinations were typical of the Founding Fathers or of Andrew Jackson. In midcentury their views resonated with a large number of Northerners, including a major branch of the Republican Party. The Blairs' intelligence, energy, and dedication to the party also gave them enormous influence.

The Blair family's early devotion to Andrew Jackson guided their political thought. It made them representative of many Republicans whose antislavery views had led them out of the Democratic Party. In the tradition of the Founders, they saw slavery as a contradiction of the American devotion to liberty. With Jackson, they had an aversion to concentrated power and aristocracy. "What the Constitution was, and what it should be," wrote one biographer, "were questions which had been answered by Jefferson and Jackson."

Jackson's foe had been the Bank of the United States. For Montgomery Blair and his family it was the Slave Power. Both represented aristocratic concentrations of power and privilege. The idea of a Slave Power—popularized by abolitionists and Republicans—held that slaveholding interests were trying to dominate the national government. Like many Republicans, the Blairs saw Southern aggression in the war with Mexico, the Compromise of 1850, and the Kansas-Nebraska Act. Step by step, the slaveholding aristocracy had extended its influence in the United States. Then it cast longing eyes on Cuba. Southern threats to disrupt the Union must be put down, just as Jackson had faced down the Nullifiers. But love of liberty and Union also meant support for states' rights, since the national government could itself become a dangerous source of concentrated power.[10]

Montgomery Blair was the older of Francis Preston Blair's two sons and would become an influential member of Lincoln's cabinet.[11] Before studying law at Transylvania University, Montgomery had graduated from West Point. He quickly left the military but for the rest of his life carried himself with a military bearing. Standing ramrod straight, he was six feet tall, "straight and spare." He could wear his West Point uniform comfortably, even to the end of his life. He had a "sharp eye and intelligent face." Sure of his own opinions, Montgomery Blair made independent choices about his appearance. He trimmed his hair closely and was always clean shaven in an era when beards were very much in fashion. Along with these personal habits went energetic dedication to his legal practice, an interest in art, and wide intellectual curiosity. The journalist Noah Brooks judged him "the best-read man in Lincoln's cabinet."[12]

Montgomery Blair argued his first case before the Supreme Court before he was thirty.[13] His reputation as an exceptional advocate preceded him from Missouri to Washington, D.C. There he became a key legal resource for the new Republican Party. It was to him that antislavery forces brought the case of a Missouri slave named Dred Scott. Scott's owner, an army surgeon named Dr. John Emerson, had taken his slave for extended periods to posts in Illinois, a free state, and in the Wisconsin Territory, where slavery had been prohibited by the Missouri Compromise. On these grounds Dred Scott and his supporters sued for his freedom. The case raised vital questions about slavery and freedom in the territories, Congress's powers, and the status of African Americans in the nation and its legal system.[14]

Blair's research for the Dred Scott case was extremely thorough. It went back to the Articles of Confederation. It continued with the Northwest Ordinance of 1787, when the Founders barred slavery from the vast area north and west of the Ohio River, and with the act of Congress in 1789 that gave full effect to that ordinance.[15] He delved deeply into both the law and history. On key historical facts his lengthy brief is far more accurate than the subsequent ruling by Chief Justice Roger Taney. Blair also was careful, in a shrewd way, to cite favorable precedents that had been argued or decided by Taney or the Court. Against the real possibility that this case would be decided on political grounds, he made an eloquent argument for the rule of law. Portions of his brief also summarized effectively the history from which the Republican Party drew its vision of the future.[16]

Blair's research was especially convincing on the question of black citizenship. He proved that from the nation's origin free black men who met local qualifications had exercised *all* the rights of citizenship in some states. That included voting, even in slaveholding North Carolina before 1835 (when a constitutional convention restricted the suffrage to whites). Three years after free black men lost the right to vote in North Carolina, the courts there nevertheless affirmed black citizenship. They ruled in 1838 that, once freed, slaves became citizens if they had been born in that state. "The essence of citizenship," said Blair, summing up legal history, "is the right of protection of life and liberty, the right to acquire and enjoy property, and equal taxation." Tests for voting or holding office were tests of fitness for the duties required, not tests of citizenship. Throughout the United States, women and children were citizens but not voters. Acts of Congress had apportioned taxes on the basis of "white and *other free citizens.*" Blair even demonstrated that Chief Justice Taney had brought suit in a case involving a Negro. That case and others seemed to prove that blacks were citizens and had the right to sue and be sued.

Did extended residence in a free state and free territory make a slave free? Blair cited cases from various states that had answered "yes." Even some Southern states had found in favor of freedom for slaves who had gained their freedom elsewhere. Missouri's courts also had ruled, in the recent past, that masters who took their slaves to free areas liberated them by doing so. But politics had changed the composition of the Missouri Supreme Court and influenced its decision. "Times now are not as they were when the previous decisions on this subject were made," claimed the Missouri court. "A dark and fell spirit against slavery," warned one Missouri judge, now threatened the institution. Blair responded against this intrusion of politics into judicial matters:

> The question for this court now is, whether it will hold valid a right to freedom based on the [Northwest] ordinance of '87, the act of '89, and the constitution of Illinois—all affirmed by a succession of judicial decisions in Missouri, covering a third of a century, and recognized as statute law—or substitute Judge Scott's principle, that the existence of what he describes "a dark and fell spirit against slavery, in other portions of the country," is sufficient to subvert the law.

"The design of the framers," Blair continued, was "against the extension of slavery." Their vote on the Northwest Ordinance had been unanimous. They had avoided use of the word "slavery" in the Constitution, given Congress power over the territories in Article 4, Section 3, and closed the international slave trade. The writings of Madison and Monroe specifically recognized Congress's power to bar slavery from the territories. Since the Supreme Court had stated that the basis for constructing the Constitution must be "the history of the times, and the state of things existing when it was framed," the decision should be easy. For that history was clearly against extending slavery. Moreover, the institution of slavery created "inequality and privilege" and would "subvert" the ideals on which the government was founded.

Despite these sound arguments, the Court's decision, handed down in 1857, was entirely proslavery. Chief Justice Taney held that Dred Scott was not free. In fact, he could not sue because African Americans could not be citizens. Taney dismissed both history and the humanity of African Americans. "For more than a century," he wrote, blacks have been "regarded as beings of an inferior order . . . so far inferior that they had no rights which the white man was bound to respect." Most important, the Court adopted John C. Calhoun's proslavery theory of the Constitution. Taney's opinion for the majority—a Southern majority on a divided Court—declared that Congress could not prohibit slavery in any territory.[17]

The decision said to Frederick Douglass that he stood "outside the pale of American humanity." To Robert Purvis, a black leader from Philadelphia, it proved that "the Government of the United States," in its "essential structure as well as in its practice, is one of the basest, meanest, most atrocious despotisms that ever saw the face of the sun."[18] The decision also appeared, on its face, to be a serious blow to the very existence of the Republican Party. Its founding principle, no extension of slavery, had been rejected by the Court. But Northerners were shocked and troubled. This decision alarmed the North as deeply as the Kansas-Nebraska Act of three years before. In the hands of Republican leaders like Abraham Lincoln, the Dred Scott case actually strengthened the Republican movement. Similarly, it increased the stature of Montgomery Blair. One justice, Benjamin Curtis, pointed out the historical errors in Taney's opinion. These were the very facts that Blair had documented in his brief for the plaintiff. Key Republicans continued to look to Montgomery Blair for legal advocacy and political guidance.

As a lawyer rather than an officeholder in the 1850s, Montgomery Blair was writing briefs rather than making speeches. The family responsibility of public speaking for the Republican Party fell to his brother, Frank. Both men and their father shared the same racial attitudes, which Frank ably expressed. Though against slavery, like most Northerners they rejected any idea of equality. The Blairs believed that blacks and other people of color were inferior. Like Jefferson, they were absolutely convinced that the two races "equally free, cannot live in the same government." The United States was to be for whites only, and Southerners could emancipate only if blacks were removed.

Frank Blair spoke out often about the need for racial separation. When

Frank went to Congress, he advocated the gradual abolition of slavery, coupled with colonization of the freed slaves in Central America. On January 14, 1857, he introduced a bill to look into "the acquisition of territory either in the Central or South American States." This land would be "colonized with colored persons from the United States . . . willing to settle in such territory as a dependency of the United States, with ample guarantees of their personal and political rights."[19]

The young congressman listed several advantages to this plan. African Americans were "a class of men . . . worse than useless to us," but in Central or South America they could foster free institutions. They "would prove themselves to be of immense advantage to those countries." Their relocation in Central or South America would block the expansion of slavery while it attracted "the wealth and energy of our best men to aid and direct them in developing the incredible riches of those regions." The United States would be able to open new lands "to our commerce." This should be America's future, instead of slavery spreading into U.S. territories or free states. The nation's territories were to be for free white men. Blair vowed to fight "the oligarchy which rests upon this servile institution" and began freeing his own slaves the next year.[20]

Frank's ideas attracted attention beyond Congress. Before the decade was out, he would carry his message of colonization to Boston, New York, and several western states. Some Republicans agreed with the Blairs that colonization would be "an enabling act to the emancipationists of the South." Others frankly desired that African Americans "shall not be left in this country." Such views were widespread in the Republican Party.[21]

THIS KIND OF supposedly benevolent racism was foreign to Charles Sumner. New England Republicans recognized that colonization was popular, especially in the western and border states, but their views were different. Sumner was the epitome of advanced New England thinking. He aimed to be the eloquent abolitionist in the Senate, an idealist and reformer, rather than a politician. He would embody the progressive, humane thinking of Massachusetts. Sumner's future depended on his reputation, and he kept his name before the people as a foe of slavery. In the middle years of the 1850s, that future was uncertain. Political parties in the Bay State were very much in flux. Sumner's new Republican Party was weak; it was struggling to make progress against various coalitions and against the sudden (though brief) popularity of the anti-immigrant American Party.

Brilliant but pedantic, **Charles Sumner** embraced abolitionist ideals and advanced Massachusetts's reformers as the conscience of the nation.

Repeatedly Sumner stressed ideals. He argued that Freedom must conquer Slavery. After passage of the Kansas-Nebraska Act, he seized several opportunities to speak out. Harriet Beecher Stowe had organized a *"united clerical protest of New England"* against Douglas's bill. Clergymen who branded the measure "a great moral wrong" signed their names to a petition inscribed on a 200-foot-long scroll. When Southerners criticized the clergymen for "desecrating the pulpit," Sumner defended his region's ministers. No man in the Senate, he said, was competent "to sit in judgment on the clergy of New England." They had risen to the moral issue. Douglas's "odious measure" put "Freedom and Slavery face to face, and bids them grapple. Who can doubt the result?" Sumner asked.[22]

One day after the Senate gave final approval to the Kansas-Nebraska Act, antislavery feeling gained power in Boston. The arrest of Anthony Burns sparked a protest outside Boston's courthouse. The protest turned into an attack on the building's entrance, and one guard was killed. Then President Franklin Pierce used federal power to return Burns to slavery. Bostonians of every political stripe were appalled.[23]

Pro-Southern newspapers blamed the trouble on *"Sumner and his infamous gang"* who counseled "treason to [the] law." Southerners targeted him for abuse. They confronted and insulted Sumner in the Washington restaurant where he regularly dined. Verbal threats, Sumner told another senator's wife, included putting "a bullet through my head." He ignored such threats, "except," as one scholar as noted, "to see that they received suitable publicity." The governor of Connecticut offered to come to the capital, personally, in order to defend the Massachusetts senator. Back in Boston, the efforts to intimidate Sumner unified "the good men of all parties in a common sentiment of hostility" to "the slave power."[24]

These events left Sumner more determined than ever to wage war on slavery and racism. Early in 1855, when Congress adjourned, he went on a speaking tour in Massachusetts and New York. In New York City the audience was "carried away" by his message as well as by his "magnificent presence" and "the grand organ-music of his voice, bearing to the heart" his "intense conviction."[25] In his speech "The Antislavery Enterprise," Sumner took the radical, abolitionist position. Despite "bigotry," the African American was "an unquestionable member of the human family, and entitled to *all the rights of man.*" Truth, he argued, often had to struggle against prejudice to be heard, but now it was winning. Eloquently he identified truth with "the cause of the slave." He denounced the "grievous" wrongs of slavery, describing "the flesh galled by the manacle or sp[u]rting blood beneath the lash . . . the sale of fathers and mothers, husbands and wives, brothers and sisters, little children—even infants—at the auction block."[26]

Sumner also found a way to dramatize personally the human suffering caused by the separation of slave families. Harriet Beecher Stowe had showed the power of this family theme in *Uncle Tom's Cabin.* The story of Eliza, the mother who risked everything to keep her child, had touched the conscience of Northern readers. A New England woman, Mary Hayden Green Pike, followed on Stowe's novel with *Ida May.* Pike's melodramatic story centered on a white child kidnapped and sold into slavery. Although less successful than *Uncle Tom's Cabin,* it sold 60,000 copies in 1854 and 1855. Soon Sumner went before the public to declare that such stories were real. He helped an escaped slave buy his daughter out of slavery in Virginia. This little girl's complexion was very white, so white that Sumner called her "another Ida May." Her story and her picture became tools to dramatize the injustice of slavery. Sumner wrote about her in Boston and New York newspapers. He passed her daguerreotype around the Massachusetts legislature and gave a copy to future governor John Andrew. He even introduced the little girl to audiences in New York, Boston, and Worcester, Massachusetts.[27]

Radical Republicans like Charles Sumner fought for freedom and equal rights despite the racism that was deeply rooted in the Northern public. Their commitment was to racial equality. For Republicans like Montgomery Blair, however, equality remained unthinkable, and the party struggled to find a common position. Black leaders like Frederick Douglass often did not know what to think of this new political organization. They saw that Republicans were becoming the "most numerous" antislavery force. Perhaps a "part of the North" would decide "to redeem *itself* from bondage"—bondage to racism. Yet Republicans refused to be "entirely just and humane to the black man."²⁸

The Republican Party's struggle to define its views on race had a personal—as well as a political—dimension for the man who would become the party's first president.

4

Lincoln's Attitudes on Slavery and Race

"IF SLAVERY IS NOT wrong, nothing is wrong. I can not remember when I did not so think, and feel."[1] Abraham Lincoln would make this statement during his presidency. As a description of his entire life, it may well have been true. In Kentucky, where he was born, his parents belonged to a fundamentalist Baptist sect that was opposed to slavery. The young Lincoln would have heard antislavery views in church, and as a boy he amused his friends by repeating and mimicking the preachers' sermons.[2]

But he also grew up in racist Kentucky, Indiana, and Illinois. As a young man he shared in racist banter and commentary. He did not always reject the casual but virulent racism around him. Humane racial feelings and settled antislavery convictions came later. They were the product of personal disappointment that led to significant moral growth. By the late 1850s they differentiated him from other politicians. They became one key part of his outlook on the challenges facing society.

The other part was always a sympathetic, tolerant feeling toward Southerners. He remembered with great affection the boys he had played with in Kentucky.[3] He knew well the farmers in Illinois for whom racism was as natural as breathing. He married into a large slaveholding family. These realities, as well as an office seeker's need to respect the widespread prejudice of the voters, gave him an understanding for Southerners and slave owners. He had an often-misplaced confidence in their patriotism and love of the Union.

Lincoln's attitudes about slavery, race, and Southerners shaped his public positions. Before he became president he was staunchly against the expansion of slavery, but he was not an abolitionist and vigorously rejected that label. Further growth amid the crisis of war would eventually make him an emancipator. Wartime experiences also deepened his sympathy for African Americans. His marriage—difficult and far from ideal—played an important role in the evolution of his feelings about race, an evolution that began in the 1850s.

EARLY IN LINCOLN'S career in Illinois state politics, there was "nothing to indicate the future reformer, either in religion, or morals, or politics."[4] In fact, racism was a standard political weapon in Illinois, and Lincoln used his wit to exploit racism on the stump and in local newspapers. African Americans made up only one-half of 1 percent of the population in Sangamon County in 1836. Yet racism was a political tool for Lincoln and his Whig Party in that year. They attacked Martin Van Buren, the Democrat who was running for president, because fifteen years earlier he had supported limited black suffrage in New York State. Van Buren's running mate was Richard M. Johnson of Kentucky, who had two children by his black mistress. Thus the Democrats' ticket was vulnerable to racist charges.

"In all likelihood" Lincoln authored a letter supposedly written by a black man to the *Sangamo Journal.* The fictional letter writer boasted that blacks would all vote for Van Buren "and that dare tudder man wat lub de nigger so." Why? Because "hese going to sen all dese poor white folks off to Library [Liberia], and let the free niggers vote . . . and den de niggers will be in town!" In the legislature Lincoln and his fellow Whigs had tricked the Democrats into opposing a long slate of resolutions, one of which slyly condemned black suffrage. Lincoln then charged that Democrats did not agree "that the elective franchise should be kept free from contamination by the admission of colored voters." In another letter, Lincoln had a fictional Democrat complain that the "people are up in arms" because "they don't like that a free negro should crowd them away from the polls." The *Sangamo Journal* warned that Illinois "is threatened to be overrun with free negroes." If Van Buren and Richard Johnson prevailed, "how long before poor white girls will become the waiting maids of sooty wenches? . . . How long before . . . the whole population of the country become[s] one huge mass of degenerate and stupid mulatoes?"[5]

Four years later "Negrophobia loomed large" in another presidential campaign between President Van Buren and the Whig's William Henry Harrison. Illinois Democrats charged that Harrison was an "Abolitionist of the first water" who would "make slaves of White men" and "free men of black slaves." In reply Lincoln charged that Van Buren was "clothed with the sable furs of Guinea" and that his "breath smells rank with devotion to the cause of Africa's sons." Debating Stephen Douglas, Lincoln engineered an ambush on the race question. He prodded Douglas into denying that the Democrat Van Buren had ever voted for limited Negro suffrage. Then he produced a letter, solicited by one of Lincoln's friends, in which Van Buren confirmed that he had done so. Surprised and frustrated, Douglas flew into a tantrum.[6]

A few weeks later Lincoln again attacked Van Buren, saying he had "advocated and supported Abolition principles." The *Sangamo Journal* charged the president with "love for free negroes," and predicted that his policies would lead to black suffrage and "one step more—too horrid to be contemplated— and that amalgamation." Lincoln published another letter in which he pretended to be a Democrat quizzing President Van Buren. "We know," the supposed Democrat asked his party's president, that "you honestly consider the negroes, particularly the fat sleek ones, superior to poor white folks; but why, in the name of *Guinea* itself, can you not suppress even your honest sentiments until after the election?"[7]

At this early date Lincoln's talent for amusing audiences with jokes and stories was often on display. Along with it went a mean streak toward political opponents. In what became known as "the skinning of [Judge Jesse B.] Thomas," Lincoln attacked the inconsistencies in a fellow legislator's record. He did so with "absolutely overwhelming and withering" remarks and with such skillful mimicking of Thomas's gestures and accent that the man was reduced to tears. In another incident Lincoln cleverly ridiculed a Democratic candidate for the state senate, Colonel Dick Taylor. Taylor, who accused Lincoln's Whig Party of elitism, was himself a stylish dresser. He "never appeared in public without a ruffled shirt, a blue coat and brass buttons, and a gold-headed cane." After Taylor criticized the Whigs as aristocrats, Lincoln spoke about his own youthful poverty and his buckskin breeches that never reached his ankles. Then he reached out, unbuttoned Taylor's vest, and caused his ruffled shirt to cascade forward "like a pile of Entrails." The crowd responded with "furious and uproarious laughter."[8]

The young Lincoln could be a rough-edged partisan. In 1840 a quarrel with a political opponent seemed likely to lead to a duel. Lincoln was able to defuse the situation. He denied that he had unkind feelings toward his opponent and expressed "sincere regret that I permitted myself to get into such an altercation." But two years later Lincoln very nearly fought a duel with the Democrat's state auditor, James Shields. Shields demanded satisfaction for Lincoln's newspaper attacks, and the two men actually crossed the Mississippi River into Missouri (to avoid an Illinois law against dueling) before their seconds arranged a compromise.[9]

Lincoln's political ambition "was a little engine that knew no rest."[10] That thirst for political success was one of the things that united Lincoln and the woman he married, Mary Todd. The two were, in many ways, an odd couple. Lincoln came from hardscrabble frontier farmers. Mary was born into a wealthy, slaveholding Kentucky family. Emotionally and physically they were mismatched. Lincoln stood six feet four inches tall, towering over Mary, who barely reached five feet. Lincoln had long limbs and a thin, lanky frame. Mary was compact and increasingly plump. Lincoln was outwardly gregarious but emotionally guarded and closed off. Those who knew him best called him "the most shut-mouthed man" in regard to his own feelings. Mary needed and wanted attention. She was self-centered, self-indulgent, and given to emotional outbursts. Among the Todd traits that she obviously shared were "determination . . . obstinacy," an inability to "govern my temper or tongue" and an unforgiving attitude toward enemies. But both hungered for his political success.[11]

Mary's family enjoyed high social position in Lexington, Kentucky. The Todd family was wealthy, had many slaves, and was on friendly terms with prominent people like Henry Clay. (As a little girl, Mary once visited and charmed the famous lawmaker.)[12] Her father and mother had six children, of whom she was the fourth. A fine education and many privileges were hers. Nevertheless, Mary described her childhood as "desolate."

When she was only six, her mother died, and her father soon remarried. This second marriage produced eight more children, but Mary and her full siblings felt excluded or ignored. She never was able to find the love and approval that her temperament craved. Her home in Kentucky seemed emotionally barren. Mary's oldest sister, Elizabeth Todd, moved to Illinois when she married Ninian Edwards Jr., who had a prominent social position there. Soon the younger girls from Mr. Todd's first marriage began making long visits to Elizabeth, their "second mother." Her home was a magnet for ambitious and rising young men, and each of the sisters met her future husband in Springfield. Mary took full advantage of this setting. She was unusually well informed about politics and so flirtatious that "she could make a bishop forget his prayers."[13]

The Edwards were politically important. Ninian Edwards Sr. had been governor of both the Illinois Territory and the state, as well as one of Illinois's first U.S. senators. Promising lawyers, legislators, and officeholders, such as Stephen A. Douglas, socialized in the Edwards home. Though Ninian Edwards Jr. considered the young Lincoln rather rough and socially awkward, he made the ambitious representative from Sangamon County welcome. There, in the winter of 1839 – 40, Lincoln met Mary Todd. There was interest on both sides, but Mary proved to be the more determined to bring their relationship to marriage. She saw Lincoln's undeveloped potential. "Mary Todd did most of the courting," recalled Orville Browning, another rising Illinois politician. She was "in earnest [in] her endeavors to get Mr. Lincoln."[14]

After almost a year, the two became engaged. Others wondered why two people whose "tastes were so different" would decide to marry. In later years Mary Lincoln herself would refer to "our opposite natures." Evidently Abraham developed serious doubts, for within a few months he broke off the engagement. "According to a friend, he had concluded that they 'were not congenial, and were incompatible.'" As public knowledge of Lincoln's decision spread, Mary was humiliated. But she released him from his commitment while telling him that she "felt as always." Her gesture threw Lincoln into a torment of guilt over his responsibility and duty. He became "crazy for a week or so" and had to be cared for by friends. But in time he recovered. The next year he proposed to another woman, Sarah Rickard, who turned him down because of "his peculiar manner and his General deportment." But Mary Todd waited for Lincoln, and after a year and a half they reconciled. On November 4, 1842, they married "with virtually no advance notice." Lincoln looked "as if he was going to the slaughter," said one of his groomsmen. While he was dressing, someone asked where he was headed. "I guess I am going to hell," he replied. His friend Joshua Speed believed "Lincoln Married her for honor."[15]

The newlyweds set up housekeeping, and in slightly less than nine months Mary gave birth to the first of their four sons. But living together was not easy. In terms of her family background, Mary had married down. Always status conscious, she had to give up the pampering and privileges she was used to and take on unaccustomed household duties. Moreover, she was emotionally needy and demanding, volatile and expressive. Abraham Lincoln, in contrast, was reserved and controlled, even unavailable emotionally. He had married up and lacked both social polish and familiarity with the domestic courtesies that his role required. He assumed some household chores, but he always dressed poorly and remained indifferent to niceties like flowers for the table or flowering shrubs for the yard. He discovered that Mary had a short and violent temper and an excessive estimation of what she deserved from the world and others.[16]

Lincoln's law partner, William Herndon, called Mary a "tigress," a "she-wolf," and the *"female wild cat of the age."* His was not the only negative opinion. A Springfield neighbor recalled that Mary sometimes had "the devil in her." When her "unusually high temper ... invariably got the better of her," Lincoln would "pick up one of the children and deliberately leave home as if to take a walk. After he had gone, the storm usually subsided, but sometimes it would break out again when he returned." A carpenter who worked at their house saw her "fret and scold a great deal," and another witness heard her "yelling & screaming at L. as if in hysterics." At times she threw cups and firewood at her husband. Years later, in the White House, Lincoln's male secretaries dubbed her "the Hell-Cat" and "Her Satanic Majesty." The wife of another Illinois politician judged Mary's behavior to be "really a species of madness." Emotional or mental instability was present among her family relations, and as the years progressed her behavior became more unbalanced. At the least, one could say that Mary had a personality disorder or certain demanding and narcissistic traits.[17]

Meanwhile, the Lincolns made progress toward their political goals. Mary urged her husband on and helped him by entertaining guests. After becoming a leader of the Whigs in the Illinois legislature, Lincoln gained his chance to run for Congress in 1846. His popularity with voters carried the day, and he began to prepare for the opening of the session, which in that era's peculiar schedule would not take place until December 1847. That summer he made a speech in Chicago at the national Harbor and River Convention. Delegates from other states heard him for the first time and learned that he was "the ablest and wittiest stump speaker on the Whig side in the State of Illinois." Lincoln also wrote for himself a memo on the tariff question. He analyzed that issue in terms of a principle that he saw as valid for all classes and races. A passage in the Bible said, "In the sweat of thy face shalt thou eat bread." Laborers, Lincoln believed, had a right to the product of their efforts. "But it has so happened in all ages of the world, that *some* have labored, and *others* have, without labour, enjoyed a large proportion of the fruits. This is wrong, and should not continue. To [secure] to each labourer the whole product of his labour, or as nearly as possible, is a most worthy object of any good government."[18]

Traveling to Washington, D.C., with his family, Lincoln had his first direct experience in the federal government. He had realized a major goal, but his single term in Congress proved less rewarding than he or Mary had dreamed. They arrived at a dingy train station that was a disgrace to the federal district. The city itself, according to Charles Dickens, was one of "magnificent" but unfulfilled intentions. It had "spacious avenues, that begin in nothing, and lead nowhere; streets, miles-long, that only want houses, roads, and inhabitants." Washington remained an "ill-arranged, rambling, scrambling village" whose thoroughfares turned into mud holes with every rain. "The houses were insufficiently heated, the hotels abominable." The capital also had a Southern feel, with an active slave market and a large black population.[19]

Racism flourished even among some who later became Radical Republicans. Ohio's senator Benjamin Wade called D.C. "a mean God forsaken Nigger rid[d]en place. . . . [T]he Nigger smell I cannot bear, yet it is on and about every thing you see." Wade complained that his food was "cooked by Niggers, until I can smell & taste the Nigger." Hired slaves served the guests at Mrs. Sprigg's boardinghouse, where the Lincolns took a room and ate their meals. Tending to two young children and finding no social life, Mary left after a few months to visit her father in Kentucky.[20]

Lincoln stayed on at Mrs. Sprigg's, which was known as "the Abolition house." Joshua Giddings of Ohio, fiery leader of antislavery forces in the House, boarded there. Another antislavery boarder from Pennsylvania was known for his "offensive" and "provoking" manner. Lincoln, by contrast, presented his views in an amiable style that defused tension around the dinner table. With his unpretentious and humorous ways, he made friends with Southerners, such as Daniel Barringer of North Carolina and Alexander Stephens of Georgia. "Fond of fun and humor," Lincoln was "ever ready to match another's story by one of his own." He became known for his vast store of yarns. Many of them were off-color. Occasionally some were racist as well, including one about an "old Virginian stropping his razor on a certain *member* of a young negro's body."[21]

But telling jokes was not all Lincoln did. In his brief term in Congress he challenged President Polk with his "spot" resolutions. By suggesting that the Democratic president had purposely started the war with Mexico, these resolutions advanced the Whig Party's goals. Lincoln also supported proposals to bar slavery from California and New Mexico. In discussions about slavery in the District of Columbia, he opposed some measures because he felt their language was too abrasive. These were the votes that caused Horace Greeley and Indiana congressman George Julian to dismiss Lincoln's antislavery convictions. Julian described him as one whose "anti-slavery education had scarcely begun." Yet it was under way. Lincoln offered the bill for gradual, compensated emancipation in the District that was described in chapter 2. It was a thoroughly moderate proposal, yet nothing came of it.[22]

Reaching Congress had been Lincoln's chief ambition. But soon his two-year term was over, and there was no possibility of reelection. An unwritten rule among Illinois's many Whig aspirants meant that someone else would gain the chance to come to Washington. Yet politics had dominated Lincoln's adult life. He was very reluctant to climb down from the small pinnacle he had reached. As his term came to an end, he angled for an appointment in the administration of newly elected Whig president Zachary Taylor. His efforts to gain a lucrative position in the Interior Department came to nothing, however. He declined an offer to become governor of the far-off Oregon Territory. Lincoln would have to return to Springfield, Illinois, as a private citizen and resume the practice of law.[23]

This began a period of personal frustration, disappointment, and, ultimately, growth. Lincoln spent four years of personal trial out of the public eye. Few human beings are ever so fortunate as to pass through life without major difficulties, defeats, or unexpected detours from their desired path. But the way one deals with personal loss and disappointment can be defining. In Lincoln's case it was exactly that.

His climb had been difficult. He had spent his youth among harsh conditions in isolated frontier farm districts. There had been little sympathy between him and his demanding, uneducated father, for whom Lincoln felt obliged to labor until he reached age twenty-one. Then, after striking out on his own, the young Lincoln had made a place for himself among his neighbors in Sangamon County. He read law, went into politics, and gained a reputation in the legislature in Springfield. He had married, perhaps unwisely, started a family, and won election to Congress. Then, at age forty, he seemed to have reached a dead end. His hopes and dreams for the future were blocked. The road ahead looked unrewarding and filled with certain frustration.

Such circumstances can sour the most optimistic personality—which would not describe the often-melancholic Lincoln. They can turn an individual against the world, fostering a bitterness and latent hostility that lurk constantly below the surface, looking for an outlet. In other, rarer cases, they can stimulate a deepening of human sympathy, nurture a broader understanding of the dilemmas of the human condition. In a figurative sense, the enormously ambitious Abraham Lincoln was trapped, or enslaved, at midcentury by seemingly iron circumstances. But he responded to them by growing as a human being.

The frustration and disappointment for Lincoln were real. With his hopes for a political future blocked, he faced a private life that was not happy. Tragedy struck the Lincolns in 1850 when Eddie, their second son, died. Only three years old, the little boy lay sick for fifty-two days before dying. Lincoln felt the loss deeply. He admitted to a friend that he "could never cease to sorrow for that one," even if he were to have twenty children. His pain was far deeper than anything he felt the next year, when his father died. Lincoln had never been close to or even liked his harsh and uneducated father. He chose not to visit his deathbed and did not attend the funeral. But his father's passing was another landmark—a signal that the term of one's life was growing shorter.[24]

Opportunities and possibilities were fewer as each birthday arrived. What had Lincoln accomplished? How close was he to realizing his ambition "of being truly esteemed of my fellow citizens?" In 1851 he told his friend Joshua Speed that "he had done nothing to make any human being remember that he had lived." To his law partner, William Herndon, he said, "How hard—oh how more than hard, it is to die and leave one's Country no better for the life of him that lived and died her child."[25]

At home, life with Mary was not becoming any easier. She suffered from headaches throughout her life, and they did nothing to sweeten her temperament. As in previous years, Lincoln handled the stress of his domestic situation largely by limiting his exposure to a difficult wife. Like other attorneys in central Illinois, Lincoln had ridden the circuit—trying cases in many small towns where the hotels were abominable and the food was poor. By the 1850s the state's growth and development had made this less necessary. "Only Lincoln continued attending courts throughout the circuit." He seemed to crave the fellowship of other lawyers and townspeople, whom he entertained during the evenings with a growing repertoire of jokes and stories. He stayed out on the circuit as long as possible and did not come home on weekends. Frequently he was gone for four months of the year. By his own reckoning, in one year (1858) he was absent for more than six months. The conversation and storytelling among the people in the Illinois small towns seemed to be a balm to his spirit. During his absences from Springfield he never wrote to Mary, and she didn't write him. Yet the loving correspondence between other lawyers and their wives survives. Back in Springfield, Lincoln spent many hours at his office by day and by night. Billy Herndon said that his law partner often left his house again at seven or eight in the evening and didn't return until midnight or later.[26]

In part, Lincoln was giving greater attention to his profession, and he gained in reputation as an advocate. He also prospered more and was on retainer for some railroads. He had an analytical mind that buttressed his talent for talking to a jury. But although he became known as an effective trial lawyer, he was not a great attorney. He rarely read reports of cases and court decisions and was somewhat disorganized. His most conscientious biographer concludes that "Lincoln was a highly capable but not outstanding lawyer." He would not make a lasting mark in the world through his profession. And he knew it.[27] He was a man who felt trapped by discouraging circumstances that he could not change. The political life that had captured his excitement seemed foreclosed to him. His marriage was difficult and often troubled by conflict. His legal career was his business, but not his vocation.

Lincoln proved to have the capacity to meet these frustrations with humane maturity. He looked inside himself and reconciled his feelings with ethical principles. He grew in these years, using them to achieve a deeper sympathy for others, especially for those who were in bondage to circumstances beyond their control. He became more humble, more tolerant, and more convinced that every person should have a fair chance to better himself. As a telling sign of his inner growth, the personal attacks and racist jokes that had marked his earlier career diminished and almost disappeared.[28] His increased stature as a human being was evident as he moved into the next phase of his life—one that was again public and political.

What reawakened Lincoln to leadership was the Kansas-Nebraska Act. He was the leader, the most eloquent voice, of those in Illinois who opposed the opening of the Great Plains to slavery. In his speech at Peoria he attacked Stephen Douglas's legislation. Lincoln's positions stopped short of being abolitionist. But his arguments about the tyranny inherent in slavery had a moral impact. He called slavery a "monstrous injustice." At the same time he appealed to Northern self-interest by citing the South's additional power in Congress, gained through slaveholding. And his insistence that the territories must be kept free of slavery spoke to the aspirations and hopes of poor white people for greater opportunity and self-improvement.

What Lincoln said about the future status of African Americans mirrored the inconsistencies of a racist society. On the one hand, his words suggested that the Negro was "a man" and therefore entitled to human rights. On the other hand, he denied that he was "contending for the establishment of political and social equality." He said, "We cannot, then, make them equals." He also was unclear about colonization. His opening remarks showed that he favored the idea but recognized that it was a difficult undertaking. Freeing and sending the slaves to Liberia was "impossible" in the short run. There were not enough ships or money, nor preparations to sustain them in Africa once they landed. But he suggested there might be "high hope" in this idea. Then he underlined that hope with the words "as I think there is."[29]

These comments reflected a long-held interest in colonization as a possible solution. Lincoln's idol, Henry Clay, had been a leading advocate of the American Colonization Society. When Lincoln eulogized Clay in 1852, he praised Clay's efforts. Colonization, he said, offered "possible redemption of the African race and the African continent. . . . May it indeed be realized!" The next year he spoke to Springfield's colonization society and in 1855 addressed the state organization. On that occasion he raised the question of race mixture and called separation "the only perfect preventive of amalgamation." After admitting that "the enterprise is a difficult one," he quoted an old adage: "'[W]hen there is a will, there is a way,' and what colonization needs most is a hearty will. Will springs from the two elements of moral sense and self-interest. Let us be brought to believe it is morally right, and, at the same time, favorable to, or, at least, not against, our interest, to transfer the African to his native clime, and we shall find a way to do it."[30] This straddle proved politically adequate in 1854 and 1855, when the public was up in arms over the Kansas-Nebraska Act.

Not only was Douglas rocked back on his heels by the Peoria speech, but Lincoln's words stimulated the political rebellion that was reshaping the party system. The Whig Party was crumbling and divided by North-South issues. The anti-immigrant American Party was rising, briefly, to prominence. Other men were organizing the new Republican Party.

Lincoln was slow to abandon his lifelong allegiance to the Whig Party. He moved cautiously toward the Republicans. But many of his principles were already clear in his mind. In an 1855 letter to Joshua Speed, who had returned to his native Kentucky, Lincoln explained where he stood—on constitutional issues, parties, and the ideals of the Declaration of Independence.

Speed, reacting defensively as a slaveholder, had declared that rather than yield his "legal right to the slave," he "would see the Union dissolved." Lincoln responded that no one was asking him to "yield that right; very certainly I am not." Slaveholders had rights, and Lincoln recognized "*my* obligations, under the constitution." But though he was no abolitionist, he informed Speed that he hated "to see the poor creatures hunted down, and caught, and carried back to their stripes, and unrewarded toils." He reminded his friend that during a river trip in 1841 they had seen slaves "shackled together with irons. That sight was a continual torment to me." Therefore Lincoln had a legitimate interest in "a thing which has, and continually exercises, the power of making me miserable." He judged that "the great body" of Northerners now felt the same way.[31]

Speed acknowledged that proslavery zealots were intent on making Kansas a slave state. Lincoln's opposition to "the extension of slavery" went beyond those zealots' actions. He saw the Kansas-Nebraska Act itself

> not as a *law,* but as *violence* from the beginning. It was conceived in violence, passed in violence, is maintained in violence, and is being executed in violence. I say it was *conceived* in violence, because the destruction of the Missouri Compromise, under the circumstances, was nothing less than violence. It was *passed* in violence, because it could not have passed at all but for the votes of many members, in violent disregard of the known will of their constituents. It is *maintained* in violence because the elections [in Kansas] since, clearly demand it's [*sic*] repeal, and this demand is openly disregarded. . . . By every principle of law, ever held by any court, North or South, every negro taken to Kansas is free; yet in utter disregard of this—in the spirit of violence merely—that beautiful Legislature gravely passes a law to hang men who shall venture to inform a negro of his legal rights.[32]

Lincoln also challenged his friend on the gap between white Southerners' private beliefs and their public behavior. Lincoln believed that privately they felt the contradiction between liberty and slaveholding. But publicly, in political contests, they let proslavery extremists "dictate the course of all of you." "The slave breeders and slave-traders," Lincoln charged, though a "small, odious and detested class, among you . . . are as completely your masters, as you are the masters of your own negroes." Though discouraged by Southern behavior, he still felt there was common ground in key values. His knowledge of Kentuckians, slaveholders, and ordinary folks in Illinois told him they were not fundamentally different.[33]

Finally, he shared with Speed his views on party organizations. Explaining why he was not a Know-Nothing (or American Party supporter), Lincoln voiced deep admiration for the ideal of equality. Since he abhorred "the oppression of negroes," how could he favor a party that wanted to degrade immigrants?

> Our progress in degeneracy appears to me to be pretty rapid. As a nation, we began by declaring that *"all men are created equal."* We now practically read it "all men are created equal, *except negroes."* When the Know-Nothings get control, it will read "all men are created equal except negroes, *and foreigners, and catholics."* When it comes to this I should prefer emigrating to some country where they make no pretence of loving liberty—to Russia, for instance, where despotism can be taken pure, and without the base alloy of hypocrisy.[34]

This letter revealed the development of Lincoln's antislavery views. They were not entirely clear or consistent. The same was certainly true for most Americans. Unquestionably, Lincoln was becoming adamantly against the expansion of slavery, but he was saying little about the future of black Americans.

Soon his values would be tested. He was disappointed not to be nominated for the Senate in 1855, but Lincoln knew his chance would come. It arrived in 1858 in the campaign for the Senate against Stephen Douglas. Lincoln wanted to oppose the spread of slavery. But how could he attack slavery without arousing the racist fears of white voters?

5

Warning Whites about Slavery

ANTISLAVERY VERSUS RACISM

As THE CAMPAIGN of 1858 approached, Abraham Lincoln faced an array of challenges. Suddenly, and surprisingly, influential Republicans were praising Illinois's Democratic senator, Stephen Douglas. Some even considered supporting Lincoln's main antagonist. If Lincoln could beat back that threat to his future, he then would face a formidable task in running against Senator Douglas. The Little Giant was a skilled and experienced debater, able to thrust and parry with the best politicos. And Douglas was sure to use racism against Lincoln. Every time Lincoln might denounce slavery, Douglas could raise fears of black equality. Lincoln's antislavery, he could say, threatened white supremacy over an inferior, offensive, and incompetent race.[1] Racist rhetoric came easily to Douglas, as it did to many politicians willing to exploit the dark potential of prejudice.

Northern attitudes were becoming more hostile to slavery, and that gave Lincoln a potential advantage. But if Douglas defined his opponent as an abolitionist, the result would be fatal. Racial equality was anathema to an overwhelming majority of voters. Those who advocated it were ostracized. Republicans needed to be antislavery in a way that distanced them from racial equality.

Lincoln met this dilemma by going on the offensive. He raised the stakes, and his rhetoric, to a higher level. In shocking new charges he pictured slavery as a menace to white America and an immediate threat to the interests of white men. He depicted slavery as invading not only the territories but the free states as well. He named Douglas as part of a conspiracy to *nationalize* human bondage. Slavery endangered free white society, Lincoln argued, and it gave the lie to America's founding values. These arguments could strike home without making Lincoln an abolitionist.

When questions about racial equality were unavoidable, Lincoln was frank: he did not support it. Even more, he favored racial separation. His brand of antislavery would respect Northern racial arrangements and Southern constitutional rights. But in dramatic fashion he warned of a dangerous Slave Power conspiracy.

IN MAY OF 1858, just one month before Illinois Republicans were due to launch their campaign for the fall elections, Stephen Douglas suddenly became popular in various Republican quarters. It was an *"incongruous"* situation, said Lincoln. It also was a dangerous one for him and for the state's Republican Party. What caused this odd reversal, which had included even prominent eastern leaders of the party?[2]

Douglas had finally broken with his party and his president over Kansas. President James Buchanan was pressuring Congress to admit Kansas to the Union under the so-called Lecompton Constitution. It had become clear that a large majority of settlers wanted Kansas to be a free state. But the Lecompton Constitution was a proslavery deception. It seemed to give settlers a chance to vote for or against slavery, but in fact that vote could only prevent *new* slaves from entering Kansas. Slavery would continue, permanently, for all slaves already in Kansas and for their descendants. This fraud on the idea of "popular sovereignty" was ultimately too much for Douglas, who rebelled.

The unexpected conversion of a leading Democrat to the cause of free soil in Kansas caused prominent Republicans to praise Douglas, even to consider an alliance with him. Lincoln knew that Horace Greeley, the influential editor of the *New York Tribune,* "would be rather pleased to see Douglas re-elected over me or any other republican." Greeley's paper was "so extensively read in Illinois" that it "is, and will continue to be, a drag upon us." Lincoln also knew that New York's "Govr. [William Henry] Seward too, feels about as Greel[e]y does." In such a situation it was crucial to stiffen the backbone of Illinois Republicans and remind them that Douglas was unreliable.[3]

Lincoln warned and counseled his party in letters and speeches, and then he seized bold ground at the Republican State Convention. His "House Divided" speech was a call to arms for Republicans in the coming campaign and an attack on Douglas. It was also a startling, alarming statement about the imminent threat that slavery supposedly posed to free white Northerners.

Lincoln began with the biblical image that "a house divided against itself

Known as "the Little Giant" and a power in the Democratic Party, **Stephen Douglas** advocated popular sovereignty for the territories and was Lincoln's great rival in Illinois.

cannot stand," a phrase he had been testing for several months.[4] Divided by slavery, the United States would not be able to "endure, permanently half *slave* and half *free.*" Not wanting to seem too radical, Lincoln declared that he did not "expect the house to *fall.*" The Union would endure. But he did expect it to "become *all* one thing or *all* the other." "Either the opponents of slavery, will arrest the further spread of it, and place it where the public mind shall rest in the belief that it is in course of ultimate extinction; or its *advocates* will push it forward, till it shall become alike lawful in *all* the States, *old* as well as *new — North* as well as *South.*"[5]

Then, unveiling the heart of his argument, Lincoln asked, "Have we no *tendency* to the latter condition?" The rest of his speech itemized the alarming progress of slavery against freedom. It arraigned Douglas as part of a diabolical Slave Power conspiracy at the highest levels of the federal government, and it charged that Illinois and all the free states might soon become slave states in one uniform slave nation. Frank Blair had recently made the same claim in Congress, but no one described the danger to freedom more convincingly than Lincoln.[6]

The Kansas-Nebraska Act and the Dred Scott decision, asserted Lincoln, were parts of a "piece of *machinery*" designed for a certain work — the spread of slavery everywhere. First Douglas's Kansas-Nebraska Act repealed

the Missouri Compromise and "opened all the national territory to slavery."
Then Dred Scott's suit for freedom moved through the courts in a manner
whose timing was highly suspicious. The Supreme Court heard arguments,
but delayed its decision until after President James Buchanan was elected. In
his inaugural address, Buchanan "exhorted the people to abide by the forth-
coming decision, *whatever it might be.*" Soon after, that decision arrived, and
its contents were shocking. It declared that residence in a free state and free
territory had not made Scott free; that no Negro could "ever be a *citizen* of
any State"; and that "neither *Congress* nor a *Territorial Legislature* can exclude
slavery from any United States territory."[7]

Lincoln painted an exaggerated but effective verbal picture of this Slave
Power conspiracy. He used the image of a house-raising, something his
western audience would understand. When different workmen—"Stephen
[Douglas], Franklin [Pierce], Roger [Taney] and James [Buchanan], for
instance"—frame timbers at different times and different places, "and when
we see these timbers joined together" to make a "house or a mill, all the tenons
and mortices exactly fitting," there must have been "preconcert." "We find it
impossible to not *believe* that Stephen and Franklin and Roger and James all
understood one another from the beginning, and all worked upon a common
plan." In this case, the plan carried out by Democratic leaders and the chief
justice was to bring about the spread of slavery and to defend it with legal and
constitutional doctrines.[8]

Stephen Douglas's role did not stop there. By repeatedly declaring that
he "*cares* not whether slavery be voted *down* or voted *up*" in the territories,
Douglas was part of an effort gradually to accustom people to the spread of
slavery. With the other conspirators, said Lincoln, Douglas used his Nebraska
doctrine "to *educate* and *mould* public opinion, at least *Northern* public opinion, to not *care* whether slavery is voted *down* or voted *up*." His legislation also
omitted any statement that the people of a territory could prohibit slavery,
and Douglas and others spoke of the people's decisions being "subject only to
the Constitution."[9]

Then Lincoln made his most radical charge. These statements and events
had created the opening for "another Supreme Court decision" which will
declare that no *state* can "exclude slavery from its limits." Another Supreme
Court decision "is all that slavery now lacks of being alike lawful in all the
States.... We shall *lie down* pleasantly dreaming that the people of *Missouri*
are on the verge of making their State *free;* and we shall *awake* to the *reality,* in-

stead, that the *Supreme* Court has made *Illinois* a *slave* State."[10] The conspiracy was going to establish slavery everywhere in the United States.

In conclusion, Lincoln drew an obvious lesson for the convention's delegates: Douglas was not the man to overthrow the power of the proslavery "dynasty." "[H]e is not *now* with us—he does not *pretend* to be—he does not *promise* to *ever* be." But Republicans should fight their battles courageously, as they did with great success in the 1856 elections. Urging his colleagues not to waver or falter, he ended his speech declaring, "We shall not fail—if we stand firm, we shall not fail. . . . sooner or later the victory is *sure* to come."[11]

Lincoln's radical and remarkable House Divided speech united the Illinois party and energized it for the coming campaign. Lincoln also prepared himself for the tests that lay ahead. He consulted with other Republicans on appeals to the electorate. As the party's nominee for the Senate, he mapped out his strategy and drafted some of his arguments for the debates with Douglas. He decided what he would emphasize, where he would attack, and how he would defend.

Frank Blair, who would campaign for Lincoln in Illinois, had advised him "to drop the Negro and go the whole hog for the white man. . . . [T]he territories should be reserved for free white men or surrendered to the slaves and their masters."[12] Lincoln took this advice in part. He emphasized over and over again the danger that slavery would become national and spoke eloquently about the need to preserve opportunity for white men and immigrants in free territories and free states. But he did not "drop the Negro" entirely. He decided to speak out about the wrong of slavery and the value of the principles of the Declaration of Independence. But at the same time he readied himself for racist attacks, deciding how he would repel charges that he favored political and social equality.

The territories and race proved to be the key issues in the Lincoln-Douglas debates, overshadowing the inevitable squabbles over who had been consistent or inconsistent, honest or misleading. Douglas quickly exploited racism. His prominent position in society did not keep him from using scurrilous racist attacks in order to strengthen his position and damage Lincoln, whom he linked to the abolitionists.

African Americans, Douglas declared, were a "barbarous race," one of the "inferior and degraded" races. Almighty God had not "made the negro capable of self-government." For that reason alone the black man "ought not to be on an equality with white men. [Immense applause.]"[13] He scorned the "abolition lecturers" who traveled about the country citing the Declaration of Independence, and he attacked Lincoln for following in their track and reading the Declaration "to prove that the negro was endowed by the Almighty with the inalienable right of equality with white men." Douglas insisted that the Founders' words

> had no reference to negroes at all. . . . They were speaking of white men. ["It's so," "it's so," and cheers.] They alluded to men of European birth and European descent—to white men, and to none others. . . . I hold that this government was established on the white basis. It was established by white men for the benefit of white men and their posterity forever, and should be administered by white men, and none others.[14]

While comparing Lincoln's actions to the abolitionists', Douglas identified Republicans as the abolition party. In the very first of seven debates he charged that Lincoln and Lyman Trumbull had agreed in 1854 to break up Illinois's Whig and Democratic Parties "and to connect the members of both into an Abolition party under the name and disguise of the Republican party." These "Black Republicans," he claimed, planned to repeal the fugitive slave law, abolish slavery in the District of Columbia, restrict slavery to states where it already existed, and oppose the acquisition of any new territory unless slavery would be prohibited there.[15]

This posed the greatest danger: racial equality. Lincoln and his "Black Republican party . . . are in favor of the citizenship of the negro." Quoting some of Lincoln's statements, Douglas asserted that Lincoln believed in "negro equality." Lincoln had declared "that all men are created free and equal." In Chicago he had said, "let us discard all this quibbling about this man and the other man—this race and that race, and the other race being inferior." But, charged Douglas, Lincoln became silent about his beliefs in the southern part of the state or wherever it was unpopular.[16]

Sexual allusions were especially inflammatory, and Douglas made them repeatedly. The famous black abolitionist Frederick Douglass, he said, did more than campaign for Lincoln. At one of the debates Douglass arrived "in a carriage driven by the white owner, the negro sitting inside with the white lady and her daughter. [Shame.]" Ought "the negro . . . to be on a social equality with your wives and daughters, and ride in a carriage with your wife, whilst you drive the team . . . ? [Good, good, and cheers, mingled with hooting and cries of white, white.]" "FRED. DOUGLASS, THE NEGRO" was "Lincoln's ally," and "another rich black negro . . . is making speeches for his friend Lincoln as the champion of the black men." These charges brought additional hostile reactions from the crowd, such as "Down with the negro."[17]

What was Lincoln going to say about African Americans? Hating slavery, he believed it was wrong, a contradiction of America's ideals, and a stain on the nation's reputation. On these grounds he could appeal to the growing antislavery ranks and even to abolitionists. The territorial issue offered him a way to appeal to the self-interest of white farmers and immigrants. But any connection to racial equality would brand him as an abolitionist, a dangerous radical. And in fact, neither Lincoln nor most Republicans believed in equal rights for black Americans.

Before his House Divided speech, Lincoln had mapped out his strategy. He developed phrases and arguments that he repeated throughout the debates. Sometimes he denied that he was "an Abolitionist, and an Amalgamationist"; at other times he explained and limited his views. The authors of the Declaration of Independence, Lincoln said, "intended to include *all* men, but they did not intend to declare all men equal *in all respects*. They did not mean to say all were equal in color, size, intellect, moral developments, or social capacity." The equality of the Declaration of Independence gave the black man or woman an equal and "natural right to eat the bread she earns with her own hands without asking leave of any one else." To counter charges that he favored amalgamation or intermarriage, Lincoln ridiculed "that counterfeit logic which concludes that, because I do not want a black woman for a *slave* I must necessarily want her for a *wife*. . . . I can just leave her alone." He held to his criticism of the Supreme Court for saying that no Negro could be a citizen. "States have the power to make a negro a citizen under the Constitution of the United States if they choose." But if the possibility of acting on that power arose in Illinois, "I should be opposed to the exercise of it."[18]

When Lincoln wanted to put a positive emphasis on equality, he said that the Founders considered all men equal "in 'certain inalienable rights, among which are life, liberty, and the pursuit of happiness.'" Equality did not exist in fact. Yet the Founders "meant to set up a standard maxim for free society, which should be familiar to all, and revered by all; constantly looked to, constantly labored for, and even though never perfectly attained, constantly approximated, and thereby constantly spreading and deepening its influence, and augmenting the happiness and value of life to all people of all colors everywhere."[19]

But when challenged too hard on equality, Lincoln was blunt. "There is a natural disgust in the minds of nearly all white people, to the idea of an indiscriminate amalgamation of the white and black races," he declared. If that "horrified" Douglas, he and Lincoln were "agreed for once—a thousand times agreed." In the fourth debate, Lincoln met his opponent's racist charges with the round assertion that "I am not, nor ever have been in favor of bringing about in any way the social and political equality of the white and black races." He was opposed to "making voters or jurors of negroes, . . . qualifying them to hold office, [or] to intermarry with white people." Lincoln went on to say that "there is a physical difference between the white and black races which I believe will for ever forbid the two races living together on terms of social and political equality." Since one race would be superior and the other "inferior, I as much as any other man am in favor of having the superior position assigned to the white race." Using his wit, Lincoln then suggested that if Douglas was so worried about interracial marriage, he should stay home and fight in the state legislature against any such measure.[20]

Going further, Lincoln declared, "What I would most desire would be the separation of the white and black races." That made him the candidate most opposed to race mixing. "Douglas pretends to be horrified at amalgamation, yet had he not opened the way for slavery in Kansas, could there have been any amalgamation there?" Separation ends all possibility of race mixing, whereas slavery is "the great source of it."[21] The year before, Lincoln had admitted that colonizing African Americans outside the United States was difficult, "but 'when there is a will there is a way;' and what colonization needs most is a hearty will."[22] Newspaper transcriptions of the debates and of speeches during the campaign indicate that three times Lincoln used the word "niggers" rather than "blacks" or "Africans."[23]

Lincoln preferred to talk about the ideals of the Declaration of Independence, and he did so eloquently. The Founding Fathers, "*all of them* greatly deplored the evil" of slavery. The Declaration's statement that all men were created equal and endowed with inalienable rights was their "noble understanding of the justice of the Creator to His creatures [Applause.] Yes, gentlemen, to *all* His creatures, to the whole great family of man." No person should be "degraded, and imbruted." The Founders had "erected a beacon to guide their children and their children's children . . . [T]hey established these great self-evident truths" against the day when some tyrant should declare "that none but rich men, or none but white men, were entitled to life, liberty and the pursuit of happiness."[24]

Republicans, as the Founders' true descendants, viewed slavery as "a moral, a social, and a political wrong." Like the Founders, they aimed to "prevent its growing any larger." Republicans acknowledged that "[w]e have no right to interfere with slavery in the States. We only want to restrict it to where it is." By putting it "back upon the basis where our fathers placed it," by keeping it out of the territories, "the public mind *will* rest in the belief that it is in the course of ultimate extinction."[25]

The Republican position, Lincoln emphasized, meant opportunity for immigrants and poor white men. The logic of enslaving people "does not stop with the negro." It had been used by kings against the many who came to America, seeking a better life. "[F]or the sake of millions of the free laborers of the north . . . he was opposed to slavery extending one inch beyond its present limits." In an eloquent passage, Lincoln declared that the territories must be free of slavery so that there

> white men may find a home — may find some spot where they can better their condition — where they can settle upon new soil and better their condition in life. [Great and continued cheering.] I am in favor of this not merely . . . for our own people who are born amongst us, but as an outlet for *free white people everywhere,* the world over — in which Hans and Baptiste and Patrick, and all other men from all the world, may find new homes and better their conditions in life. [Loud and long continued applause.][26]

Douglas, on the other hand, was part "of a conspiracy to perpetuate and nationalize slavery." Leaders of the "Slave States" had made an "open confession" that they wanted slavery to become "perpetual and national." In support of them, Douglas was "ingeniously and powerfully preparing the public mind" to accept that development. "[I]n his assertions that he 'don't care whether Slavery is voted up or voted down;' . . . that 'upon principles of equality it should be allowed to go everywhere;' that 'there is no inconsistency between free and slave institutions'" he was preparing "the way for making the institution of Slavery national! [Cries of 'Yes,' 'Yes,' 'That's so.']" Douglas was "blowing out the moral lights around us," eradicating "the love of liberty in this American people." And when he had succeeded, all that would be "necessary for the nationalization of slavery . . . is simply the next Dred Scott decision. It is merely for the Supreme Court to decide that no *State,* under the Constitution can exclude [slavery]." Then slavery would be "alike lawful in all the States — old as well as new, North as well as South."[27]

Slavery was an imminent threat, claimed Lincoln, to free white men in Illinois, a menace to them and the nation's future. Abolitionists were alternately encouraged and then discouraged by the racism in such arguments. The Democratic Party, said Frederick Douglass, wanted to "admit the black man into Kansas as a *slave*," and Republicans "wish to exclude him as a *freeman*." Yet the territorial question had become "the great question of the age." It was threatening the Slave Power. Republicans shrank from "true ground on which to meet slavery," but perhaps they could advance the cause of freedom and "achieve a valuable victory."[28]

With such arguments Lincoln waged an effective campaign against Stephen Douglas. However, the Democratic Party had an advantage in the Illinois state legislature, and that body sent Douglas back to the U.S. Senate. Nevertheless, Abraham Lincoln had made his mark as a Republican of national stature, a future leader. Such leaders would be needed as the conflict over slavery grew more intense and more violent.

6

Violence

VIOLENCE, FUELED BY passions over race and slavery, invaded American politics during the 1850s. It changed society and left its mark on most of the principals of this story. "When faced with its dilemma over slavery, American society . . . responded with violence."[1]

The nation had too many proslavery extremists like John Wilkes Booth. Violence ran like a bright thread through his life. Attracted to the style of the slaveholding aristocracy, he made hot-tempered pretension part of his social identity. When he was only sixteen he had attacked a tenant who rented some of the family's land and then boasted about the thrashing he had given him. His mother allowed hired laborers to eat at the family table, but Booth repelled any familiarity. He would not deign to sit down with them.[2]

Coming from a distinguished theatrical family, he soon built his identity around a career on the stage, and again violence proved important. Aspiring to be "essentially a Southern actor," Booth entered the world of theater through violent roles. His debut came in August 1855, when he was only seventeen years old. The play was Shakespeare's tragedy *Richard III.*[3]

The play begins in treachery. Richard, then a duke, determines "to prove a villain" in conformity with "a prophecy." Through plots and "inductions dangerous," he schemes "to set my brother Clarence and the king / In deadly hate the one against the other." The unattractive Richard, "cheated of feature by dissembling nature," resolves to be the murderer "of [King] Edward's heirs" and gain the throne.[4] In later years, the role of Richard III would be one of John Wilkes Booth's favorites.

In his debut, however, the young Booth played the Earl of Richmond, who slays Richard at the end of the play. In an England that "has long been mad," where "the brother blindly shed the brother's blood," violence is justified. King

John Wilkes Booth's acting won
the admiration of Abraham Lincoln, but Booth hated everything
Republicans stood for, loved the
South, and shared its racial and
social values.

Richard's "cruel deeds," the Earl of Richmond tells him, "have stampt thee tyrant." He adds, "In peace, there's nothing so becomes a man / as mild behavior
and humility; / But, when the blast of war blows in our ears, / Let us be tigers."[5] Twice in 1858 John Wilkes performed this role with his brother Edwin
in Baltimore. Later that year he appeared again as the slayer of King Richard
in Richmond, Virginia.[6] Many of Booth's most celebrated roles would involve
bloodshed and multiple murders.

Booth's stage persona reinforced suspicions that his destiny was a violent
one. For one thing, a strain of insanity seemed to threaten the family. His
younger brother seemed "not of sound mind," and his older brother Junius
feared the tendency toward madness "which father in his highest had and
which I fear runs more or less thro' the male portion of our family."[7] In addition, John Wilkes's destiny seemed especially dark. When he was a young
boy a gypsy had read his fortune. Her blunt prophecy stayed with the family.
"You'll make a bad end," she declared. "I've never seen a worse hand."[8]

But at first Booth seemed destined for theatrical success. As his skills on
the stage developed, his handsome looks increased his popularity. Though

he was not tall, John Wilkes Booth seemed to many an "Adonis, with high forehead, ascetic face corrected by rather full lips, sweeping black hair, a figure of perfect proportions and the most wonderful black eyes in the world." His eyes had a riveting quality that helped to give him "extraordinary presence and magnetism." After a short apprenticeship in Philadelphia in 1857, he moved to Virginia's Richmond Theatre the next year. In the Old Dominion he indulged his love of the South and pursued his dream to become the region's favorite actor.[9]

Eager to show his Southern attitudes, Booth raced to Harper's Ferry in 1859 when news broke of John Brown's raid. This fanatic's attempt to free some of Virginia's slaves failed completely. Many of the raiders were killed; Brown himself was wounded, arrested, tried, and condemned to death. The attack on slavery—the attempt to put blacks on a level with whites—enraged Booth. "Donning the uniform of the city's elite militia regiment, the Richmond Grays," he arrived in time to aid the execution. He "stood in the ranks of armed men arrayed around the scaffold . . . ," ready to block any attempt to free the abolitionist. Booth was proud of his role in the execution. But he also was impressed by Brown's courage and his "bold gamble at changing history with a single violent act."[10]

By 1860 the actor known then as "Wilkes Booth" was gaining fame. As the Civil War began, he was earning princely sums and touring in the South. In the fall of 1860, as the nation headed toward war, accidental violence interrupted Booth's stage tour of Georgia. In Columbus he was chatting in his dressing room with his agent, who was toying with a pistol. Somehow the gun went off, wounding Booth in the leg or buttocks. Canceling several appearances, he had to recuperate for several days before he could travel on to Montgomery, Alabama, where the Confederacy would soon be formed.[11]

When secession occurred, Booth quickly displayed a passionate loyalty to the South. He happened to be in Philadelphia in December 1860 when residents were meeting in the streets to debate the nation's crisis. This was his opportunity to condemn the abolitionists and praise the South. According to a draft of his remarks, Booth argued that those "who preach the Abolition doctrine" have "nigh destroyed our country. I call them tra[i]tors." They should be "stamped to death." Booth declared that if he had them "in my grasp" with "the power to crush," he would "grind them into dust." Boasting that "I saw John Brown hung . . . I may say I helped to hang John Brown," he urged the elimination of traitors and suppression of their ideas. The abolitionists' abuse of free speech, Booth claimed, "should not be tolerated. . . . Men have no right to entertain opinions which endanger the safety of the country."[12]

He blamed all the nation's troubles on "Northern fanaticism." The South was "the brightest half of our stars upon the nation[']s banner." "She has been wronged." To solve the crisis, people must "revenge to right the states . . . prove to the south . . . that she shall have those rights which she demands, *those rights which are her due.*" South Carolina had seceded before a Republican president could even take office, but Booth declared that such precipitous action was justified. South Carolina "is fighting in a just cause with God himself upon their side." To oppose her would be tyrannical. Southerners had a constitutional right to hold slaves and to take slaves into the territories. That institution was not a "sin" but "a happiness for themselves and a social and political blessing for us." Racism, states' rights, opposition to "a great central government," and hatred of reform "agitation" shaped his attitudes.[13]

In Philadelphia John Wilkes Booth's words were violent. Incidents of actual violence would follow him during the war. In some situations he was the hot-blooded aggressor. At other times he dramatized injuries or chose to describe surgical scars as bullet wounds. Rash displays of his growing hostility to the Lincoln administration would also put him in danger, even though he remained far from the battlefields where hundreds of thousands were dying from the organized violence of war.

VIOLENCE, ONE MIGHT suppose, would be totally foreign to the life of a highly educated, literary Bostonian like Charles Sumner. His erudition and references to literature suited him for the lyceum or the lecture hall. But the sectional crisis fed extremism in both North and South and invaded the halls of Congress. Slaveholders described human bondage as a "positive good" and praised slave society as superior to a society of free labor. Abolitionists used strong words and images to warn Northerners about the Slave Power that was deeply entrenched in American institutions. Sumner, in his role as a moralistic reformer in politics, never hesitated to be outspoken, even offensive in the cause of morality. His claims to moral superiority often irritated other legislators, who knew "that he was perfectly willing to compromise or equivocate when it suited him."[14]

The Kansas-Nebraska bill had shocked Sumner, as it did the thousands of Northerners who began to coalesce into the Republican Party. Sumner protested that the bill opened to slavery an area "larger than the original thirteen states" and overturned a sacred "compact" between the sections. The United States should not do less, he insisted, than Russia, which had refused to extend serfdom, and the South should honor its "solemn obligations" dating from the Missouri Compromise in 1820. Recalling the Founders' policy of prohibiting slavery *"in all the national domain,"* Sumner had ended his "Landmark of Freedom" speech with a moral declaration. *"Nothing can be settled which is not right.* Nothing can be settled which is adverse to freedom."[15]

Sumner's words proved to be prophetic. Nothing *was* settled by the passage of Douglas's bill. Lincoln's contests with Douglas were only one example of this fact. The new law proved to be only the beginning of controversy over Kansas, as violence and disorder spread rapidly over the territory. Although some men fought each other over land claims, most conflict centered on slavery, and extremism sowed the seeds of violence.

Slaveholders were intent on making Kansas a slave state. Thousands of men from western Missouri armed themselves and crossed the border into Kansas to elect proslavery officials. A U.S. senator, David Rice Atchison, personally led the illegal invasion of these "Border Ruffians," who captured the election for a territorial legislature. Antislavery forces fought back to make Kansas a free state settled only by whites. Henry Ward Beecher, the prominent New York minister, contributed money to buy Sharps carbines, as antislavery groups sent "Beecher's Bibles" to arm free-state settlers. The territorial governor could not maintain control. Soon rival governments, proslavery and antislavery, vied for power.

"Bleeding Kansas" became an absorbing issue as violence grew. Border Ruffians killed a free-state settler and later sacked the town of Lawrence. In retaliation, John Brown led an attack on the proslavery settlement at Pottawatomie Creek, where he and his sons killed five people. Little except violence and a racist hatred of African Americans united Kansas's settlers.[16] Every month news from the territory magnified tensions throughout the nation and in Washington. In this situation, Charles Sumner spoke out again, addressing the Senate on May 19, 1856.

"The Crime against Kansas" was a fiery, combative, judgmental speech. Sumner spoke for three hours and still had to return on a second day to conclude his oration. In addition to his customary use of Latin quotations, historical examples, and literary allusions to writers such as Molière and Shakespeare, he laced this address with extreme language and insulting imagery.

He attacked the Kansas-Nebraska Act, the South, and individual legislators with venom. Violence in Kansas had produced violent rhetoric. Observing the speech, an irritated Stephen Douglas remarked, "That damn fool will get himself killed by some other damned fool."[17]

Sumner denounced the Kansas-Nebraska Act as a perversion of American institutions and principles. The "madness for slavery" had corrupted the government "from the President to the lowest border postmaster." The law itself was a "swindle," followed by biased appointments, illegal proslavery invasions of Kansas, and the suppression of all kinds of liberties in order to impose slavery in the territory. Douglas's principle of "popular sovereignty" had turned out to be "Nothing for the People." Sumner defended abolitionists and the Emigrant Aid society, which recruited and aided free-soil settlers to Kansas, denying that it had sent arms. Free-soilers and Northerners "inspired by a noble cause" were resisting the "Tyranny" of the Slave Power. Again he emphasized the Missouri Compromise and predicted that "the aroused masses of the country" will "overthrow this Tyranny."[18]

More pointed still was his imagery. Sumner drew on sexual language to attack the South. Its "depraved longing for a new slave State" had produced the violent "rape of a virgin territory." Kansas had been forced into "the hateful embrace of Slavery," and this violation of free soil could only produce a "hideous offspring" that would augment slavery's power. Then he likened South Carolina's senator Andrew Butler, formerly his friend, to Don Quixote, and described Stephen Douglas as Butler's Sancho Panza. Just as Don Quixote had worshiped Dulcinea, Senator Butler "has chosen a mistress to whom he has made his vows, and who, though ugly to others, is always lovely to him . . . the harlot, Slavery." Douglas was "the squire of Slavery . . . ready to do all its humiliating offices."[19] After years of publicity by abolitionists on the sexual abuse of female slaves, these words carried a powerful charge.

As he concluded, Sumner again assailed individual senators, singling out James Mason, Stephen Douglas, and Andrew Butler. Mason represented Virginia, but now, said Sumner, it was "that other Virginia, from which Washington and Jefferson avert their faces, where human beings are bred as cattle." By authoring the fugitive slave law, Mason had identified himself forever "with a special act of [flawed] humanity and tyranny." For Stephen Douglas it was necessary to invent a new word worse than "traitor," because Douglas had betrayed "all the cherished sentiments of the fathers and the spirit of the Constitution, in order to give new spread to slavery." Senator Butler, Sumner declared, "shows an incapacity of accuracy" on all topics. There was no "possible deviation from truth which he did not make. . . . [T]he Senator touches nothing which he does not disfigure—with error, sometimes of principle, sometimes of fact." Then, alluding to a slight paralysis that affected Butler's lips, Sumner charged that the South Carolinian "with incoherent phrases, discharged the loose expectoration of his speech" against a free Kansas. As for the state of South Carolina, Sumner made clear that little would be lost if all its history were "blotted out of existence."[20]

The antislavery *New York Tribune* praised Sumner for adding to his stature as a principled reformer. Abolitionists also reacted with praise. Seasoned politicians, however, were more critical of Sumner's tone, and Southern leaders were enraged. They resented the challenge to their honor.[21] Reaction to his speech would soon reveal the explosive nature of divisions over slavery and race.

Two days later Congressman Preston Brooks went to the Senate chamber to seek out Sumner. Brooks represented South Carolina and was a cousin of Senator Butler. Although he was not regarded as hotheaded or a Southern firebrand, Brooks despised the abolitionists and deeply resented criticism of his kinsman and his state. He had determined to deal with Sumner according to the Southern code of honor.

The Senate adjourned early that day, and Brooks loitered at the rear of the chamber until a female visitor had left. Then he approached the desk where Charles Sumner sat writing. With little warning he began to beat Sumner over the head with his gutta-percha walking stick—a punishment reserved under the Southern code for inferiors. Sumner threw up his hands to defend himself and struggled to stand. But his desk was bolted to the floor, and by the time he had wrenched it loose, he had absorbed a severe beating that eventually shattered Preston Brook's cane. By Brook's own estimate, the South Carolinian had given "him about 30 first rate stripes." Reeling and staggering about, Sumner fell to the floor, bloody and "as senseless as a corpse for several minutes."[22]

The Congress had seen fistfights and dangerous altercations in its chambers before but nothing as violent as this. Even more shocking to some was the attitude of three or four other senators from the South, who had encouraged Brooks and blocked others from restraining him. South Carolina's Lawrence M. Keitt had shouted, "Let them alone, God damn you," and Robert Toombs of Georgia later affirmed, "I approved it."[23]

Public reaction throughout the country was vociferous and polarized.

"Virtually every Northern city held a public meeting to protest the assault." The editor of the *New York Evening Post* asked, "Has it come to this, that we must speak with bated breath in the presence of our southern masters?" A prominent Southern journal, the *Richmond Enquirer,* seemed to give a direct reply, charging that "vulgar Abolitionists in the Senate" had been "suffered to run too long without collars. They must be lashed into submission." While voters in Massachusetts rallied strongly behind Sumner, South Carolinians sent Preston Brooks dozens of new canes.[24]

Sumner's injuries were severe but not fatal. Bruised and shaken, he had deep cuts on his head, one of which became infected and led to blood poisoning. Feverish and without appetite, Sumner lost weight and began to complain of pain in his head and weakness in his back. He had difficulty walking. Francis Preston Blair intervened to help. In the middle of June he moved Sumner to the restful and cooler environment of Silver Spring. At first Sumner spent all but two hours of every day lying flat on his back, but in a week or so he was able to walk slowly and began to gain strength. On July 5 he was able to leave the Blairs' house to go to the cooler North. Later he traveled to Europe, where he sought the advice of physicians; some magnified fears over his health, and others administered treatments that probably did more harm than good. For more than three years, Sumner did not feel able to return to full-time work in the Senate.[25]

Neither his wounding nor his absence reduced the growing hostility in Congress. The violence of Kansas had spread to Washington and was infecting the nation.

Violent emotions surfaced in Missouri as well. Montgomery Blair escaped dangerous confrontations once he had left the state, since battle in the courts customarily turned on legal reasoning and precedents. His brother Frank, however, remained in the cockpit of border-state electoral violence. Politics in Missouri were rent by factionalism and personal ambition, but many voters became most enraged over the slavery issue. Frank was always outspoken, and his opposition to slavery made him anathema to proslavery men. In 1860 he was highly visible as the only Republican elected to Congress from a border state.[26]

The atmosphere there was tense, but Frank campaigned vigorously for the Republican ticket. He also answered calls to speak outside Missouri, making an extensive tour of Indiana, Ohio, and Pennsylvania, "with a stopover in Springfield to confer with Lincoln." But it was in Missouri that he came closest to danger. Before an engagement in the town of Ironton, opponents announced in advance that he would be mobbed. As Frank approached the courthouse to give his address, he saw that armed men awaited him. His "few friends" and guards "became greatly alarmed for his safety." But Frank faced down the hostility. "When he rose to address the meeting," his friends' "fears were soon dissipated when they saw how calm and collected he was, and heard him boldly declare that any man who came armed to the meeting, with the intention to use violence against him, was too great a coward to attempt it." Frank then spoke for two hours, and when he finished many opponents congratulated him and shook his hand.[27]

Frank Blair's personal courage, which proved indispensable that day, was well known. It was a trait of the Blair family that earned the respect of many, including Abraham Lincoln and Gideon Welles, who would become his secretary of the navy. Welles admired the directness and courage of the Blairs: "Warfare with them is open, bold, and unsparing." Lincoln expressed his admiration one year later, in 1861. Frank, Montgomery, and their father were pressing for the removal of General John C. Frémont as military commander in Missouri. Abolitionists like Charles Sumner sprang to Frémont's defense, but the Blairs prevailed. The president explained to Sumner why he supported Frank Blair over Frémont. "Now Mr. Sumner," said Lincoln, "the Blairs are brave people and never whine—but are always ready to fight their enemies and very generally whip them." He also described Frank Blair as "the most honest & best man of the two."[28]

ABRAHAM LINCOLN ADMIRED the Blairs' combativeness, but personally he favored what he called "short statutes of limitation" for political quarrels.[29] Only once, early in his political career, had Lincoln come close to violence—in 1842, when his anonymous, satirical letters enraged James Shields, who demanded an apology and a retraction. Poorly advised by a friend who relished dueling, Lincoln replied in an unsatisfactory way and received a challenge to a duel. Lincoln tried to minimize the danger by choosing heavy broadswords as the weapons.[30] Although the dispute was resolved without fighting, for the rest of his life Lincoln remained embarrassed over this affair.[31] Yet, ironically, he could not escape violence, both organized and personal, as president. "The violent confrontation of the Civil War . . . was a logical outcome" of the passions loosed by slavery and race.[32] Lincoln would have to make decisions that led to the slaughter of hundreds of thousands of men, and his own life would end in an act of violence incited by racism. At the end of the 1850s he moved toward that destiny by shrewdly positioning himself to win the presidency.

7

Ambition, Triumph, and Crisis

THE STATURE LINCOLN gained through his debates with Douglas changed him. It stimulated that ambition which his law partner, Billy Herndon, said was "a little engine that knew no rest." Now his political career, which had once seemed over, might reach new heights.

But to climb higher, Lincoln would have to deal with problems both practical and fundamental. The practical problems were themselves daunting. The Republican Party was a mixture of differing elements, only partially cohered. The turbulent events of 1859 and 1860 posed unexpected challenges even for the most seasoned politicians, and the political arena was rife with maneuvering and individuals seeking advantage.

Beyond that, as an aspiring Republican, Lincoln needed to solve the party's basic dilemma. How could he and the party sharpen antislavery fears without seeming to advocate racial equality or threaten the Union? How could he be a safe antislavery candidate? Lincoln would need to be a shrewd strategist and a leader who seemed both combative and reassuring.

IN THE SPRING of 1860 Lincoln sent a confidential letter to his Illinois colleague Senator Lyman Trumbull. In it Lincoln reviewed political trends and the chances of various candidates. Then he admitted, "I will be entirely frank. The taste *is* in my mouth a little."[1] By this time Lincoln's friends were actively promoting his prospects. But Lincoln's efforts to gain the presidential nomination had begun long before.

How to be safely antislavery was very much on his mind throughout 1859. Arguments against slavery struck a chord in the North, but the idea of racial equality raised fears and hostility. Many other Republicans worried about this dilemma, and some were convinced that they had the solution. Among them were former Democrats like Montgomery Blair who were accustomed to speaking out strongly against equality. The entire Blair family denounced slavery. But at the same time it believed in colonization to remove freed black people from the United States. Only separation, they argued, would remove the danger of equality.

Montgomery Blair was actively promoting colonization in 1859. He reminded Pennsylvania Republicans that Thomas Jefferson had believed in the necessity of separating the two races. He urged Wisconsin's senator James Doolittle to convince the governors of Ohio, Iowa, and Wisconsin to advocate colonization in their legislatures. This appeal met with success, since Senator Doolittle and the governor of Iowa both spoke out in favor of colonization. Soon the governors of Ohio, Wisconsin, and Illinois followed suit. Montgomery Blair believed that any "policy of casting out free negroes from the Slave States upon the Northern States" required removal of African Americans. To him colonization abroad would have three benefits. It would allow the freed slaves to develop their "manhood" under favorable circumstances while it would "rally the North, as one man, to our ranks." In addition, Blair thought that it would "disabuse" Southerners of the notion "that the Republicans wish to set negroes free among them to be their equals and consequently their rulers when they are numerous."[2]

Montgomery's brother Frank carried the family's beliefs into Missouri, Ohio, Iowa, and New Hampshire.[3] In January 1859 Frank made the case for colonization in a visit to Massachusetts, perhaps the state most favorable to abolition. For a group of young Boston merchants, he developed the ideas he shared with his brother and their father. He argued that removing black people would "exalt the destiny of all the races of this continent." It was "a *sine qua non* in every State that looks to deliverance from Slavery" because it eliminated the specter of racial equality. His address, which was reprinted for wider circulation, combined the idea of racial separation with commercial advantage, imperial influence in Central America, and supposed benefits for blacks.

It was necessary to sever the "unnatural connection" between blacks and whites, Blair said. There were "indelible marks of difference" between the races, which had different adaptation "to the various climates of the earth." African Americans "cannot assimilate with our people," and their presence "is a blot on the fair prospect of our country." But slavery was wrong, and Chief Justice Taney's denial of all rights to blacks was "a monstrous doctrine." The "true mission of a superior and enlightened race" was to protect "the feebler races." Blair argued that the United States should acquire land "within our tropics to make a permanent home" for blacks. Then "emancipation will take place rapidly all along the line of slave States bordering on the free." Since whites would not tolerate free blacks living among them, federal funds should assist in the "removal of the enfranchised race to the tropics."

In this plan African Americans received freedom "in regions congenial to their natures," and could enjoy a "government of their own . . . without ceasing to be part of this country." For whites this would mean "a new empire" for "commerce within the tropics of America" and the spreading of "people of our own race across the great temperate zone." The United States would extend its influence to the south, while a transcontinental railway to the west would attract white immigrants. Freed of blacks, "the Southern States will fill up with people of our own race," the image of the United States would improve, and the nation would gain vast new commercial power.[4] Frank's influential father would urge Lincoln in 1860 to propose colonization as a necessary step and the antidote to fears about emancipation.[5]

LINCOLN HAD LONG been a supporter of colonization. But in 1859 he was taking a different approach to being antislavery while improving his own and his party's prospects. First he hoped to limit disagreements among Republicans. In June of that year he wrote to Governor Salmon P. Chase of Ohio about strategy. Anger over the fugitive slave law burned brighter in Ohio than in Illinois. Republicans there had adopted a party platform that demanded the repeal of this "atrocious" law. Lincoln warned Chase that the Ohio stand would damage Republican chances in Illinois; it was simply too radical. He urged that the party needed to be unified. Similarly he counseled Republican leaders in Indiana to avoid "apples of discord." Conservatives and radicals in the new party saw many things differently, but Lincoln urged Republicans to "at least say *nothing* on points where it is probable we shall disagree."[6]

That fall Lincoln went on a speaking tour where the second element of his approach was on display. He promoted moderate and carefully framed antislavery views. Stephen Douglas had just published a long article in *Harper's Magazine* to defend his position on the territories. In Columbus, the Ohio capital, Lincoln attacked Douglas's faulty grasp of history and drove home the point that Douglas did not care about the cruelty of human bondage. Senator

Douglas basically felt that nobody had "a right to object" if "one man chooses to make a slave of another man." Douglas's ideas would prepare the way for legalizing slavery everywhere, even for reopening the African slave trade. But Lincoln also denied that he supported voting rights for black men. He also put down interracial marriage with characteristic wry humor. "I shall never marry a negress," Lincoln said. "If a white man wants to marry a negro woman, let him do it — *if the negro woman can stand it.*"[7]

In Cincinnati Lincoln spoke primarily to slaveholding Kentuckians across the Ohio River. After he admitted to being what others called a "Black Republican," he explained that slaveholders' rights were safe with the Republican Party. "We mean to leave you alone, and in no way interfere with your institution, to abide by all and every compromise of the constitution." Going further, Lincoln added that "you are as good as we; that there is no difference between us other than the difference of circumstances." Praising the "good hearts" of Kentuckians, Lincoln reminded his audience that he had married a Kentucky girl. Reiterating his understanding of what equality for blacks meant in the Declaration of Independence, he insisted that "whatever any one man earns with his hands and the sweat of his brow, he shall enjoy in peace." All men should have the opportunity to raise themselves through hard work. That was the "progress that human nature is entitled to."[8]

In Indiana Lincoln attacked an argument that Douglas had made to minimize the historic importance of the Northwest Ordinance. Douglas claimed that realities of soil and climate, rather than a law, had kept slavery out of Indiana and Ohio. But in fact, parts of both states were farther south than parts of Kentucky. The Northwest Ordinance had been necessary and effective. Denying that the interests of blacks and whites were in conflict, Lincoln argued that they were aligned. Slavery was a cruelty to blacks, but it also injured "the mass of white men," because plantations and slavery damaged free laborers.[9]

Lincoln's speeches were well received, and Republicans in other states, including Frank and Montgomery Blair, took notice. Frank called one of Lincoln's speeches "the most complete overthrow Mr. Douglass [*sic*] ever received," and other leaders were impressed. Rank-and-file people began to talk about him as a possible candidate for the presidency. To further such discussion, Lincoln had 75,000 copies of his speeches in Ohio distributed throughout that state.[10]

He also showed Ohio Republicans the text of all his debates with Stephen Douglas, and they were eager to publish them. A printed edition of the debates eventually appeared, to Lincoln's benefit, despite being delayed by Governor Chase, who also hungered for the presidential nomination. Traveling on to Wisconsin, Lincoln gave three or four speeches in which he underlined his standard arguments and emphasized free labor. The "mud-sill" theory of South Carolina senator James Henry Hammond held that every society needed an exploited class. In contrast, Lincoln insisted that free labor in the United States allowed the "prudent, penniless beginner in the world" to work, save, and improve himself. American society must have an economic system that "opens the way for all—gives hope to all, and energy, and progress, and improvement of condition to all."[11]

To promote his own chances, Lincoln was corresponding with Republican leaders in states he did not visit. But dramatic events soon interrupted this quiet politicking behind the scenes. Extremism of the antislavery variety shocked the nation. John Brown, the abolitionist zealot who had murdered proslavery men in Kansas, launched an ill-conceived attack on the federal armory and arsenal at Harper's Ferry, Virginia. Brown believed in violence as the means to destroy slavery. Apparently he hoped to make a dramatic strike, flee into the Appalachian Mountains, and inspire Southern slaves to join him there. His plan to assault the slave system had financial backing from several high-status Northern abolitionists. With twenty-one men, mostly white, Brown invaded Harper's Ferry on October 16, 1859.

Brown captured the armory. But soon he was surrounded by local militia, even before the arrival of federal marines, who were ordered to Harper's Ferry by President Buchanan and commanded by Colonel Robert E. Lee. Ten men in Brown's party were killed, and Brown himself was wounded. Tried for treason against Virginia, Brown was condemned to die by hanging at the beginning of December. Rumors flourished that armed men from the North would attempt to free him, but no attempt was made.[12] He went to the gallows saying, "I, John Brown, am now quite *certain* that the crimes of this *guilty land will* never be purged away, but by Blood."

His failed raid had two main consequences. Though most citizens in the North condemned Brown, his zeal and his composure as he went to his death inspired some Republicans and prominent intellectuals. John A. Andrew, then a Massachusetts legislator and soon to be the state's governor, organized legal aid for Brown; he contacted Montgomery Blair, who sent a Virginia lawyer to mount a defense.[13] Henry David Thoreau wrote that Brown died in "a righteous cause" and had "a spark of divinity in him." Ralph Waldo Emerson declared that Brown's "martyrdom" would make "the gallows as glorious as the cross."[14] Such reactions, plus the revelation that several wealthy and prominent Northerners had supported Brown, enraged the slave South. Southern states began to strengthen their neglected militias. Southern political leaders attacked the Republican Party, charging that Republicans had incited Brown's violence and encouraged all the evils of abolitionism.

What would Lincoln and Republican leaders do? On another speaking tour in Kansas, Lincoln acknowledged that "Old John Brown . . . agreed with us in thinking slavery wrong." But, Lincoln immediately and sternly added, "That cannot excuse violence, bloodshed, and treason." In another Kansas town he labeled attempts "to identify the Republican party with the John Brown business" as an "electioneering dodge." No Republican supported Brown's uprising, said Lincoln; rather, his party denounced it. Lincoln also congratulated Kansans for desiring to be a free state and emphasized that the proper way to deal with slavery was "through the ballot box—the peaceful method provided by the Constitution."[15]

But Lincoln also found a way to go on the offensive against Southern leaders and their threats. The real cause of slave revolts, he said, was not Republican principles but slavery's cruelty. The bloodiest slave uprising in U.S. history, Nat Turner's rebellion, had occurred in 1831, long before the Republican Party existed. The principal elements of the Republican Party, Lincoln argued, were not abolitionists but political conservatives: former Democrats and "*eminently* conservative Whigs." If voters "constitutionally elect a [Republican] President" and the slaveholding South tries "to destroy the Union," Lincoln stated, "it will be our duty" to deal with the secessionists "as old John Brown has been dealt with." Though he hoped no "extreme measures" would be necessary, he announced, "We shall try to do our duty."[16]

On the whole, the shock of John Brown's raid aided Lincoln by hurting the man seen as the leading Republican candidate: New York's William Henry Seward. Though Senator Seward was actually moderate in his instincts and disposition, he had acquired a reputation as a radical. In some of his speeches he had spoken of a "higher law" than the federal Constitution. His statement in 1858 that there was an "irrepressible conflict" between North and South deepened that reputation for extremism. As threats to the Union increased, Seward's past rhetoric became a problem for his presidential ambitions. Lincoln, on the other hand, was on middle ground. Although Democrats claimed he was a dangerous abolitionist and one newspaper called him "an imbecile" of "one idea . . . nigger, nigger, nigger," most Republicans saw him as an effective, but moderate, advocate.[17]

At the beginning of 1860 younger Republicans in New York City gave Lincoln an opportunity to impress an influential eastern audience. The Young Men's Central Republican Union organized a series of speeches by rising or prominent Republicans at the Cooper Institute. The purpose was a standard political one—to rouse up the party faithful and fire their enthusiasm for the coming elections. But the series was also a means for the young party to assess its leaders and begin to identify who might best head the ticket.

Frank Blair led off with a speech in January 1860. He repeated his arguments for colonization, but with greater emphasis on how Republicans would help the South. "The destiny of the colored people of this continent is to carry freedom and improvement to its rich tropics," he declared. A Republican president would respect slavery where it existed, support a reasonable fugitive slave law, aid colonization, and extend U.S. prosperity and power to the isthmus. Southerners would actually benefit from these Republican policies. Thinking of Kentuckians like his relatives and some of Lincoln's friends, Blair said that many planters viewed slavery as an "evil, thrust upon us." Slave labor was inferior to "free labor." Under a Republican administration, planters could "rid themselves of the human beings whose fate is in their hands" and gain prosperity from "new avenues of commerce."

Blair's tone grew harsher when he discussed the influence that slavery was gaining over the national government. He saw "a settled design against the Union . . . to impose a slave Constitution upon a resisting people." The slavery interest was dominating the government and insisting that everything be "shaped, tinged, and controlled by it." Echoing Charles Sumner, Blair argued that slavery was supposed to be "a local institution," tolerated only where it already existed. Reflecting his family's Jacksonian heritage, he labeled Southern leaders as "nullifiers" who wanted slavery to become "the foundation of an oligarchy." Such ideas were "at war" with America's basic "elements of freedom."

Frank Blair also developed the now standard Republican themes about the nation's history. He quoted Washington's and Jefferson's views against slavery. Like other Founders, they had expected an undesirable institution to fade away as the nation grew and more white labor arrived. Early policies of the new nation had been wise; they aimed to limit slavery and restrict its influence. In contrast, the repeal of the Missouri Compromise reversed history, broke faith with the North, and was a tragic mistake. These were themes that Charles Sumner, Salmon Chase, and many others had voiced. Since 1854 Abraham Lincoln had done as much as anyone to develop and refine them.[18]

The next month, in February 1860, Lincoln had his chance to speak. Realizing that easterners were skeptical of a little-known politician from the Illinois frontier, Lincoln took his opportunity seriously. He bought a new suit for the occasion — one that was still too short in the arms and legs. He arrived in New York early, to rest, prepare, and collect himself for his speech. But what could Lincoln say that was new? How could he make a mark as a potential leader for the party?

Lincoln used skills he had developed as a lawyer to amplify the standard Republican themes, and he again found a way to attack where he might seem weak. First, through exhaustive research he documented the antislavery views of the Founding Fathers. He studied the entire careers of the thirty-nine men who signed the Constitution and the seventy-six members of the Congress that proposed the Bill of Rights. What he found deepened and reinforced the Republican interpretation of American history. Even more, it legitimated the party's central principle — opposition to the extension of slavery.

In various legislatures and political arenas these men had supported measures to restrict the spread of slavery. None had questioned Congress's power to keep slavery out of the territories. "I defy any man," concluded Lincoln, "to show that any one" of the 115 Founders "ever, in his whole life, declared" that "the Constitution forbade the Federal Government to control as to slavery in the federal territories." The conclusion was obvious. Slavery should *"be again marked, as an evil not to be extended"* just *"as those fathers marked it."* Lincoln acknowledged that the Constitution recognized slavery. But the true policy was to tolerate and protect slavery *"only because of and so far as its actual presence among us makes that toleration and protection a necessity."*[19]

Then Lincoln confronted the idea that Republicans were endangering the Union. Rather than being on the defensive, he attacked. Addressing "a few words to the southern people," he challenged every criticism of his party. Were Republicans sectional? "We deny it," he said. Republicans wanted Southern votes and had no policies that "would wrong your section." Were Republicans radical? It was not radical to follow the policy of the Founders, a policy that Southerners "spit upon." In place of the wise views of men like Washington, Southerners "insist on substituting something new." Had Republicans made the slavery question more prominent? No, it was the "innovation" and new demands of the South that had disturbed "the peace of the old times." What about insurrection? "John Brown was no Republican," and Southerners had "failed to implicate a single Republican" in his raid. Republicans continually protested "against any interference whatever with your slaves" and could not be accused of encouraging slave revolts. Only states can emancipate, but "we insist" that the federal government "has the power of restraining the extension" of slavery.[20]

Then Lincoln sharpened his offensive. "But you will break up the Union rather than submit to a denial of your Constitutional rights." In fact, there is "no such right" to take slaves into the territories. The Dred Scott decision was a mistaken judgment, "made in a divided Court, by a bare majority of the Judges, and they not quite agreeing with one another in the reasons for making it." Besides, the Founders "decided this same Constitutional question in our favor, long ago." The Southern attitude amounted to "rule or ruin." Should they break up the Union because a Republican wins the presidency, the responsibility would be theirs, not the Republicans'.[21]

Lincoln also had "a few words now to Republicans." He urged calm and as much consideration for Southern demands as was constitutional and proper. But he warned that the Southerners did not want to hear Republican reassurances. They believed slavery was right and insisted on "its full recognition, as being right." But Republicans should not surrender their principles. They should not allow slavery "to spread into the National Territories" and "overrun us here in these Free States." There was, in fact, no "middle ground between the right and the wrong." In closing, Lincoln called on his audience to "HAVE FAITH THAT RIGHT MAKES MIGHT" and "DARE TO DO OUR DUTY AS WE UNDERSTAND IT."[22]

The Cooper Institute speech was a success. The audience forgot about Lincoln's high-pitched voice and unsophisticated frontier pronunciations. As so often happened, his clearly expressed arguments captured people's attention and carried them along with him. Lincoln emerged as a contender for the party's nomination, someone who should be considered. Taking advantage of his progress, he gave speeches in New Hampshire, Connecticut, Rhode Island, and New York before returning to Illinois.[23] Still, his success was far from sure.

Lincoln himself recognized the weakness of his position. "I am not the *first* choice of a very great many," he admitted. His name was still "new in the field" and he was not as well known as several others. Therefore Lincoln had to hope that he might emerge as a compromise candidate. "Our policy is to give no offence to others—leave them in a mood to come to us, if they shall be compelled to give up their first love."[24] If Lincoln could be everyone's second choice, he might prevail.

His friends and supporters understood that strategy, but they also knew other ways to gain an advantage. Chicago was the site of the Republican Party's national convention, and Lincoln's Illinois delegates knew how to pack the hall, a new building called the Wigwam. Enthusiastic Lincoln supporters created an atmosphere of excitement for the Railsplitter. Meanwhile, seasoned Illinois politicians worked hotel rooms and hallways, making deals and convincing delegates to vote for Lincoln. On the first ballot, William Seward predictably was far in the lead, but Lincoln and three others together outpolled the New Yorker. On the second ballot Lincoln pulled almost even with Seward. On the third he gained the nomination.[25]

The candidate had stayed home in Springfield. When a dispatch reached the newspaper office where he was waiting, an assembled crowd gave three cheers for "the next President of the United States." Lincoln commented, "I must go home; there is a little short woman there that is more interested in this matter than I am."[26] He and Mary had reached a pinnacle of their political ambitions. Only one more summit remained on the path ahead.

Lincoln stayed in Springfield during the campaign, as was customary then. But he followed events closely. Racism was one of the chief barriers to victory. Democratic candidates and newspapers charged that Republicans wanted only to elevate the black man and degrade the white. The Chicago *Herald* warned that a Republican victory meant Negro equality, and equality meant that "monkey-headed, muskrat-scented cannibals from Congo and Guinea" would arrive "in hoards." A St. Louis paper declared that "negro equality" was the central Republican principle. Since African Americans could never reach the "moral and intellectual level" of whites, equality would be achieved by "dragging the whites down." The Democratic *Illinois State Register* said that "worthless negro[es]" would push into "your family circle" and marry "your sisters and daughters." Western racism had its match in New York City. There Democratic papers pictured black men hugging white girls and warned of "Free Love and Free Niggers."[27]

Most Republicans countered these charges in the manner of the *New York Times*. That Republican paper accurately stated that more than 90 percent of Republicans at the Chicago convention opposed racial equality. The party was "pretty thoroughly a white man's party." An Indianapolis newspaper added that charging "'nigger equality'" was absurd "against a party, the first cardinal principle of whose creed is, exclusion of Niggers from the Territories." Conservative Republican leaders, like the Blairs, used racism against their Democratic opponents. Frank Blair assured voters that Lincoln would "respect the rights of the whites."[28]

On the other side most abolitionists roundly castigated Lincoln. He was a "craven wretch . . . against negro equality . . . not to be classified with men." He would be a "slave-catching President" and would support "the ostracism, socially and politically, of the blacks at the North." Wendell Phillips, the outspoken Massachusetts orator, labeled Lincoln "the slave hound of Illinois," a "knave," and a "huckster in politics." The *Weekly Anglo-African,* aware of Republicans' interest in colonization, denounced the party for "look[ing] to the expulsion of the free black American from his native land." Frederick Douglass was a rather lonely dissenter, seeing Lincoln as a man of "great firmness of will . . . fully committed to the doctrine of the 'irrepressible conflict'" between slavery and freedom.[29]

The Republican senators from the Bay State joined in Lincoln's defense. Henry Wilson said that during Lincoln's time in Congress he had been "ahead of the Anti-Slavery sentiment of the Republican party" and that he had grown rapidly "in intellectual stature." Charles Sumner defended Lincoln's character and judged that his "heart is large enough to embrace the broad Republic and all its people."[30]

Sumner did not know Lincoln but hoped to influence him. To strengthen Lincoln's grasp of Republican principles, he sent the new nominee a copy of his speech "The Barbarism of Slavery," delivered in the Senate on June 4. That speech underlined the violent, brutalizing impact that the "character of Slavery" had on the "character of the Slave-masters" and slavery's defenders. Sumner's words were harsh, but they could have described John Wilkes Booth: "The swagger of a bully is called chivalry; a swiftness to quarrel is called courage; the bludgeon is adopted as the substitute for argument; and assassination is lifted to be one of the Fine Arts." This speech provoked so many threats from Southern partisans that friends guarded Sumner, night and day, for three weeks.[31]

The 1860 election was unusually complex and tension-filled. Southern Democrats, not willing to trust Stephen Douglas, walked out of their party's convention and nominated John C. Breckinridge of Kentucky as a States' Rights Democrat. Douglas was left with the empty prize of a northern Democratic Party nomination. Some politicians in the upper South, fearing that the

Union was doomed, organized the Constitutional Union Party and nominated Tennessee's John Bell. In fact it was their new party that was doomed, hoping as it did to preserve the Union by ignoring the slavery issue.

When the votes were counted, Abraham Lincoln and the Republicans had triumphed. He won less than 40 percent of the popular vote and had almost no support whatever in the South. But the Republicans had swept the free states of the North. In the Electoral College Lincoln's victory was clear and decisive. The new party, still an unstable amalgam of former Democrats and former Whigs, would take control of the government. Lincoln, the former one-term congressman from Illinois, would realize the highest ambition that he and Mary Todd had ever considered. His was a triumph to be savored.

Yet victory also meant crisis, for almost immediately Lincoln confronted the very real danger that he would have no Union to lead on Inauguration Day. Angry Southern leaders began to talk more loudly about secession. One after another, prominent Southerners declared that they would not accept a Republican president. South Carolina seemed the most agitated and called a convention for December. Before he even left Springfield, Lincoln faced several weeks in which the Union was in danger. The pressures of that crisis would intensify up to and beyond his inauguration in March.

8

Secession

THERE WAS LITTLE time for celebration. Surely Lincoln and the "little short woman" who was interested in his success shared some quiet moments of wonder. After all, they had reached the highest goal of their dreams. But there was no opportunity to relax. Friends, allies, and office seekers demanded attention. The cabinet had to be selected, various appointments made, and an inaugural address written. On top of the many customary and important duties, a greater question imposed itself. What would the president-elect do to save the Union?

It was immediately clear that the Republican victory heightened the danger of secession. Frederick Douglass had predicted that "[t]he slaveholders know that ... their power is over when a Republican President is elected."[1] Now those Southern leaders warned that they would not live under "Black Republicans." They saw little difference between Lincoln's party and the abolitionists and feared any change in racial arrangements. Before Christmas arrived, South Carolina would decide its future, and that action would probably influence other states. Time to save the Union, many believed, was short.

The pressure on Lincoln came from all sides. Northern Democrats, moderate Southerners, newspaper editors, all wanted him to act, and act quickly. Even within the Republican Party there were powerful elements, mainly eastern business interests, that urged some measure of compromise to avert a disaster.[2] All these groups looked anxiously to Lincoln for some statement or plan.

Congressman John A. Gilmer of North Carolina was one of those who wrote, pleading "the present perilous condition of the Country." Gilmer admitted that he and his constituents had done "all we could" to defeat Lincoln, but now he appealed to the president-elect to save the Union. "[A]pprehensions of real danger and harm to them and their peculiar institution . . . have seized the people of my section," Gilmer wrote. He hoped that "the dangers of the crisis" would excuse his urgent request that Lincoln give assurances about his intentions toward slavery.[3]

From the beginning Lincoln resisted such pleas and arguments. He wanted to stand by the positions he had so painstakingly defined. Beyond that, he discounted the reality of Southern threats. Told by a fellow Republican that there were "men honestly alarmed" in the South who feared he would attack slavery, he immediately objected: "There are no such men." Such claims were merely "the trick by which the South breaks down every Northern man." Lincoln felt his "first duty to the Country would be to stand by the men who elected me." If he betrayed them he would arrive in Washington "as powerless as a block of buckeye wood."[4]

Judge Daniel Breck of Kentucky was another visitor to Springfield. Breck was both a member of the Kentucky Supreme Court and a distant in-law of Lincoln's. He urged the president-elect to appoint conservatives to his cabinet, including some non-Republicans from the South. Lincoln replied that no "prominent public Republican had justly made himself obnoxious to the South." Breck wanted Republicans to "surrender the Government into the hands of the men they had just conquered." Efforts to placate the South meant "that the cause should take to its bosom the enemy who had always fought it and who would still continue to fight and oppose it."[5]

Lincoln took a similar tone with John Gilmer (who was offered a cabinet seat, which he declined). "Is it desired that I shall shift the ground on which I have been elected?" Lincoln pointedly asked. "I can not do it." Besides, he told Gilmer, to relieve Southern fears "[y]ou need only to acquaint yourself with that ground, and press it upon the attention of the South." Lincoln believed he had taken no positions contrary to the South's constitutional rights. Repeating his views now would allow his enemies to claim that he repented "for the crime of being elected." He asked if Gilmer had even read his speeches or the Republican Party platform. He referred Gilmer to the Republican platform and to specific pages in a published version of his debates with Douglas.[6]

After making his point, Lincoln privately assured Gilmer on several issues. He had "no thought" of recommending abolition either of slavery in the District of Columbia or of the slave trade among the states. Nor did he plan to give patronage jobs to Republicans throughout the slave states or put slaves to work in arsenals or dockyards. Lincoln could not imagine himself ever being in "a mood of harassing the people, either North or South." But he added, "On the territorial question, I am inflexible." That issue revealed "the only substantial difference" between white Southerners and Republicans. "You think slavery is right and ought to be extended; we think it is wrong and ought to be restricted. For this, neither has any just occasion to be angry with the other."[7]

Lincoln's instinct for firmness troubled Republicans like Henry Raymond, editor of the *New York Times.* But it received strong support from the Blair family. Both Frank Blair and his father, Francis Preston Blair, visited Springfield and conferred with Lincoln. For reasons of history and temperament, the Blairs believed in a tough line against threats to the Union. Andrew Jackson was their exemplar, and they admired his determination to enforce the tariff against South Carolina's nullification in 1832. The domination of the federal government by Southern aristocrats, they believed, had to end. Lincoln shared their unwillingness to give in to what seemed an unending series of Southern threats.[8]

But nationwide anxiety over the destruction of the Union continued to build. In Washington both houses of Congress struggled to draft a compromise. The House formed a special Committee of Thirty-three; the Senate created its own blue-ribbon Committee of Thirteen. In both committees attention soon focused on a proposal by Kentucky's John J. Crittenden. The key element of Crittenden's compromise was to divide all U.S. territories, "now held or hereafter acquired," at 36 degrees, 30 minutes (the Missouri Compromise line). Slavery would be permitted south of that line but prohibited above it. Public opinion seemed to favor Crittenden's proposal. Massive petitions and letters favoring it poured into Congress.[9]

On the territorial question, however, Lincoln was unshakable. Illinois's William Kellogg served on the Committee of Thirty-three, which was considering Crittenden's idea. On December 11 Lincoln wrote to him in unequivocal terms. "Entertain no proposition for a compromise in regard to the *extension* of slavery. The instant you do, they have us under again; all our labor is lost. . . . The tug has to come & better now than later."[10]

Nor would Lincoln bend before Southerners on the Senate's Committee of Thirteen. Jefferson Davis of Mississippi and Robert Toombs of Georgia were among the committee's most influential members, along with Northerners Stephen Douglas and William H. Seward. In December Jefferson Davis made it known that he and Toombs would support Crittenden's compromise, *if* the committee's Republicans would agree to it.[11] This went further than senators from the Deep South had previously been willing to go. The possibility of reaching a compromise now depended on the Republicans.

To learn Lincoln's views, they sent a veteran New York editor and strategist, Thurlow Weed, to Springfield. Lincoln and Weed spent almost an entire day together. At the end of their meeting Lincoln drafted some resolutions to be shared with Seward and the Republican senators.[12] Lincoln made sure that "they do not touch the territorial question." Instead, he offered three proposals. First, the fugitive slave law should be enforced by a law of Congress "not obliging private persons to assist in its execution, but punishing all who resist it" and with "safeguards" against a free man being wrongly sent into slavery. Second, state laws in conflict with that law should be repealed. Third, "the Federal Union must be preserved." By the time Republicans on the committee discussed these proposals, Seward had already offered slightly different proposals, without winning agreement.[13] The efforts of the Committee of Thirteen came to nothing.

On the very day that Thurlow Weed conferred with Lincoln, South Carolina seceded from the Union. In a proclamation explaining its action, the Palmetto State's secession convention complained of the North's failure to enforce the fugitive slave law. Then it enumerated its fears for the future of slavery. The entire North was guilty of "increasing hostility . . . to the institution of slavery," which it "denounced as sinful." A "sectional party" possessed "the means of subverting the Constitution." A man "hostile to slavery" had won the office of president. Moreover, some Northern states had "elevat[ed] to citizenship, persons who, by the supreme law of the land, are incapable of becoming citizens." Charging that Republicans had announced "that a war must be waged against slavery until it shall cease throughout the United States," South Carolina declared the Union "dissolved."[14]

Though unwelcome, this action did not change Lincoln's course. Two days later, on December 22, 1860, he replied to a note from Alexander Stephens of Georgia. From his term in Congress Lincoln remembered Stephens as "a friend." For that reason he offered some reassurance, but it was "for your own eye only" and was concise, even terse. "Do the people of the South really entertain fears that a Republican administration would, *directly,* or *indirectly,* interfere with their slaves, or with them, about their slaves?" Lincoln asked. There was "no cause for such fears." Then he added the words he had used with John Gilmer: "You think slavery is *right* and ought to be extended; while we think it is *wrong* and ought to be restricted. That I suppose is the rub. It certainly is the only substantial difference between us."[15]

As the new year began, Lincoln remained in Springfield, but hardly in isolation from national events. Letters and visitors arrived as frequently as news of important events. The mail brought many threats of "assassination, mayhem, fire and brimstone." John Nicolay said that Lincoln's "mail is infested with brutal and vulgar menace." One man who actually signed his name wrote "God damn you" over and over, while "A young creole" told Lincoln, "You will be shot on the 4th of March . . . we are decided and our aim is sure." Lincoln tried to ignore these threats, but when Major David Hunter repeatedly sent warnings, Lincoln took him more seriously.[16] Hunter would accompany the president-elect on his route to Washington.

Letters with a friendly tone came from the Blair family. Francis Preston Blair Sr. wrote from Washington and offered to send reports on the developing situation in the nation's capital. Looking ahead to February, Montgomery Blair invited Mr. and Mrs. Lincoln to stay with him, rather than in a hotel, before the inauguration. Blair House contained the room that "General Jackson intended to occupy after leaving the White house," and Lincoln could "begin where he left."[17] From various quarters, advice on appointments poured in. Work on the staffing of the new administration continued, but little about the situation was normal.

The dismantling of the Union gathered speed. On January 9 Mississippi adopted an ordinance of secession. Florida followed the next day, and Alabama the day after that. At intervals of about a week, Georgia and then Louisiana seceded, and on February 1 Texas began its process of leaving the Union. Lincoln saw that before he could take the oath of office on March 4, the states of the Deep South would have left the Union.

Most of these states chose to issue declarations about their actions. Like South Carolina, they named slavery and race as their central concerns. "Our position," proclaimed Mississippi's convention, "is thoroughly identified with the institution of slavery." "None but the black race can bear exposure to the tropical sun," claimed the convention, which saw no choice but "submission to the mandates of abolition, or a dissolution of the Union." Alabama complained that the victory of "a sectional party, avowedly hostile" to slavery was "insulting and menacing." Georgia insisted on "the political and social inequality of the African race" and condemned the Republican Party as "antislavery in its mission and its purpose." Georgia was seceding "to avoid the desolation of our homes, our altars, and our firesides." Texans declared "as undeniable truths" that the nation was "established exclusively by the white race," that African Americans "were rightfully held and regarded as an inferior and dependent race," and that slavery was "justified" by "the revealed will of the Almighty Creator."[18]

Still a private citizen with no governmental authority, Lincoln could do little except to comment or advise. The deteriorating situation softened his stance only a little. On maintaining the Union and arresting the spread of slavery Lincoln remained adamant. When Francis Preston Blair sent information about General Winfield Scott's view of the military situation, Lincoln gratefully replied. It gave him an opportunity to stiffen military thinking. If forts were "given up before the inaugeration [*sic*]," Lincoln wrote, "the General must retake them afterwards." On February 1 he told Seward that the territories were key. He was inflexible on the territories but cared comparatively little about such issues as fugitive slaves, the District of Columbia, the slave trade in the slave states, "and whatever springs of necessity from the fact that the institution is amongst us." Consequently, he was exasperated when Congress, just days before the inauguration, organized the Colorado, Nevada, and Dakota territories with no provision excluding slavery. "I only wish I could have got there," said Lincoln, "to lock the door before the horse was stolen."[19]

His work on cabinet appointments continued. Sensitive egos and the demands of various states and party factions turned this task into a delicate and protracted minuet. Lincoln was determined from the outset to bring major Republican figures into his cabinet. A balance of former Democrats and former Whigs also seemed essential in such a new, diverse, and compound political organization. From December into the first days of March, Lincoln consulted, planned, flattered, and balanced interests to get the cabinet he wanted.

Seward was so prominent that from the start Lincoln thought of him for secretary of state. He also wanted Salmon Chase, whose record Lincoln admired though he had never actually met the vain and ambitious Ohioan. As secretary of the treasury Chase would handle a difficult task rather well while scheming for higher office. Edward Bates of Missouri agreed to be attorney general, and Gideon Welles of Connecticut accepted the post of secretary of the navy. Indiana's Caleb Smith agreed to be interior secretary, but naming the Pennsylvania political boss Simon Cameron to the War Department proved contentious (and soon unwise).[20]

The many who recommended Montgomery Blair for a position in the cabinet noted the importance of melding the diverse elements of the Republican Party. As early as November 20, Ohio's Benjamin Wade joined with New York's Preston King in urging that Blair should have an appointment. "The

A rival for the Republican nomination, **Edward Bates** was one of many Republicans who could not imagine a nation in which the races were equal.

zeal and ability with which that whole family" had promoted the Republican Party weighed heavily in their favor. "An additional and powerful reason why the appointment should be made" was "the fact that they live in a Slave State [Maryland] and are from the old Democratic party." In the middle of December Lyman Trumbull argued that "besides his personal fitness," Montgomery Blair came "from the South" and had "Democratic antecedents." Others pointed out that he "represent[ed] the views of the old Jackson portion of the Republican party," and Maryland Republicans stressed the race issue. "He has the addition[al] qualification of having studied the great social question of slavery more thoroughly than almost any man in America, always excepting Mr. Jefferson." Like Jefferson, Montgomery Blair recognized "the importance of providing homes for the emancipated as an essential and indispensable counterpoint to emancipation."[21] Blair become postmaster general, a post from which he would give Lincoln staunch support.

Before the cabinet was fully set, the Lincolns set out for Washington. Their trip consumed twelve days, and everything Lincoln said or did went under a microscope. Cheering crowds in Springfield, Indianapolis, Indiana, and Columbus, Ohio, buoyed his spirits. At most stops he tried to say little and be optimistic in what he did say. But in Philadelphia, at Independence Hall, he grew more serious. He identified the Declaration of Independence as the source of all his political feelings. The Declaration gave "hope to the world for all future time . . . [and] promise that in due time the weights should be lifted from the shoulders of all men, and that *all* should have an equal chance." Immediately a Democratic newspaper charged that this meant emancipation and enfranchisement for African Americans.[22]

Such extreme charges did not trouble Lincoln, who said he would "rather be assassinated" than surrender that principle of the Declaration. Talk of assassination had loomed up as the presidential party planned its route to Baltimore, where pro-Southern sentiment was strong. The detective Allan Pinkerton sent undercover agents to the city. There he found reason to doubt the loyalty of the police force and soon learned of a serious plot. Pinkerton himself heard the group's leader declare, "If I alone must do it, I shall. Lincoln shall die in this city."[23]

Warnings of violence from Pinkerton and others convinced Lincoln to travel quietly by night through the city, arriving in Washington one day earlier than planned. This change of plans succeeded without incident, except for the anger and belligerent noncooperation of Mary Todd Lincoln. Enraged that she was to stay behind on the original schedule, she argued loudly and publicly, compromising the secrecy of the arrangements. The Pennsylvania editor and politician Alexander K. McClure decided she was "a hopeless fool" and never spoke to her again.[24]

The atmosphere in Washington was little better than Baltimore. The nation's capital had always been a Southern city, and now the crisis had heightened pro-Southern sentiment. Democrats had dominated the city's social life through the 1850s. The "Black Republicans" were not welcome with the "resident elite," many of whom "were Secessionists or in sympathy with Secessionists." Secretary of the Navy Gideon Welles described the atmosphere as "thick with treason." The *New York Tribune* would praise Lincoln for ignoring "villains who had threatened to shoot him." Even as Southern Democrats left Congress, some Northern Democrats sympathized with the rebels and wanted Lincoln's administration to fail.[25]

It was in this climate that Lincoln put the finishing touches on his Inaugural Address. In the Union's crisis, with secession well under way, it was sure to be an unusually important statement. His words could foster unity or further division. Lincoln needed to defend and uphold the Union, but could he do it in a way that would not precipitate war? How far should he go to calm Southern fears and allay discontent in the upper South?

A misperception shaped part of Lincoln's approach and colored many of his later actions. Knowing border state Southerners as he did and feeling some connection to them, Lincoln believed that there was a deep vein of Unionism in the South. He hoped that Virginia and other border states would remain in the Union. If they did, sentiment then might shift in the states that had already seceded, as Unionism and sober second thoughts emerged.[26]

Lincoln showed his text to only three men. Francis Blair Sr. counseled him on content and tone, along with Secretary of State Seward and Illinois Republican Orville Browning. A key word of advice that Lincoln received from these advisers was that if conflict were to occur, "it is very important that the traitors shall be the aggressors." For that reason the president said, "The government will not assail you. You can have no conflict, without being yourselves the aggressors." To this he added, "*You* have no oath registered in Heaven to destroy the government, while *I* shall have the most solemn one to 'preserve, protect and defend' it."[27]

Lincoln used the very beginning of his address to offer reassurance to the people of the South. "Nearly all" his published speeches contained "ample evidence" that Southerners had no reason to fear that "their property, and their peace, and personal security" would be endangered. He quoted one of these earlier statements: "I have no purpose, directly or indirectly, to interfere with the institution of slavery in the States where it exists. I believe I have no lawful right to do so, and I have no inclination to do so." In addition, he cited the Republican Party's platform, which stated that "the right of each State to order and control its own domestic institutions according to its own judgment exclusively" was "essential to that balance of power on which the perfection and endurance of our political fabric depend." This platform, Lincoln added, was "a law" to Republicans "and to me."

Later in his speech he went even further. Congress had proposed a constitutional amendment providing "that the federal government, shall never interfere with the domestic institutions of the States, including that of persons held to service." This proposed amendment would now go before the states for rejection or ratification. The president had no constitutional role in this process. Yet Lincoln went "so far as to say that, holding such a provision to now be implied constitutional law, I have no objection to its being made express, and irrevocable."

On the most controversial issues, he appealed to reason and to reasonable men. Southerners had no need to fear his administration, as the Founders had limited the power of the central government. Elected officials had "but little power for mischief," and the people had the power to change that government "at very short intervals." Surely a fugitive slave law could be drawn that would safeguard liberty and respect the rights of citizens of all the states. Slavery in the territories was one of those questions on which the Constitution gave no "express" and clear statement. Discussion, even of Supreme Court decisions, would necessarily continue in a government controlled by the people. Again he acknowledged that Northerners and Southerners disagreed over the morality of slavery. Such differences over slavery "cannot be perfectly cured," but they would "be *worse* . . . after the separation of the sections than before."

Lincoln's words on the Union were strong and unequivocal. "[T]he Union of these States is perpetual," he declared. Not only did the Founders and the Constitution intend for the government to "endure forever," but "the central idea of secession, is the essence of anarchy." Majority rule was "the only true sovereign of a free people." Secession, by contrast, would breed further secession by any dissatisfied minority. Lincoln's oath required him to "take care . . . that the laws of the Union be faithfully executed in all the States." And his duty was not only to administer the government but also "to transmit it, unimpaired" to his successor.

Lincoln promised "to hold, occupy, and possess the property, and places belonging to the government, and to collect the duties and imposts." But he sought to avoid collision and offered conciliatory words. There would be "no invasion—no using of force against . . . the people anywhere" and no forcing of "obnoxious strangers among the people." He would try to promote "a peaceful solution of the national troubles, and a restoration of fraternal sympathies and affections." His closing words about the "mystic chords of memory" that might "yet swell the chorus of the Union" testified to his hope for peace.

The fate of that hope depended on events in the days ahead. Lincoln knew that they would be trying days, days that would spell the difference between peace in a slaveholding nation and a civil war of untold consequences. The inauguration was over and the responsibilities of office had begun.

9

Making War and Alliances

"THE FIRST THING that was handed to me when I came from the inauguration," said Abraham Lincoln, "was the letter from Maj. Anderson [in Fort Sumter] saying that their provisions would be exhausted before an expedition could be sent to their relief." The new president told Senator Orville Browning, "Of all the trials I have had since I came here, none begin to compare with those I had between the inauguration and the fall of Fort Sumter. They were so great that could I have anticipated them, I would not have believed it possible to survive them."[1]

Lincoln's first weeks in office were a time of tense strategy and diplomacy. They involved contests for influence within the administration, and they culminated in war. Once armed hostilities began, new questions about the goals of the war came into play. The anxious president focused on the immediate difficulties of preserving the Union. Some, however, looked far beyond 1861 and saw great opportunities in the crisis: both Charles Sumner and Montgomery Blair pressed for new, ambitious, and radically different agendas. In this period of crisis Lincoln strengthened his relationship with both of them. Little did he imagine how much the war would change many accepted ways of thinking, including his own. Neither he nor others foresaw how destructive the war would be.

AS HE TOOK OFFICE, Lincoln remained hopeful that war could be avoided. He thought he knew and understood slaveholding Southerners, at least the Southerners who were his friends in the border states. Joshua Speed, his "only truly intimate friend," lived in Kentucky. They had roomed together in Springfield when Lincoln began his legal career, and Speed had supported the young

Lincoln in times of personal crisis. The Todds of Kentucky and the Blairs of Maryland and Missouri were further examples of antislavery Southerners with whom Lincoln shared a mutual understanding. He got on well with many of the Todds. Ben Hardin Helm, the son of a Kentucky governor and the husband of Mary's sister Emilie, was on close terms with Lincoln. In 1857 he had spent a week with the Lincolns, and the two men "developed a genuine rapport." Ben Helm believed Kentuckians would "go for compensated emancipation," the only kind of emancipation that Lincoln had ever endorsed. The men in the Blair family owned slaves, but they were liberating them, acting on their antislavery principles. Their beliefs and the political skills they demonstrated as they built the Republican Party had gained Lincoln's confidence. Lincoln even felt a tie to Southerners that was deeply personal. He always believed that his intelligence came from a planter, a "nobleman — so called of Virginia," who had taken advantage of Lincoln's maternal grandmother and fathered his mother, Nancy Hanks.[2]

Lincoln believed that there were deep reservoirs of Unionism in the South. Pride in the United States had been strong throughout the country in the prewar decades. Surely these sentiments could still come to the surface and counter the hasty overreaction of Deep South states. He had special confidence in Virginia. Once the constitutionally responsible character of his administration became clear, a reaction would begin. With eight of the fifteen slaveholding states still in the Union, those Southerners who had seceded might begin to reconsider their hasty, premature secession. In that way Lincoln thought that a return to the Union was possible.[3]

The president was mistaken. He overestimated the loyalty of Virginia and the upper South, particularly once fighting began. Lincoln's old rival Stephen Douglas had a truer estimate of Southern feelings and was desperate about the danger to the Union. In April, as he was driving in his carriage, Douglas caught sight of Gideon Welles, secretary of the navy. Hoping to alert the administration, Douglas jumped to the ground and seized Welles's attention. "The whole South," he warned him, was "united and in earnest." Douglas was convinced that Southerners planned to attack Fort Sumter in Charleston harbor, and would do so soon.[4]

William Henry Seward was both less worried and dangerously overconfident. More than Lincoln, he believed that war could be averted, and he was determined to be the peacemaker. Seward suffered at this point from a wildly inflated opinion of himself. Throughout the 1850s he had been the nation's most prominent Republican, the man who should have received the party's nomination. It seemed outrageous to him that a lesser-known politician from frontier Illinois had displaced him. The new president was "a clown, a clod," someone to be outmaneuvered.[5] When Seward visited Lincoln in Springfield, he was rather rude, and their meeting was awkward. Though he accepted the post of secretary of state, Seward was not prepared to be subordinate. He intended to dominate the administration.

Seward told a foreign diplomat that the United States' president was like a constitutional monarch in Europe. As "leader of the ruling party," Seward would direct affairs. Before the inauguration he set to work to do just that. On the floor of Congress and in conferences with Southern leaders, he worked to remove anything that might "stand in the way of the restoration of the American Union." He even predicted, shortly before the inauguration, that he would have "this whole matter . . . satisfactorily settled within sixty days." If not, he told a Southerner, "I will give you my head for a football."[6]

To achieve this result he thought "the negro question must be dropped" and concessions made to the seceded states. Abolitionist Republicans like Charles Sumner distrusted Seward. Earlier, as Southern states seceded, the Massachusetts abolitionist had "almost hysterically denounced" Seward's efforts at compromise. But few knew for certain what the secretary of state was doing. Behind Lincoln's back he communicated indirectly with envoys from the newly formed Confederate government and promised that Fort Sumter would be evacuated.[7]

Lincoln's intentions were very different. At his first cabinet meeting he was astonished and upset to be informed that Fort Sumter "*must* be evacuated." The army's highest officer, General Winfield Scott, declared that there was no way to defend the fort. Although Lincoln instructed him to "exercise all possible vigilance for the maintenance of all" military installations, Scott did nothing. The time to save Sumter "had passed away nearly a month ago," said Scott, and on March 11 he drafted an order to its commander, Major Robert Anderson, to evacuate.[8]

At this crucial juncture Montgomery Blair gave Lincoln strong and timely support. He objected strenuously in the cabinet meeting and prepared to resign in protest if Fort Sumter were abandoned. He also talked with his father, who thought General Scott's attitude was craven. The very next day Francis Preston Blair called at the White House. He told Lincoln that "the surrender of Fort Sumter was virtually a surrender of the Union unless under irresistible

Well-read and a skillful lawyer, **Montgomery Blair** proved to be one of the most loyal supporters Lincoln had during his presidency.

force." To lose the fort would be to "lose . . . irrevocably the public confidence" and give to secession "a recognition of its constitutionality." He even warned of impeachment. The elder Blair feared that he might have gone too far and been "impertinent."[9] But he need not have worried. The will to defend the fort was a sentiment that Lincoln welcomed.

Even better, Montgomery Blair offered an alternative to General Scott's attitude of resignation. On March 12 he met with his brother-in-law Gustavus Fox, a former naval officer who had a plan to supply the needed provisions to Fort Sumter. The next day he and Fox briefed the president and then the cabinet. Lincoln requested an opinion in writing from every cabinet member. Only Montgomery Blair gave unconditional support to Fox's plan. Lincoln was impressed but decided, in the face of such reactions, to wait, sending Fox to Charleston to gather more information.[10] Still, these events were the first of several that solidified and deepened the mutual confidence between Lincoln and the Blairs. They would agree almost totally on policy for more than three years.

Gustavus Fox returned from Charleston and reported that his plan would work. At the same time Lincoln began planning to reinforce Fort Pickens in Florida. Then, on March 27 General Scott urged the abandonment of *both* Fort Pickens and Fort Sumter. Lincoln was shocked and called a cabinet meeting for the next day. In that meeting Montgomery Blair again played a major role. He broke "a very oppressive silence" in the room to denounce Scott for giving political rather than military advice. It was undeniable, after all, that Fort Pickens was located well offshore and was easily defended. Lincoln chose to ignore Scott's advice. Preparations for naval missions to both forts went forward. When an angry Seward privately announced to Lincoln that he, Seward, should run the administration, the president quietly and calmly put Seward in his place. Soon the secretary of state learned to be a loyal subordinate to his chief.[11]

Lincoln still had faith in Virginia's Unionism. "For more than a month after his inauguration," noted Secretary of the Navy Gideon Welles, "President Lincoln indulged the hope, I may say a felt confidence" that Virginia would ultimately not secede but would "adhere to the Union." He wanted "to conciliate the people and strengthen their attachment to the Government." On April 3 Lincoln sent a message to Unionists in the Virginia convention and requested a meeting. It is certain that he gave assurance on three points: he would enforce the fugitive slave law "better than it has ever been"; he would protect slavery in the states where it existed; and he would let Southerners staff federal offices in the South. Most evidence indicates that he also offered to abandon Fort Sumter if Virginia's convention would adjourn *sine die,* keeping that important state in the Union.[12] But the convention stayed in session.

On April 6 Lincoln sent word to South Carolina's governor that a peaceful attempt to resupply Fort Sumter would be made. At the same time he ordered another mission to Fort Pickens. But Seward's overreaching caused a serious problem at this point. Because Seward had gone around the secretary of the navy, miscommunications occurred and a vessel vital to the Charleston expedition instead headed to Florida. The extent of Seward's earlier meddling became clear, but Lincoln generously "took upon himself the whole blame." In the end, the mix-up did not matter, because on April 12, before the resupply expedition could reach Charleston, Confederates opened fire on the fort. Major Anderson surrendered the next day, and the war had begun.[13]

On April 15 Lincoln called on the states to furnish 75,000 militia to put down "combinations too powerful to be suppressed by the ordinary course of judicial proceedings." By law these militiamen could serve for only thirty days after Congress assembled. Despite indicating that "the perpetuity of popular government" was in question, Lincoln still extended an olive branch, saying that "the utmost care will be observed" in reclaiming federal property "to avoid any . . . disturbance of peaceful citizens in any part of the country."[14]

That conciliatory gesture accomplished nothing. On April 17 Virginia seceded. Lincoln was in disbelief and said he was "not yet prepared to believe that one of the founders of the Union, and the mother of so many of its rulers, was yet ready to break down her own work and blast her own glorious history by this act of treason." He had Francis Preston Blair meet with Robert E. Lee to see whether the general would be willing to command the federal army. But Lee refused, and the state of Virginia was not alone. In short order Arkansas, North Carolina, and Tennessee also seceded and joined the Confederacy.[15] Among slave states, only Missouri, Kentucky, Maryland, and Delaware remained in the Union—barely so, in the case of the first three.

Washington, D.C., now endured weeks of great anxiety and near panic. Surrounded as it was by Virginia and the slave state of Maryland, the nation's capital was virtually without military protection. On April 18 telegraph wires were cut, leaving the city in isolation. Kansas's senator Jim Lane improvised some "Frontier Guards" who drilled "in the East Room" of the White House and "bivouac[ed] on the velvet carpet among stacks of new muskets and freshly opened ammunition boxes." Yet for days no additional soldiers arrived. "Why don't they come! Why don't they come!" said Lincoln. By April 24 Lincoln anxiously watched for any sign of ships steaming up the Potomac to bring help. Despairingly he told a few volunteers who were present, "I don't believe there is any North. . . . R[hode] Island is not known in our geography any longer. *You* are the only Northern realities." When New York's Seventh Regiment finally arrived the next day, Lincoln was "the happiest-looking man in town."[16]

As frenzied efforts began to raise, equip, and train an army, Lincoln started to build a surprisingly close relationship with Charles Sumner. Two men could hardly be more different in background, education, and temperament, yet they would meet frequently and see much of each other both socially and in the public's business.

The issue that initially brought them together was foreign policy. Secretary of State Seward was in a blustering and bellicose mood in the early days of the war, and Lincoln wisely sensed that he needed to restrain Seward and tone down his communications with European powers. For assistance he naturally looked to Sumner, the chairman of the Senate Foreign Relations Committee. Sumner was more than just the appropriate legislator. The Massachusetts abolitionist also had legal expertise in international law and considerable influence in the Republican Party. In addition, Sumner may have been the single American with the most high-level friendships and contacts abroad. When Lincoln turned to Sumner for advice, his efforts were quickly rewarded. Sumner informed Seward that the Senate must be consulted on issues of peace and war; the secretary of state's "every statement . . . concerning European powers will be carefully watched." In the White House Sumner told Lincoln, "You must watch him and overrule him."[17]

Being influential in foreign policy was important, but Charles Sumner had a larger agenda. The abolition of slavery was his paramount goal, and he now saw a god-given opportunity. As soon as the war began, he went to the White House and met with Lincoln in person. Pledging his complete support, "heart and soul," Sumner urged Lincoln to remember that he would be able, as commander in chief, to destroy slavery as a military measure. "I . . . told him . . . that under the war power the right had come to him to emancipate the slaves." This was not a new insight. Two decades earlier another prominent Massachusetts politician, John Quincy Adams, had predicted that such would be the ultimate fate of slavery. But Sumner acted quickly to be sure that the idea was in Lincoln's head, and he had the wisdom and patience to let events develop this possibility. When in July Congress passed resolutions emphasizing that the only purpose of the war was to restore the Union, and *not* to attack slavery, Sumner bided his time. He did not immediately press the president.[18]

Lincoln was far from imagining great changes in May 1861. In amazement he told John Hay, one of his secretaries, "Some of our northerners seem bewildered and dazzled by the excitement of the hour." Senators Orville Browning and James Doolittle and others were advocating strange and far-reaching steps. "Doolittle seems inclined to think that this war is to result in the entire abolition of Slavery. Old Col. Hamilton a venerable and most respected gentleman, impresses upon me most earnestly the propriety of enlisting the slaves in our army."[19] It was hard for Lincoln to understand what had possessed them. At this point his conception of his constitutional powers and duties was much more limited.

Montgomery Blair, on the other hand, was thinking as far ahead as Charles Sumner. But for Blair and his family the great goal was the removal of African Americans from the United States. Their idea of colonization had gained support among some African Americans, who were dismayed by the progress of the Slave Power in the 1850s. Henry Highland Garnet, an influential minister and speaker, was actively promoting ideas of emigration, and a pro-emigration correspondent to the *Anglo-African* newspaper complained, "[W]e must have a strong nationality somewhere." But most black leaders disagreed. James McCune Smith called on Garnet to abandon "these migrating phantasms," and the Massachusetts lawyer John Rock declared, "This being our country, we have made up our minds to remain in it, and to try to make it worth living in."[20]

The Blairs acted quickly. They now had a position in government that allowed them to advance colonization. Therefore they lost no time in presenting Lincoln with a practical option to accomplish this purpose. On April 12, just hours before Southerners opened fire on Fort Sumter, Lincoln met with a representative of a colonization venture that the Blairs were promoting. The enterprise was called the Chiriqui Improvement Company. It took its name from a Central American province in what is now Panama.[21]

Ambrose W. Thompson, a Philadelphia businessman who had made a fortune in shipbuilding, headed the company. He had acquired a claim to several hundred thousand acres of land "located at what was likely to be the terminus of a projected railroad across the isthmus." Thompson and his supporters argued that Chiriqui could serve the government in several important ways. Its lagoon was deep enough to be a naval base, admirably positioned to expand American influence. Rich deposits of coal lay nearby, to fuel American ships. The land was fertile for the cultivation of cotton. The Blairs were convinced that the government could benefit from collaboration with the Chiriqui Improvement Company. More important, Chiriqui could become a home for freed African Americans.[22]

Lincoln was intrigued. He appointed his brother-in-law Ninian Edwards Jr. to examine various documents, including the company's prospectus, and then report. Four months later Edwards would inform Lincoln that the company's claims were "fully verified" and that the United States "may be vastly benefited." The previous year, by act of Congress, money had been spent to survey the harbor, have a geologist evaluate the prospects for coal, and study the possibility of building a railroad across the isthmus. On all points the results had been extremely positive. The harbor was "grand and incomparable"; the coal was "inexhaustible in quantity . . . of the best kind and highly desirable for steam purposes"; a railroad was "eminently practicable."[23]

Frank Blair, the best orator in his influential family, would hold important positions during the Civil War both in the army and in the House of Representatives.

Lincoln turned to his secretary of the navy and secretary of the treasury, but with both he encountered a lack of enthusiasm. Gideon Welles was simply opposed to colonization, and Salmon Chase said he was impressed but too busy to study the matter thoroughly. Lincoln then referred the matter to his secretary of the interior, Caleb Smith. Since Smith was an advocate of colonization, the proposal would remain viable.[24]

Meanwhile, the Blair family aided Lincoln in another vitally important way. Frank Blair personally took the lead in political and military efforts to keep Missouri in the Union. That state's governor, Claiborne Jackson, favored secession. He had immediately denounced Lincoln's call for troops as "illegal, unconstitutional . . . inhuman and diabolical." Next he asked Jefferson Davis for siege guns and mortars and called out the militia.

Frank Blair sprang into action, organizing volunteers for the Union and using his influence in Washington to ensure that Captain Nathaniel Lyon had control of the St. Louis arsenal. In May, Frank and his troops helped Lyon capture a pro-secession militia encampment just outside St. Louis. In June, after Governor Jackson called Missourians to arms under General Sterling Price,

Frank and Lyon launched a military offensive that drove the secession forces into the southwest corner of the state. Missouri, one of the crucial border states, was safe for the Union. Frank Blair, who had helped Lincoln build the Republican Party in the West, now had done important service for the Union. Except for Blair, the president said, "he hardly knew how he could have managed successfully the affairs of Government in Missouri." The younger Blair also had military abilities and was chairman of the House Military Affairs Committee. Lincoln knew that Frank would give his all for the Union cause.[25]

10

Shocking Defeat, Alternate Paths

THE UNION'S CRISIS soon deepened. The Battle of Bull Run occurred in July, and it was a shocking defeat that sobered the North. Officeholders and ordinary citizens began to glimpse the difficulty of the task ahead. Preparing for war was one thing; suffering a humiliating defeat, something quite different. When Lincoln moved to put the North on a war footing, public opinion had rallied. But Northerners recoiled in dismay when their raw, untrained army was routed at Bull Run. Immediately, thoughts turned to new measures, and lawmakers and citizens began to discard some conventional ways of thinking.

After Bull Run, during the late summer and fall of 1861, there was more recruiting and training of armies than fighting. But these months were important, despite their relative quiet. The chief priority for Lincoln was to hold on to the remaining border states. He recognized that their resources could have a decisive impact in support of either the North or the South. Even with Missouri apparently safe in the Union fold, he could not afford to lose Kentucky or Maryland. But already slavery, in the aftermath of Bull Run, was commanding attention. Not only was it the key to the rebellion, it also represented strength for the rebellious Confederacy. Perhaps the Union would have to do something about slavery.

Both Charles Sumner and Montgomery Blair saw slavery as crucial to the war and to the nation's future. In 1861 both men strengthened their ties to Abraham Lincoln. But they used those connections to advocate very different paths to the future. Emancipation and equality were Sumner's goals, whereas the Blairs believed colonization was required by emancipation and essential to Northern unity. Influential Republicans in Congress began to move toward Sumner's positions, as the power of those who would be called Radical

Independent-minded but a workhorse at the War Department, **Edwin Stanton** developed views on policy that moved him ever closer to the Radical Republicans.

Republicans began to grow. The Blairs, on the other hand, advanced their agenda within the White House through the president.

GEOGRAPHIC REALITIES forced Lincoln to take some strong measures at the beginning of the war. The nation's capital was nearly surrounded by one seceded state, Virginia, and another of doubtful loyalty, Maryland. Therefore, he decided "to authorize the Commanding General . . . to suspend the privilege of the writ of habeas corpus" and to arrest or detain individuals who were "dangerous to the public safety." That action was promptly questioned as both unnecessary and unconstitutional. When the special session of Congress that Lincoln had summoned met in July 1861, the president set out to explain himself.[1]

Lincoln poured over this address for weeks and reviewed it with his cabinet. Then he read it aloud to Charles Sumner.[2] The resulting message called for 400,000 new troops, in hopeful expectation of making "this contest a short, and a decisive one." It also explained his actions, assailed the South for beginning the war, and praised the North's patriotic reaction. Lincoln openly described his astonishment that Virginia had seceded—and had done so after electing a convention with "a large majority of *professed* Union men." He pledged to "recognize and protect" its loyal citizens "as being Virginia." As to habeas corpus, he observed that the Constitution prohibited its suspension except "when, in cases of rebellion or invasion, the public safety may require it." Rebellion was a fact, he argued, and the public safety had required it. True, the Constitution discussed habeas corpus in a section describing the powers of Congress, but the Constitution "is silent as to which, or who, is to exercise the power." Lincoln felt his action had been necessary to protect the country. "Are all the laws, *but one,* to go unexecuted . . . lest that one be violated?"[3]

The influence of Charles Sumner appeared in the section where Lincoln refuted arguments legitimizing secession. Such arguments, the president claimed, reversed the intentions of the Founders. For years and in similar fashion, Sumner had insisted that Southern theories about their rights reversed the Founders' views. History, Sumner maintained, showed that freedom was national and slavery merely local. Lincoln now used history to demonstrate that unity was fundamental and states' rights merely secondary.

The Union of the Founders, argued Lincoln, was prior to, and the "political superior" of, the states. Colonies of Britain had first declared themselves "United Colonies" and then started calling themselves states. As "dependent colonies [they] made the Union; and, in turn, the Union threw off their old dependence." Later additions to the Union, except Texas, had never been independent, and none of them, including Texas, had called themselves states before they were part of the Union.[4]

What, he asked, was the basis of "this magical omnipotence of 'State rights'?" How could it be entitled to "lawfully destroy the Union itself?" The powers of states were "neither more, nor less" than those specified in the Constitution. Since "sovereignty" means "a political community, without a political superior," no state was ever sovereign except Texas, which "gave up the character on coming into the Union." Lincoln also argued that ballots and elections, not bullets, are the rightful basis of a republican form of government. Near his close, he used language that must have thrilled and encouraged Sumner: "This is essentially a People's contest. On the side of the Union, it is a struggle for maintaining in the world, that form, and substance of government, whose leading object is, to elevate the condition of men— to lift artificial weights from all shoulders—to clear the paths of laudable pursuit for all—to afford all, an unfettered start, and a fair chance, in the race of life."[5]

Charles Sumner wanted to lift weights from the shoulders of those most oppressed—African Americans, both free and enslaved. For him, the war was not merely to restore the Union. It was *the* opportunity to end both slavery and racial injustice. Soon, in an address to Massachusetts Republicans, he publicly urged that emancipation be a war policy. Black leaders were making the same argument. The *Anglo-African* newspaper declared that "the key" to winning the war was "the abolition of slavery."[6]

Racist Republicans, like the Blairs, had very different aims. Sumner and the Blairs were still "dear friends," and for some months their opposed beliefs did not seriously divide the party's ranks. The need to unite the North and prosecute the war was too pressing. Still, a sign of future differences came as early as May, when governors were raising troops to answer Lincoln's initial call for militia. Massachusetts's governor John Andrew, who was less of an abolitionist than Sumner, sought advice from friends in Washington. He wanted to know what tone he should adopt in addressing a special session of his state's legislature. "Montgomery Blair's blunt reply was to 'drop the nigger.'"[7] Blair wanted no crusade for equality and human rights. Looking coldly at Northern public opinion, he also knew that white support would be greater if Republicans limited their appeal to preserving the Union.

Enthusiastic support was desperately needed after July 21, 1861, when the Battle of Bull Run took place. This first major engagement of the war was a rout—a humiliation and a wake-up call for the North. For several weeks previously Lincoln had struggled to get information from the commanding general of the army. Winfield Scott was at the end of his career—aged, gouty, and so obese at three hundred pounds that he could no longer mount a horse. As July 21 neared, callers noticed that the president had a "wearied and worried appearance." Almost everyone else, however, was wildly optimistic. "Senator Sumner was radiant with the assurance of great success, and spoke of taking Richmond" in two days. Scores of Washingtonians packed picnic baskets and traveled into the Virginia countryside, expecting to watch a Union victory.[8]

Back in Washington, Lincoln received some troubling dispatches once the fighting began. These prompted him to go "over to see Gen. Scott, whom he found asleep." Scott discounted Lincoln's concerns and then "composed himself for another nap when the President left." The truth was not long in coming, however. At six o'clock in the evening "an excited, frightened-looking

Seward" rushed to the Executive Mansion. "Where is the President?" he barked. Confederate reinforcements, which arrived in the afternoon, had sent Union troops into panicked flight. General Irvin McDowell, the Union commander, reported that his army had become "a confused mob, entirely demoralized. . . . [N]o stand could be made this side of the Potomac." Congressmen and Washington residents fled back to the capital in fear. Lincoln "did not go to bed all night," and when Illinois congressman Elihu Washburne found the president and his advisers, he never saw "a more sober set of men." Fortunately for the Union, Confederate troops were too exhausted to advance toward the capital. Still, the war's first major battle was "an overwhelming defeat" for the Union, "a total and disgraceful rout."[9]

The disaster had immediate consequences in Congress. Majorities in both houses reversed the stand they had just taken in the Crittenden-Johnson Resolutions. Those resolutions solemnly declared that the war was not being fought to interfere "with rights or established institutions" of the states. Its only purpose was to save "the Union, with all the dignity, equality, and rights of the several States unimpaired." Now, less than two weeks later, Congress did an about-face and decided to strike a blow at slavery. The lawmakers passed the First Confiscation Act, which declared that any slave used in direct support of the rebellion would be free.[10]

Charles Sumner and others who would soon be called Radicals eagerly promoted this change of attitude, and the Republican majority agreed. Only two days after Bull Run, Sumner and Michigan's senator Zachariah Chandler called at the White House, accompanied by Vice President Hannibal Hamlin. The war must be a contest between Freedom and Slavery, they told Lincoln. Chandler argued that freeing the slaves would disorganize the South and cause its collapse. Sumner made the case that emancipation was a military necessity, as well as an act of justice. From this point forward, the Radicals agitated for emancipation, and soon the atmosphere "around the Capitol . . . was sulphurous with the rage of the radical Republicans." Sumner began a campaign to end slavery in D.C. and to outlaw discrimination against African Americans on its streetcars.[11]

Lincoln did not act on Sumner's advice, but their relationship in 1861 steadily became closer. Cooperation between the two was surprising, given their different personalities. The well-educated, sophisticated, cosmopolitan Sumner naturally considered Lincoln a bit uncultured, even uncouth, undignified, and socially inept. The unpretentious Lincoln, coming from frontier

Illinois, had rarely encountered a pretentious man like Sumner. He once remarked, "I have never had much to do with bishops where I live, but, do you know, Sumner is my idea of a bishop." Before long Lincoln suspected that the two got along because "Sumner thinks he runs me." Still, both men recognized the sincere antislavery feelings of the other.[12]

In addition, that fall Sumner proved his value to Lincoln in a diplomatic crisis. A Union ship stopped a British vessel, the RMS *Trent,* and took into custody two Confederate diplomats. James Mason and John Slidell were on their way to Britain and France, where they planned to seek recognition of the Confederacy. When news of their capture reached the North, there was an outpouring of patriotic enthusiasm, magnified by hostility toward secessionist traitors and Great Britain. Gradually, however, it dawned on cooler heads that the United States faced a potentially disastrous crisis. British leaders were enraged, and the United States had violated its long-standing position on the maritime rights of neutral nations. Clearly, the North could ill afford a war with Britain while its resources were consumed with the Southern rebellion.

Charles Sumner immediately recognized that the government needed to release the Confederate diplomats. Drawing on his contacts with prominent and powerful Englishmen, he gave Lincoln vital information on the state of feeling among British leaders. Sumner attended a cabinet meeting to deal with the crisis on Christmas Day, 1861, and as chairman of the Senate Foreign Relations Committee he played a key role in helping the administration to defuse and resolve the crisis. His aid was important, and Sumner sought to capitalize on it to promote freedom. After the Trent affair was over, he told Lincoln that if the United States had declared emancipation previously, support for America in the diplomatic crisis would have been much greater throughout Europe.[13]

But if Sumner never missed an opportunity to press for freedom and equality, the Blairs benefited from events at home that strengthened their approach to race. Issues of slavery and emancipation in the border states soon took priority for Lincoln and solidified his personal inclination to cooperate closely with the Blairs. Holding on to the border states was vital, and Lincoln knew it. They possessed 50 percent of Southern industrial capacity and 37 percent of the slaveholding states' population.[14] But no sooner had Frank Blair apparently secured Missouri for the Union than Confederate forces made worrisome gains. Then General John C. Frémont created a series of new problems.

The Blairs had supported Frémont for his post as commanding general in Missouri; Montgomery had been his attorney for years.[15] But they soon learned that he was not up to the task. Military contracts were going to swindlers, while Frémont was living large, accomplishing little, and offending many. Then, on August 30, 1861, Frémont issued a proclamation. To take control of the state, he declared martial law, announced that he would confiscate the property of any who opposed the Union, and declared their slaves to be free. This surprising declaration delighted abolitionists and Radical Republicans. Many Northern newspapers, including the pro-administration *New York Times,* initially praised Frémont's action, for it seemed to them a promising and practical step. Its effect on border states like Kentucky, however, was dangerously negative. Angry Kentuckians called it "an abominable, atrocious, and infamous usurpation." Lincoln's close friend Joshua Speed warned him that the proclamation "will crush out every vestage [*sic*] of a union party in the state" and ignite fears of slave rebellion. Speed himself was "so upset that he could neither eat nor sleep."[16]

Swiftly Lincoln advised Frémont to rescind his order. When the general insisted on an official order to do so, Lincoln issued the order—and then faced the ire of abolitionists. Sumner felt that the president was acting like "a dictator, Imperator," and lamented that it was "vain to have the power of a God if not to use it God-like." Even Lincoln's Illinois friend Senator Orville Browning took Lincoln to task. Previously, Browning's views had been rather conservative. His protest showed how strongly pro-emancipation sentiment was running in the wake of Bull Run. Lincoln's reply showed how much his conception of the powers of the commander in chief would have to develop before he was willing to strike against slavery on his own authority.

Frémont's proclamation, Lincoln said, had gone far beyond "*military* law" and entered into the "*purely political.*" Lincoln felt that a general had the right to seize property when such action was "within military necessity" and hold it "as long as the necessity lasts." But seizing property forever exceeded military law, and liberating slaves was a matter to be "settled according to laws made by law-makers, and not by military proclamations." Lincoln seemed to rule out presidential emancipation. If a general "or a President may make permanent rules of property by proclamation," then there was no longer "any government of Constitution and laws." Lincoln was amazed that harsh criticism came from Browning, who "less than a month" earlier had supported the more limited First Confiscation Act. Freeing all the slaves might please abolitionists, Lincoln admitted, but that was a "reckless position," and Frémont's proclamation would probably have caused the Union to lose Kentucky, and then Missouri and Maryland in Kentucky's wake.[17] Fortunately for Lincoln and for the Union, the clumsy invasion of Kentucky by Confederate General Leonidas Polk in September 1861 tied the state (often resentfully) to the North for the rest of the war.

Lincoln had ended his letter to Browning by saying there was "no thought" of removing General Frémont. But concerns over the general persisted. Turning again to the trusted Blair family, Lincoln sent Montgomery Blair to Missouri, accompanied by Quartermaster General Montgomery Meigs, who had been recommended for his post by Frank Blair. After investigating and meeting with Frémont, Blair recommended the general's removal. Frémont was spending funds unwisely, "living in state with bodyguards [and] sentinels," and accomplishing "absolutely nothing." As soon as Montgomery Blair left Missouri, Frémont arrested his brother Frank. Something had to be done.[18]

Lincoln followed Blair's advice and sacked the general. Frémont's spirited wife, Jessie, traveled to Washington and challenged Lincoln, but the president rebuked her in response. The war was for the Union, he said sternly, and "General Frémont should not have dragged the Negro into it . . . he never would if he had consulted with Frank Blair. I sent Frank to advise him." Before long Frémont tried to turn Lincoln against his postmaster general by leaking to the press a letter in which Montgomery Blair had criticized the president. But his tactic failed and even highlighted the loyalty that Lincoln valued. Blair promptly offered to resign, but Lincoln assured him that there was no issue between them, for at the time of the criticism Blair had been completely frank to Lincoln about his views.[19]

In November, Lincoln and the Blairs initiated new policies toward the war's central issue. They began moving in close coordination to address questions of slavery, emancipation, and colonization. Their views and aims were identical. At virtually the same time,[20] Lincoln focused his attention on Delaware while the Blairs focused on Central America.

Delaware had fewer than two thousand slaves; in fact, it could be called a "free Negro" state, rather than a slave state, since the vast majority of its African Americans were already free. Lincoln felt that slavery was receiving "a mortal wound" due to the war. He hoped to accelerate the movement toward liberty and make Delaware a model for the border states. Lincoln believed that if border states like Delaware emancipated, the Confederacy would lose all hope of gaining their support and winning the war. Accordingly, he drew up a proposal for a gradual emancipation that was entirely voluntary, based on the decision of the slaveholding state. Gradual emancipation would include both compensation from the federal government and apprenticeship, to cushion the economic loss perceived by slaveholders. The president wrote out and had printed two schemes, which a member of the Delaware legislature who was a strong Union supporter distributed to his colleagues. Since Delaware lawmakers had stopped only one vote short of adopting such a plan in 1847, Lincoln had high hopes.[21]

The first version of Lincoln's proposal called for one-fifth of Delaware's slaves to be freed each year, beginning in 1862, so that slavery would end in 1867. Children whose mothers were not free at their birth would have to serve an apprenticeship lasting until age twenty-one for males and eighteen for females. The federal government would pay, in five installments, compensation of four hundred dollars for every slave in the form of U.S. bonds. The second version—and Lincoln said, "I like No. 2 the better"—envisioned a much longer process of emancipation, lasting until 1893. If an act were passed in 1862, all who were over thirty-five would become free immediately. Others would become free at age thirty-five or in 1893. Children born after the act would be born free but would serve apprenticeships until twenty-one or eighteen. Thus male children born to a slave as late as 1892 would have to serve their masters until 1913. Compensation would be the same. Although these plans did not specifically mention colonization, the president was on record as a longtime supporter of colonization abroad, and his other comments would soon show that colonization was part of his plan.[22]

The Blairs were eager to put colonization into practice and believed that the war made the task more urgent. They had continued working with Ambrose Thompson on the Chiriqui project in Central America. Now they came forward with a detailed proposal and an action plan. Congress had spent funds in 1858 to confirm Chiriqui's potential, and Ninian Edwards Jr. had given Lincoln a favorable report on the project. The time was right, they argued, to go forward in cooperation with Thompson, the Philadelphia shipbuilder and businessman.

On November 16 Francis Preston Blair delivered to Lincoln a detailed prospectus and proposed contract with the United States. The first of these documents furnished an outline to convince Congress of the benefits of this project. From the commercial, military, and geopolitical standpoints, it argued, the nation stood to gain enormously. Because the Chiriqui project encompassed ports on both oceans connected by a railroad, it would speed American routes to China, Japan, and other Asian countries. In the tropics and South America, vast new markets would open for "our manufacturing interests" and extend U.S. commerce. Meanwhile, Chiriqui itself would produce cotton, coffee, sugar cane, and other valuable crops, while its vast coal deposits could be mined for sale and for use by American vessels. Militarily the project gave the United States, in the days before a transcontinental railroad, "a well protected route to California and Oregon." Development of Chiriqui was also an "instrument of commercial power" and geopolitical influence. Through Chiriqui, the United States could extend "its power in the Mexican Gulf and Caribbean Sea."[23]

Just as important and even more vital were the supposed racial advantages. The war had made urgent the question, "what shall be done with the freed negroes? How shall we remove them humanely, kindly, with profit to themselves, and in accordance with the spirit of the age?" It was clear, the document argued, that the fertile but "now uninhabited" lands of Chiriqui "may become the place of residence for the Freed Negroes of the United States." In fact, it was "the only true place for their Colonization." "*For this race we must provide a home, separate and apart from our own. They are a festering sore in our body politic. They have caused the present war, a war that is to cost us four hundred millions of dollars.*" The solution was to "aid them in their passage thither by establishing a line of steamers, which shall remain, a means of communication with their protectors. Encourage them to produce Cotton, Sugar, Coffee, Rice, by their free labor, and thus raise them to the dignity of manhood—dependence upon themselves."[24] The similarity of this vision to Frank Blair's speeches in Boston and in Congress was plain.

The proposed agreement with Ambrose Thompson promised great potential benefits to the United States. It also gave generous encouragement to Thompson, since funding for construction would come upfront through contracts paid for in government bonds, which Thompson could sell. His company would contract to supply coal for the Gulf and Pacific Squadrons at half price. It would also run a line of steamers that would guarantee mail and transport service to government departments at half price. These steamers would give the United States priority in transporting colonists, and the nation would have an option to buy up to 500,000 acres at only $1.25 per acre. To fund construction of ships, ports, and the railroad, the United States was to advance one-half of its scheduled contract payments for the next sixty years.

To protect the United States' financial interests, bonds would be advanced only as the steamers were built and as five-mile sections of the railroad were completed.[25]

Francis Blair Sr. urged Montgomery to make an additional argument to the president: privateer ships of the Union could carry African Americans to Chiriqui and then be in perfect location for catching Confederate vessels or pirates. Meanwhile, Ambrose Thompson suggested to Blair Sr. that he arrange for a government ship to pick up Henry Taylor Blow, the minister to Venezuela. Blow, formerly a Missouri legislator known to the Blairs, had made a fortune in mining and therefore was well qualified to travel to Chiriqui and produce an additional, reliable evaluation of its resources. Lincoln could sign a provisional contract, subject to favorable findings by Blow. Thompson would contact black preachers in the North to start a "numerous immigration of the free negroes from the cities." This would induce others to follow, "and thus the great work would be half completed before the next summer." Francis Blair Sr. drafted orders that Secretary of the Navy Welles could use for this purpose, and in December Frank Blair gave his brother additional papers to assure and convince Lincoln.[26]

The initial results of both these initiatives were disappointing. Lincoln had told Orville Browning that he was very hopeful of success in Delaware. To David Davis of Illinois he had predicted "that if Congress will pass a law authorizing the issue of bonds" to pay for his plan, Delaware, Missouri, Kentucky, and Maryland would "all accept the terms." But Delaware's legislature was evenly divided on party lines, and by a one-vote margin the gradual emancipation idea failed. More disturbing was Delaware's next step. The legislature passed a resolution essentially telling Lincoln to keep out and keep his hands off. When "the people of Delaware desire to abolish slavery . . . they will do so in their own way." "Any interference from without, and all suggestions of saving expense to the people . . . are improper to be made to an honorable people such as we represent, and are hereby repelled."[27]

Whites in Delaware were signaling an attitude that was strong in the border states. Slavery was more than an economic interest. It also was the linchpin of racial control, the basis of superior white status. Members of the state's legislature had voiced their objections to "nigger" equality.[28] Even in a state with very few slaves, whites "repelled" any tampering with their institution, because they feared that it might open the door to racial equality.

Disappointment also met the Chiriqui plan. It ran into opposition in

Lincoln's cabinet. Chase wanted a better price for coal; Seward favored direct arrangements with New Granada, the government in that region; and Welles suspected a "fraud and cheat in the affair." Thaddeus Stevens, powerful chairman of the Ways and Means Committee of the House, also was negative. Henry Blow then resigned his post in Venezuela to return to Illinois, and the project stalled.[29] But Lincoln did not give up on colonization or dismiss Chiriqui from his thoughts.

In December the president sent his first annual message to Congress. Of necessity it reviewed many matters and covered the various departments of government. But toward the end of the message Lincoln noted that the First Confiscation Act and the tides of war had, in practice, liberated many slaves. Fleeing bondage, they were pouring into the District of Columbia and into Union lines. The government needed to take notice of this fact and respond. Lincoln proposed that some form of compensation be made to the states from which they came and that they "be at once deemed free." He urged that "in any event, steps be taken for colonizing" such persons "at some place, or places, in a climate congenial to them." Free black people should be included: "It might be well to consider, too,—whether the free colored people already in the United States could not, so far as individuals may desire, be included in such colonization." To make that possible, he recommended that money be appropriated for the possible purchase of territory. Some might object "that the only legitimate object of acquiring territory is to furnish homes for white men." Lincoln answered such objections by saying that removing blacks created "additional room" for whites. Then he closed the topic by suggesting that "this whole proposition" amounted to an "absolute necessity, that without which the government itself cannot be perpetuated." The power of racism could not be ignored, and he was anxious that the war "not degenerate into a violent and remorseless revolutionary struggle."[30]

Finding a way to colonize freed African Americans abroad would address the central problem: what one of Delaware's senators called "the antagonism of race."[31] Lincoln wanted slavery to end. So too, in their different ways, did Charles Sumner and Montgomery Blair. Sumner, wary of offending the president, urged him at this point only to propose gradual emancipation.[32] But Sumner believed in racial equality and would work for it as quickly as practicable. For the Blairs and the large majority of racist whites, emancipation created at least as many problems as it might solve. The end of slavery, thought most whites, would introduce the serious, unmanageable problems of race.

For those who believed that equality was impossible—and their number was legion—separation was a necessity. Lincoln shared their fears and their belief in the desirability of separation. His policy followed the vision of the Blairs.

Between Lincoln's views and Sumner's, at the end of 1861, there was a gulf. This was apparent in the president's reaction to the annual report of Simon Cameron, the soon-to-be-replaced secretary of war. Cameron recommended that the government arm the slaves in order to defeat the rebellion. "This will never do!" exclaimed Lincoln. As soon as he saw the report, he tried to change and repress it, but the recommendation found its way into some newspapers. Lincoln feared the power of a racist white reaction. "Arm the slaves," he said, "and we shall have more of them than white men in our army." Already in 1861 the war was seriously undermining slavery. But the problems that racism posed for the future were immense.[33]

11

Obstacles

THE CHOICE OF Cameron's replacement as secretary of war was "a surprise, not only to the country but to every member of the Administration except the Secretary of State." The appointment of Edwin M. Stanton as secretary of war would end up surprising Abraham Lincoln as well. The president was trying "to conciliate and draw in as much of the Democratic element as possible," and Seward had recommended this Democratic attorney who had once treated Lincoln rudely. "Fond of power and of its exercise," Stanton was someone who "took pleasure in being ungracious and rough towards those who were under his control." But he was also "industrious and driving," a workhorse in the War Department, where one was needed.[1] Soon Stanton became a Radical in his opinions, more radical than Cameron had been. A president who still favored conservative approaches had not expected Stanton to advocate freeing and arming the slaves.

Lincoln's plans, and his ideas, were closely tied to those of Montgomery and Frank Blair. The president was pushing forward and had decided to encourage change. But in a wartime atmosphere that was rapidly evolving, his ideas still had a strongly conservative cast. Charles Sumner tried to counter the Blairs' influence by advocating strong measures of emancipation to the president and in Congress. But Lincoln and the Blairs chose a path that respected states' rights, colonization, and white racial fears. Early in 1862 and deep into the hot, oppressive Washington summer, Lincoln courted the border states with proposals he believed were wise and fair for whites. The formidable obstacles that he met eventually aided Sumner, Stanton, and the Radicals. In time they would force Lincoln to broaden his approach.

ON MARCH 6, 1862, Lincoln sent a message to Congress, launching a new initiative carefully coordinated with the Blairs. In December he had pointed out that slaves were taking advantage of the disruptions of war to gain their freedom, and he had urged colonization and compensation to the affected states. Now he renewed his proposal with greater detail and resolve. He urged the passage of a joint resolution committing the nation "to co-operate with any state which may adopt gradual abolishment of slavery." The federal government would give "pecuniary aid, to be used by such state in it's [*sic*] discretion, to compensate for the inconveniences public and private, produced by such change of system."[2]

Lincoln hastened to emphasize that he was not claiming any "right, by federal authority, to interfere with slavery within state limits." The states retained "the absolute control of the subject" and a "perfectly free choice." But if the slave states still in the Union would act on this offer, it would "deprive" the rebels of all hope that more states would join the Confederacy. Losing that hope, Lincoln believed, "substantially ends the rebellion." Compensation was cheap; the huge cost of the war would soon surpass the bill for compensation. And "in my judgment, gradual, and not sudden emancipation, is better for all."[3]

Leaving emancipation completely in the states' hands had been Republican doctrine at the beginning of the war. Even the vigorously antislavery Salmon Chase supported that view as late as December 1861. At the end of that month he gave Lincoln a draft proposal for gradual, compensated emancipation. Feeling that Republicans must obey "every Constitutional obligation," Chase's proposal held that "slavery within State limits" was outside national jurisdiction. If the rebel states were to return to Congress, "they would find themselves at peace, with no institution changed." Their influence would be "unabridged and unimpaired."[4] But opinions were rapidly changing in Congress. The First Confiscation Act had declared freedom for slaves used in direct support of the rebellion. A growing number of lawmakers now wanted to go further.

Charles Sumner kept up his efforts to influence the president, and he had significant input on the message to Congress. He convinced Lincoln to omit a sentence that had made explicit the fact that rebel states could return to the Union and keep slavery. Though Lincoln's proposal was less than Sumner wanted, he saw progress and judged it a "great event of history." The president was moving toward emancipation.[5]

Montgomery Blair worked energetically in a racially conservative direction. He had urged Lincoln to include a specific provision for colonization, like the one in December's annual message to Congress. Lincoln did not take

Blair's advice, though his support for colonization was already a matter of record. Instead he reminded the seceded states of his annual message, where he had stated that "all indispensable means must be employed" to save the Union. Now he warned that it was "impossible to foresee" what the war might make indispensable or to predict "all the ruin" that it might bring.[6]

Prodding the border slave states to take action, Lincoln called on his allies to support this agenda. He sent a letter to Henry Raymond, the editor of the *New York Times* and one of the founders of the Republican Party. Raymond had not been supporting gradual emancipation, but Lincoln urged him to change his view and back this proposal. It would shorten the war and be far less costly, in lives and money, than battles. The president also called in Montgomery Blair and asked him to set up a meeting with border state congressmen. Montgomery's brother Frank lent a hand in trying to arrange such a meeting, so that the president could try face-to-face persuasion. Turning to their father, Francis Preston Blair, Lincoln asked him to try to enlist the support of Kentucky's John J. Crittenden.[7]

Montgomery Blair was also prominent in efforts at public persuasion. On the same day that Lincoln sent his message to Congress, a hostile meeting of citizens at New York's Cooper Institute listened to the reading of an address sent by Blair, who was too busy to leave Washington. Boldly and in detail, Blair made the case for colonization. It was essential to reunion, because it had a direct relation to what the war was all about. It was "the non-slaveholders" of the South, Blair pointed out, who "fill[ed] the armies of rebellion." Politics had awakened in them "the jealousy of caste." They went to war because they had heard "that the election of Mr. Lincoln involved emancipation, equality of the negroes with them, and consequently amalgamation." Therefore, "the difficult question with which we have to deal is, then, the question of race."[8]

Racism, or "the jealousy of race," was not the product of "ignorance and bad passion," Blair argued. Rather, it belonged "to all races" and involved "the highest wisdom"; it was "the instinct of self-preservation which revolts at hybridism." Thomas Jefferson had understood how "indispensable" the "separation of races" was to America's future. All possibility of fraternal reunion would be destroyed if emancipation "left the negroes on the soil." As Jefferson had counseled, the nation must provide "for the separation of the races, providing suitable homes for the blacks, as we have for the Indians." "To insure the cooperation of the non-slaveholders in their emancipation," it was necessary to convince them that "homes for the blacks" would be provided "elsewhere."[9]

Nor would colonization be an injustice to African Americans, Blair claimed. Their race "has not maintained and cannot maintain itself in the temperate zone." "In contact and in competition with the race to which that region belongs," freed slaves would "quickly" disappear. Colonization would "give real freedom to the black race, which cannot otherwise exist. . . . Nor would [blacks] require immediate, universal, or involuntary transportation," for "the more enterprising would soon emigrate, and multitudes of less energy would follow."[10]

Coming to Lincoln's defense, Blair rejected the charge that motivated the Cooper Institute meeting: "that certain States have been 'recently overturned and wholly subverted as members of the Federal Union.'" Those who attacked the administration on these grounds, Blair said, were "actual aiders and abettors of the confederates." He, and by implication the president, "never believed that the abolition of slavery . . . could or ought to be effected except by lawful and constitutional modes." Lincoln's proposals met that condition. They had left all initiative up to the states. The rest of Blair's address affirmed that leaders who desired "an end to slavery" would "avoid all questionable" measures and would act constitutionally.[11]

One month later, in April, Frank Blair took the defense of Lincoln and colonization to the floor of the House. As the difficulties of war increased, critics were demanding that Lincoln should make war on slavery; Blair himself had introduced a bill back in January to bar the military from returning slaves who came into Union lines. Others wanted Lincoln to use his power as commander in chief to decree emancipation, now. Frank Blair instead urged attention to race.

"This is not 'a slaveholders' rebellion,'" he declared. Rather, what made the rebellion was "the *negro question* and not the *slavery question*." "The rebellion originated chiefly among the non-slaveholders resident in the strongholds of the institution." Its cause was "an antagonism of race and hostility to the idea of equality with the blacks involved in simple emancipation." To emancipate without colonization "would make rebels of the whole of the non-slaveholders of the South," but Lincoln wisely took steps "to disarm the jealousy of race." His annual message in December 1861 had proposed colonization. His policy of colonization and compensation was "conciliation by separation of the races." It would win the war and break the Southern aristocracy's previous hold on the federal government. As for African Americans, it was "but a question of time" before they gravitated "to the tropics," where they could benefit from governing themselves.[12]

The administration's offensive for compensated emancipation with coloni-
zation succeeded in Congress. Early in April both houses agreed on a resolution to support any state that adopted gradual, compensated emancipation.
Many prominent citizens agreed that colonization was wise or necessary. The
list included *New York Tribune* editor Horace Greeley; Republicans Benjamin
Wade, Samuel Pomeroy, Lyman Trumbull, and Henry Wilson; abolitionists
Gerrit Smith and James G. Birney; and well-known figures such as Harriet
Beecher Stowe and Henry Ward Beecher. In recent years a number of black
leaders had also endorsed colonization.[13]

But outside Congress many were not convinced. The *New York Times* continued to criticize colonization as "impracticable" as well as undesirable. The
labor of a "humble, submissive, docile race" was needed in the United States, it
said. *Harper's Weekly* recommended that Congress declare the slaves' freedom
and aid "their advance to citizenship at . . . graduated times." This popular
journal admitted that "most people wish to shut their eyes" to that question,
but the editors condemned "exportation" as "not practicable" and believed
that "after due lapse of time" blacks could become "competent citizens." The
Republican *Cincinnati Daily Gazette* described colonization as a "very com-
fortable" but impractical idea, and agreed that black labor was essential to
the South's economy. Remarkably, within a few months *Harper's Weekly* even
concluded that the basic problem was prejudice: "We have got . . . to go on
unlearning prejudices, acquiring toleration."[14]

None of the border states thought that way. Lincoln's initial meeting with
border state representatives was discouraging. Lincoln did all he could to allay
the fears and resistance that he encountered. He emphasized that he had no
"intent to injure the interests or wound the sensibilities of the slave States."
Likewise, he was not trying to coerce the border states or infringe their rights.
But the war was going to give slaves new opportunities to come into Union
camps, causing slaveholders to complain "that their rights were interfered
with." He wanted his proposal to "be accepted, if at all, voluntarily," since
"emancipation was a subject exclusively under the control of the States." Even
though he personally believed slavery was wrong, he had "no designs" to punish the states if they rejected the plan. All these pledges did not visibly move
the representatives.[15]

Others in Congress were taking bolder action, as the idea of emancipation gained momentum. The District of Columbia was directly governed
by Congress. Lawmakers had unquestionable jurisdiction over slavery there.

Therefore, Massachusetts's senator Henry Wilson sponsored a bill to emancipate the District's slaves, compensate loyal owners, and provide for colonization, and on April 16 Lincoln signed it into law. Slaves in the District gained their freedom immediately. Loyal slave owners could request compensation of three hundred dollars per slave from commissioners who were appointed to evaluate these claims. One hundred thousand dollars were set aside for the president "to aid in the colonization and settlement" of blacks "beyond the limits of the United States." Some owners decided to spirit slaves out of the District, but eventually approximately three thousand human beings gained their freedom, to the delight of abolitionists and Radical Republicans. Lincoln declared, "I am gratified that the two principles of compensation, and colonization, are both recognized." Still, Congress's action did him no good with the border states.[16] Meanwhile, Charles Sumner immediately began working to end discrimination in the District's streetcars.

A new problem arose in May. General David Hunter declared "forever free" the slaves in his department, which covered Georgia, Florida, and South Carolina. Hunter had informed Secretary of War Stanton of his plan as far back as January. Hoping to prod the president into action, Hunter had promised to "bear the blame" for his actions. He had also begun arming and training slaves to fight in the U.S. army. To Hunter, who knew Lincoln and had accompanied the president-elect from Springfield to Washington, it was obvious that the government needed to strike at slavery. Equally clear was the wisdom of enlisting African Americans to fight in the Union cause, rather than letting the Confederacy benefit from their labor. In another sign that attitudes were changing in Washington, Salmon Chase now strongly urged the president not to overturn Hunter's decree.[17]

But Lincoln feared the impact of Hunter's decree on the border states. He quickly countermanded the general's proclamation, declaring it "void." But Lincoln's declaration revealed that his views on presidential powers were beginning to evolve. Again he said that a general could not declare freedom for the slaves. But now he no longer said that issue rested with "laws made by law-makers." Instead, whether the commander in chief could declare freedom, and whether such action had "become a necessity indispensable to the maintenance of the government," were questions "I reserve to myself." Then he appealed again to the border slave states to act on his suggestion of voluntary, gradual emancipation. They could not be "blind to the signs of the times," and their action could do immense good.[18]

That same day Charles Sumner delivered a speech in the Senate, arguing for much stronger measures. Sumner spoke of the "suicide" of the rebel states and called them "enemies" and "criminals." Citing ancient and modern authorities in his learned, often pedantic manner, he argued that the United States had the power to punish the rebels as criminals under the Constitution, and as enemies under the "Rights of War." On both counts "Congress, in conjunction with the President," could confiscate and liberate property, including slave property. The "extensive plantations" of the rebellion's leaders should be seized and "partitioned into small estates," so that they could become "homes to many who are now homeless." Northern soldiers could fill the South "with northern industry and northern principles." Freeing the slaves offered a noble prospect to the Union. It was a chance to "change from Barbarism to Civilization." Sumner urged the North to "punish" rebels and "elevate a race . . . change this national calamity into a sacred triumph." Meeting with Lincoln personally, Sumner urged using Independence Day, July 4, to free the slaves.[19]

Lincoln listened but held back. Instead of readying a proclamation of freedom, he returned to his ideas of gradual emancipation and colonization. He drafted a public appeal to the border state representatives. On July 12, out of a sense of "duty," he issued this appeal, calling on them to voluntarily adopt gradual emancipation, with compensation and colonization. The rebellion, he argued, would not stop "so long as you show a determination to perpetuate the institution within your own states." However, emancipation by the border states would end the war. If the war were allowed to continue, slavery "will be extinguished by mere friction and abrasion—by the mere incidents of war." Much of slavery's value "is gone already," he said. Wasn't it better to secure "substantial compensation for that which is sure to be wholly lost" and save money, lives, and the nation? Then Lincoln emphasized that he did not ask for "emancipation *at once,* but a *decision* at once to emancipate *gradually.* Room in South America for colonization, can be obtained cheaply, and in abundance," and he was confident that once colonization began, "the freed people will not be so reluctant to go." In closing, Lincoln warned that his overruling General Hunter had upset "many whose support the country can not afford to lose. And this is not the end of it. The pressure, in this direction, is still upon me, and is increasing."[20]

The "patriots and statesmen" whom Lincoln politely addressed answered him promptly. And they answered him not with "the loftiest views, and boldest action" he had requested, but with racist anger and resentment. The majority explained that they had opposed Lincoln's original proposal for several reasons. It "proposed a radical change of our social system." Its costs, for compensation and colonization, would add an immense, crushing debt to the Union's already enormous financial obligations. In addition, they did not trust the Congress to make the promised support real. Then, turning to the present issue, they declared that "no one is authorized to question the right" to hold slaves. Contrary to Lincoln's view, their giving up slavery would have no effect on the rebellion. The great body of ordinary Southerners were fighting "to maintain and preserve the rights of property and domestic slavery." They believed they "are assailed by this Government."[21]

The rebellion's leaders would fight on because they "seek to break down national independence." But ordinary Southerners would "gladly return to their allegiance" if they could believe "that no harm is intended to them and their institutions." Instead Congress had abandoned the Crittenden-Johnson resolutions and embraced antislavery "doctrines subversive of the principles of the Constitution." Generals had tried to declare freedom for the slaves. Such progress of antislavery measures was alarming. The border states were not going to "give up slavery to the end that the Hunter proclamation may be let loose on the Southern people." They directed President Lincoln to "[c]onfine yourself to your constitutional authority; confine your subordinates within the same limits; conduct this war solely for the purpose of restoring the constitution to its legitimate authority." In closing, they indicated that the border states would not consider Lincoln's proposal unless Congress first appropriated all the funds necessary for "abolishment . . . deportation and colonization." A minority report expressed sincere sympathy for Lincoln's dilemma, but did no more than pledge to "ask the people of the border states . . . to consider your recommendations."[22]

Thus, the obstacles to Lincoln's plan had proved formidable. Always slow to move until it became necessary, he did not abandon his support for colonization and gradual, voluntary emancipation. But with the "pressure" to act against slavery continuing to increase, he also was considering additional steps. On Sunday, July 13, 1862, Lincoln was riding in a carriage with Secretary of the Navy Gideon Welles, Secretary of State Seward, and Seward's daughter-in-law. For the first time to anyone he mentioned possibilities that had been weighing on his mind. He had given "much thought" to "the subject of emancipating the slaves by proclamation." It was an important, grave, and delicate question. But Lincoln shared that he "had about come to the conclusion that it was a military necessity absolutely essential for the salvation of the Union, that we must free the slaves or be ourselves subdued." Welles was somewhat taken aback. He noted in his diary that "every member of the Cabinet . . . including the President" had "considered it a local, domestic question appertaining to the States respectively, who had never parted with their authority over it." But now even Welles admitted that the rebels were using slaves for military advantage.[23]

Three days later Congress increased the pressure, though in line with Lincoln's plan. A special committee endorsed emancipation and colonization and recommended an appropriation of $20 million to support the emigration of African Americans. Colonization was needed because "a large portion of our people" opposes "the intermixture of the races" and fears the competition from black labor. "This is a question of color," stated the committee. The greatest challenge to emancipation was "the belief . . . that if the negroes shall become free, they must still continue in our midst, and . . . in some measure be made equal to the Anglo-Saxon race." Whites would "never consent . . . to such equality." The committee believed that "the whole country should be held and occupied" by whites alone, and therefore a place "must be sought for the African beyond our own limits," probably in warmer regions, "which doubtless the Almighty intended the colored races should inhabit and cultivate."[24]

The next day Congress went further and in some more radical directions. Its Second Confiscation Act gave sixty days' warning to those in rebel states to return to their allegiance. If they did not, all their property could be seized. Slaves of rebels would be "forever free of their servitude," and this included slaves of all persons who "in any way" gave "aid and comfort" to the rebellion. Thus everyone living in the Confederacy and paying taxes there was included. No longer would escaping slaves "be hindered" in gaining their liberty. Lincoln was authorized to provide for the "transportation, colonization, and settlement, in some tropical country" of all freed blacks willing to emigrate, and Congress appropriated $500,000 to make this possible. In a dramatic addition to anything Lincoln had previously discussed, the new law also authorized him to "employ as many persons of African descent as he may deem necessary and proper for the suppression of this rebellion, and for this purpose he may organize and use them in such manner as he may judge best for the public welfare."

A few days later Lincoln told his cabinet that he "was unwilling" to arm slaves. Henry Halleck, general in chief of the U.S. army, agreed and told the president, "I do not think much of the negro."[25] The fact remained, however, that the war was producing new views on policy. Attitudes toward slavery were changing. Just as clearly, racist hostility and fears were not. But the pressure to move in new directions continued to grow, as an enormously destructive war went badly.

12

Suffering

"WHAT SHALL I DO?" cried Lincoln. "The people are impatient; Chase has no money and he tells me he can raise no more; the General of the Army has typhoid fever. The bottom is out of the tub."[1] It was the military situation that caused the people's impatience at the beginning of 1862. But at this point Lincoln was troubled merely by lack of progress, rather than by defeats and death on a vast scale. Much worse was soon to come.

The tides of war beat roughly against Lincoln and an overconfident Northern public. They brought grief and mental anguish as well as physical pain. They encouraged a desperation that led to stronger policies. Deep personal sorrows—family tragedies—afflicted ordinary citizens and added their weight to the president and key policy makers. In Washington and throughout the North, suffering was the dark and lowering cloud that sometimes obscured the crucial policy dilemmas of slavery and race.

After the debacle at Bull Run, Northern citizens yearned for victory in 1862. They looked hopefully toward the nearby Virginia theater for signs of success. But the huge Army of the Potomac, growing to over 100,000 men and entrusted to General George B. McClellan, did nothing. Men trained and units drilled, but there was no fighting. In frustration Lincoln issued the "President's General War Order No. 1." It required all forces and all commanders to advance on February 22. The order was widely ignored. Considering himself a rank amateur among professional warriors, Lincoln bit his tongue and left decisions in the hands of the generals.

His chief general, George McClellan, appeared to be a military prodigy. Only thirty-four years old when the war began, he already had enjoyed a distinguished career. Son of a prominent Philadelphia family, he graduated second in his class at West Point and fought bravely in the war with Mexico. Subsequently he received important assignments and rose in the ranks. He authored official manuals on bayonet and cavalry tactics and served as the U.S. army's observer to the Crimean War before resigning to become chief engineer and vice president of the Illinois Central Railroad. Back in service, McClellan was popular with his troops and well respected by other officers.

But few could match this young general's high opinion of himself. Proudly he told his wife, "I receive letter after letter, have conversation after conversation, calling on me to save the nation, alluding to the presidency, dictatorship, etc." "I seem to have become the power of the land." He believed that "God has placed a great work in my hands." It fed his self-regard that "the men brighten up when I go among them. . . . You never heard such yelling. . . . I can see every eye glisten." When McClellan finally went into the field on a campaign, he needed six four-horse wagons to carry his personal items. (By contrast, Ulysses S. Grant often took to the field only a spare shirt, a hairbrush, and a toothbrush.)

Sure of himself, McClellan had scorn for his superiors, whether civilian or military. Winfield Scott, whom he maneuvered out of the top spot of general in chief, was "in his dotage." President Lincoln was "an idiot," a "baboon," or "the gorilla," and on more than one occasion the general skipped appointments or refused to meet with the president. The cabinet consisted of "some of the greatest geese . . . I have ever seen—enough to tax the patience of Job." Seward was "a meddling, officious, incompetent little puppy." Welles was "weaker than the most garrulous old woman." Bates was "an old fool." Such men, McClellan felt, "thwarted and deceived" him "at every turn." On top of these personal opinions, McClellan held the views of a partisan Democrat and believed that the war should touch Southern society as little as possible. Currying political favor, he entertained like-minded politicians with lavish dinners at his Washington residence.[2]

But on the battlefield McClellan accomplished little. Perhaps success and high position had come too quickly to this general, for he seemed afraid to take risks. Everything had to be perfect before he would act. Never did he feel he had sufficient troops or adequate support. Always the enemy seemed, to McClellan, to outnumber his army by a wide margin. Delay and hesitation marked his style, rather than decisiveness and action. In February 1862 Lincoln finally prodded him into action to secure the upper Potomac and nearby rail lines, but some canal boats necessary for the operation proved to be six inches too wide to enter the locks. "Why in hell didn't he measure first!" shouted the exasperated president.[3]

The grand offensive planned for 1862 was put off month after month while

McClellan demanded reinforcements. When he finally moved in June, he ferried a far superior army by boat to the James River peninsula and advanced within a few miles of Richmond. But then, as Robert E. Lee attacked, McClellan steadily fell back. With the expedition a failure, Little Mac dictated a telegram to Washington, claiming "a few thousand more men would have changed this battle from a defeat to a victory." The president should have supplied more troops, McClellan told Stanton (and by extension the president). "If I save this Army now," he wired his superiors, "I tell you plainly that I owe no thanks to you or any other persons in Washington—you have done your best to sacrifice this Army."[4]

The public reaction was severe, and Lincoln got the blame. The capital had been "almost wild with rumors and suspense," and failure made "everybody . . . "terribl[y] blue about it for several days." Republican senator William P. Fessenden of Maine, a responsible legislator, lamented that "Seward's vanity & folly & Lincoln's weakness & obstinacy have not yet quite ruined us, but I fear they will." For weeks the president looked "as if he had no friend on earth." Lincoln said he was "as nearly inconsolable as I could be and live."[5]

The only news of victory came from the West, and it was accompanied by truly sobering casualty statistics. In February General Grant captured Forts Henry and Donelson, which opened the Cumberland and Tennessee Rivers for future Union invasions. Grant became a hero when he demanded "unconditional surrender" at Fort Donelson. Rapturously happy Northerners sent him thousands of cigars. But in April, when he pushed downriver into southern Tennessee, the praise turned into harsh criticism. Grant was stopped in the shockingly bloody Battle of Shiloh. Two days of fighting produced 23,000 casualties—by far the bloodiest battle in U.S. history to that point. Grieving families suffered for their dead, wounded, or permanently maimed fathers and sons. Northerners could not ignore how costly the war would be and how badly it was going. Even the capture of New Orleans by elderly but vigorous Admiral David Farragut could not dispel the gloom.[6]

Meanwhile Washington had suffered another scare. Confederates had armored a scuttled Union frigate and renamed it the CSS *Virginia*. This ironclad promptly destroyed two federal ships and threatened to break the Union blockade. Frightened cabinet officials feared that the *Virginia* might prove invincible and wreak havoc all along the East Coast. Secretary of War Stanton "scurried from room to room" and "swung his arms about while raving and scolding." Fortunately, a new and strange-looking Union ironclad, the *Moni-*

tor, soon arrived to challenge the *Virginia.* It fought the Confederate ship to a draw and forced it to return to its base. Later the *Virginia* was scuttled so that it would not fall into federal hands.[7]

Summer brought more depressing news from the battlefields of Virginia. Secretary of the Treasury Chase had demanded McClellan's removal. Other cabinet officials and many in the public agreed that "he was not a fighting general." Sharing their frustration, Lincoln appointed General John Pope to command the newly organized Army of Virginia, and Pope promptly boasted that his policy would be "attack and not defense." But in August he was out-maneuvered and trapped between the forces of Stonewall Jackson and Rob-ert E. Lee at Second Manassas. Fear gripped Washington, and the War Office prepared to evacuate. Pope lost 16,000 men to the Confederates' 9,000, plus a huge quantity of supplies. Lincoln was distraught: "We had the enemy in the hollow of our hands," he said. Secretary of the Navy Welles saw the country as "very desponding and much disheartened," with "a perceptibly growing dis-trust of the administration and of its ability to conduct the war."[8]

To make matters worse, quarreling among the army's generals had con-tributed to this latest debacle. When called upon to send reinforcements to Pope, George McClellan had replied that Pope should "be allowed to get out of his own scrape his own way." Shocked, Secretary Seward said that he had never imagined "what military jealousy is." Lincoln complained that "all of our present difficulties and reverses have been brought upon us by these quar-rels of the generals." They had acted "without regard of the consequences to the country." But Lincoln's troubles redoubled, as Confederates launched an invasion of Maryland. This new rebel offensive "brought panic and terror to Northern cities, and war governors demanded that Lincoln oust McClellan, emancipate the slaves, and reorganize his cabinet."[9]

Who should lead the Union's defense? Lincoln had no faith in McClel-lan, but the army was "demoralized," and he believed that "McClellan has the army with him." Only McClellan, he feared, could "reorganize the army and bring it out of chaos." The president let General Halleck give the command to McClellan, since "I could not have done it, for I can never feel confident that he will do anything effectual."[10]

Lincoln could have cited additional reasons to mistrust McClellan, for the hostile attitudes and Democratic politics of the general had infected much of his army. General Burnside, joining McClellan's staff beside an evening's campfire, was so shocked to hear the views they expressed that he blurted out, "I don't know what you fellows call this talk, but I call it flat Treason, by God!" Word reached the cabinet that McClellan "had no particular desire to close this war immediately." One of his subordinates, Major John Key, openly explained that the goal was not to destroy the rebel army but to pursue a policy of "exhaustion" that would end in "compromise." As the troops marched through Washington to meet Lee in Maryland, their officers led them by McClellan's house. "They cheered the General lustily, instead of passing by the White House and honoring the President."[11]

Union forces met Robert E. Lee's army at Antietam. They might have gained a great victory, but McClellan made many mistakes. A copy of Lee's marching orders fell into his hands, but instead of attacking the separated, vulnerable rebel forces, McClellan did nothing for eighteen hours and let the "opportunity of a lifetime" slip away. Once the battle was joined, he failed to use his larger forces simultaneously and declined to throw in fresh troops at a critical moment. Only two-thirds of his army saw battle. After the first day's fighting he sat, inert, and did not attack the weakened Confederates, whom he then allowed to return back across the Potomac. In vain did Lincoln implore him to pursue and destroy Lee's force. McClellan, Lincoln groaned, "never embraces his opportunities."[12]

Washington, D.C., saw and felt the terrible human costs of combat. In the war's first days, the capital "had been a camp" for recruits. By the summer of 1862 it had "been transformed into a hospital—the vast base hospital of the Army of the Potomac." Now huge new additions to the number of wounded poured into Washington. Antietam was the bloodiest battle in all of U.S. history. The casualties exceeded those at Shiloh, and almost 8,000 men died in that single day of fighting. Morale sank lower, even among western troops, who saw that the "Campaign on the Potomac is another failure on our part."[13]

Even more appalling military news brought 1862 to a close. Fed up, Lincoln sacked McClellan and turned to General Ambrose Burnside. Attacking Fredericksburg, Burnside foolishly attempted an assault against enemy forces positioned behind a stone wall on Marye's Heights. Burnside's men would have to advance over a half mile of open ground. One Confederate officer surveyed the scene and said, "A chicken could not live on that field when we open on it." He was right. Union troops were trying "to take Hell," and General Lee made a famous comment as he watched the carnage: "It is well that war is so terrible; we should grow too fond of it." Burnside's casualties were almost 13,000 men, two and a half times those suffered by the enemy. "The shock is great," wrote Secretary Welles in his diary. It produced deep "discontent in the public mind." Lincoln moaned that "if there is a worse place than hell I am in it."[14]

The stress on Lincoln and his chief advisers was correspondingly great. One of the few outlets that the president had, to escape the weight of his responsibilities, were the moments when he played with his children. Lincoln was a notoriously permissive and lenient father. He wanted his children to enjoy themselves, and he raised few obstacles to their games and pranks, even when they infringed on work or official ceremonies. Lincoln's two boys, Willie and Tad, often played on the White House lawn with Montgomery Blair's children. Parents and children also enjoyed opportunities to relax at Silver Spring.

> When the President wished to obtain relief from his exacting and arduous duties he sometimes drove out to Silver Spring. There he found quiet, rest, and sage advice, and there he played town-ball with the boys. The strongest impression which remains as a memory to Woodbury Blair, one of the participants in those ball games, is that created by the sight of the president's long legs and arms reaching for distance while he ran about the bases, his long coat-tail flying behind like a flag.[15]

In February 1862 the Lincolns hosted a grand reception at the White House. Mary Lincoln decided to break with social custom and give a large, by-invitation-only party. All Washington gossiped over who was on and who was off the substantial guest list. The preparations were elaborate and many delicacies awaited the evening's guests. But even before the reception began, the evening's hosts were worried and distracted.

Both the Lincoln boys—Willie and Tad—had fallen ill. Doctors of that day called their sickness a "bilious fever." In fact, it was probably a waterborne disease, which they may have contracted by living in the White House. The Potomac River, an often-polluted channel, provided the drinking water for the first family, and it may have been the source of their illness. Mary Lincoln's reception was a social success—guests pronounced it "remarkable and brilliant," or "splendid and dazzling"—but she could not focus on her social triumph. Several times during the evening she went upstairs to check on the suffering children.[16]

The boys' conditions grew worse, and two weeks later the older son, Willie, died. Willie had been a very bright and intelligent boy. Visitors called him

The stress and tragedies of the Civil War took a terrible toll on **Abraham Lincoln,** both politically and personally.

"sprightly, sweet tempered and mild mannered," "the most lovable boy," "ambitious to *know* everything, always asking questions, always busy." Many felt that he "faithfully resembled his father," and his tutor described Willie as "the exact counterpart of his father." He even carried his head slightly to the left, as Lincoln often did. The connection between father and son was very close. Watching Willie think through a problem, the president once remarked, "I know every step of the process by which that boy arrived at his satisfactory solution . . . as it is by just such slow methods I attain results."[17]

For nine days before Willie died, the children's illness "absorbed pretty much all [Lincoln's] attention," noted his secretary John G. Nicolay. Then, late in the afternoon of February 20, 1862, Lincoln rushed into Nicolay's office. "'Well, Nicolay,' said he choking with emotion, 'my boy is gone—he is actually gone!' and bursting into tears, turned and went into his own office." For days Illinois's Orville Browning sat up with Lincoln "a portion of each night" as they watched over Tad, who eventually recovered. But Lincoln's grief for Willie was deep and long lasting. Journalists saw a "marked change" in the president, so marked that "it would move the heart of his bitterest political enemy." For two days he was absorbed by grief and paid little attention to public affairs. At Willie's funeral he was "bowed over & sobbing audibly." Lincoln himself said, "This is the hardest trial of my life. Why is it? Oh, why is it?" Two weeks later an observer commented, "I certainly never saw a more impressive picture of sorrow." For several weeks Lincoln marked Thursdays, the day on which Willie died, by taking time from work to be by himself and mourn.[18]

The president's son was not the only well-loved child mourned by members of the cabinet. In July the infant son of Secretary of War Edwin Stanton died, and Lincoln was among those who attended the funeral. He probably felt more deeply and personally another loss, one suffered by the Blair family. Not only had Lincoln played with the Blair children at Silver Spring and turned to the Blairs frequently for counsel. In addition he relied on them for their loyal support. Postmaster General Montgomery Blair was, said Mary Lincoln, the only cabinet member who "did not stab her husband" daily. At the beginning of September Lincoln received this note from the conscientious and loyal Montgomery Blair: "My little sufferer [his daughter] died yesterday at Philadelphia where I sent her for medical aid. I shall go tonight to bring her body home for interment, unless you think it impossible for me to leave the city now for 24 hours."[19]

Willie's death was crushing for Lincoln, but it hit the high-strung and emotionally unstable Mary Todd Lincoln even harder. She blamed herself and her social ambitions for Willie's death. "Utterly unable to control her feelings," she could not even give much attention to Tad's recovery. She took to her bed and for months was inconsolable. Never again did she enter "the guest room where he died, or the Green Room, where he was embalmed." Mrs. Lincoln gave no more parties, except official functions that she absolutely could not avoid. For two years she remained in mourning and began visiting hospitals with her dressmaker, Elizabeth Keckley. A former slave, Keckley became the Washington confidante of Mary Lincoln, whose childhood in a slaveholding family helped her draw close, in a domestic setting, to an African American employee. Keckley later recalled that Mary's emotional state led Lincoln to say to her, "Try to control your grief, or it will drive you mad."[20]

Unfortunately, Mary's behavior was a trial for Lincoln in several other ways. Narcissistic and craving attention, she bought expensive things in a vain attempt to gain the personal attention and pleasure she needed. She spent lavishly on gloves, clothing, and other personal items, and she grossly over-spent government accounts to refurbish an admittedly threadbare White House. More seriously, she accepted expensive gifts from people who sought to use her influence to obtain appointments or government contracts. To get her way on such appointments she threw tantrums, threatening to roll on the sidewalk or lock herself in her room for days. With the collusion of the White House gardener, she padded expense accounts to try to cover her excessive expenditures. Lincoln tried to reimburse the government for her unauthorized spending and asked the Treasury Department to monitor and flag padded accounts. He confided to Orville Browning "about his domestic troubles." "Several times," Browning said, Lincoln "told me . . . that he was constantly under great apprehension lest his wife should do something which would bring him into disgrace."[21]

The burdens of office were extremely heavy for Lincoln and for Montgomery Blair and other members of the government. In matters of policy, the larger, richer, more powerful North was making little or no progress in suppressing the rebellion. The costs of the war—financial but especially human—were stunningly large, unexpected, and painful. In addition, personal tragedies invaded the homes of both leaders and citizens and increased their suffering. The pain of loss that was so deeply felt in the White House mirrored the suffering that was reaching an ever larger number of soldiers' families. Without victory over the rebellion it was impossible to justify such suffering. Something had to be done to turn the tide of battle.

13

Military Necessity and a Covenant with God

NOW, IN THE latter half of 1862, events and feelings were converging for Abraham Lincoln. As commander in chief he had to find a way to make progress on the battlefield. As a man of antislavery principles, his personal desire was for freedom. The nation's crisis was swiftly changing attitudes, as Republicans and many ordinary citizens increasingly believed that, to win the war, the government must strike a blow at slavery. Lincoln had lagged far behind these shifts in opinion. But he now decided to act. In his characteristic manner, however, he acted in a complex way, moving forward on separate fronts, keeping his options open.

Charles Sumner and the Radical Republicans had pressured Lincoln to emancipate in July. Sumner argued that July 4 was the perfect day for a declaration of freedom, and he, Thaddeus Stevens, and Henry Wilson lobbied Lincoln at the White House every chance they could. Those three, said Lincoln, "simply haunt me with their importunities for a Proclamation of Emancipation." He said he felt like the little boy who couldn't pronounce the names of Shadrach, Meshach, and Abednego from the Bible. When his teacher called on him to read another passage containing these difficult names, the boy broke into tears. "There come them same damned fellows again," wailed the boy.[1]

Religious groups and antislavery delegations were equally importunate. A delegation of Quakers met with Lincoln and asked him to emancipate. Lincoln tried to be sympathetic but noncommittal. He said that he would try to seek "light from above," but he bristled when they suggested that he was ignoring the thrust of his House Divided speech. Before an antislavery group from Connecticut, he became more irritated. Exasperated, he barked out, "I suppose what your people want is more nigger."[2]

Lincoln put Sumner off more politely, saying, "[W]ait; time is essential."

But he did initiate discussions in the cabinet. "We had about played our last card," Lincoln felt, "and must change our tactics, or lose the game!" On July 21 he announced to his advisers that harsher measures were necessary. He mentioned using slaves as laborers and again brought up colonization. The next day there was a discussion about arming slaves. Chase, along with Stanton and Seward, argued in favor of this step, but Lincoln did not approve. Not to be silenced, Chase then urged that generals in the field should be allowed to issue emancipation proclamations. Instead, Lincoln said that *he* might issue a proclamation, based on the Second Confiscation Act. That law gave the rebels sixty days to return to the Union or lose their slaves. Lincoln added that he would renew his proposal to Congress for gradual, compensated emancipation. In addition, he proposed declaring slaves emancipated wherever the rebellion continued on January 1, 1863.[3]

The cabinet did not balk at the idea of such presidential action—another sign of the war's transforming impact on thinking. It seemed wise, however, to wait for a Union victory, so that the proclamation would not be read as a sign of desperation. On August 14 Lincoln met in the White House with five black leaders from the Washington, D.C., area. To them he made his strongest pitch for colonization, extolling the advantages of Central America. It was not one of his finest hours. He seemed to blame the war on African Americans— saying "but for your race among us" white men would not be "cutting one another's throats"—and he emphasized that "on this broad continent, not a single man of your race is made the equal of a single man of ours." It was better "for us both," Lincoln concluded, "to be separated." Even worse, he lectured these men—native-born Americans who had made successful lives for themselves—that to decline emigration would be "an extremely selfish view of the case.... [Y]ou ought to do something to help those who are not so fortunate as yourselves."[4]

Black leaders were understandably offended. Robert Purvis, a wealthy Philadelphian, blasted Lincoln for talking about "two races." There "is but one race, and that is the *human* race," said Purvis. He added that "this is our country as much as it is yours, and we will not leave it." Frederick Douglass criticized Lincoln for "his pride of race and blood, his contempt for negroes and his canting hypocrisy." To this point, Douglass concluded, the Republican president was acting as "a genuine representative of American prejudice and negro hatred." Radical Republicans agreed, and Salmon Chase wrote, "How much better would be a manly protest against prejudice against color!" Leading Republican newspapers, such as the *Chicago Tribune* and the *New York Times* also scoffed at the proposal. Of the five black Washington leaders, all but one rejected Lincoln's proposal out of hand.[5]

On August 20 Horace Greeley, editor of the widely read *New York Tribune*, lectured Lincoln by publishing an open letter titled "The Prayer of Twenty Millions." Greeley called on Lincoln to "EXECUTE THE LAWS." It was his duty to emancipate in accordance with the Second Confiscation Act. He should cast aside "timid counsels" and the concerns of "fossil politicians" in the border states and act. It was "preposterous and futile" to try to put down the rebellion while "uphold its inciting cause" — slavery. In fact, "the Rebellion, if crushed out tomorrow, would be renewed within a year if Slavery were left in full vigor." Lincoln, responding cautiously and publicly, insisted that his "paramount" goal was "to save the Union, and is not either to save or to destroy slavery. . . . What I do about slavery, and the colored race, I do because I believe it helps to save the Union." In closing, however, he added that his own "oft-expressed *personal* wish" was "that all men every where could be free."[6]

On September 22, after the battle of Antietam, Lincoln was ready to act. He told the cabinet that "he had made a vow, a covenant, that if God gave us the victory in the approaching battle, he would consider it an indication of Divine will, and that it was his duty to move forward in the cause of emancipation." He invited comments from the cabinet but made it clear that his decision was firm. No one objected to Lincoln's proposed proclamation. Montgomery Blair, though in favor of "immediate emancipation," worried about timing. At this point he "was afraid of the influence of the Proclamation on the Border States and on the Army." He also worried about the impact on the fall elections. Others, in previous discussions, had made minor suggestions on wording. Attorney General Edward Bates had argued strongly for deportation of freed slaves, saying that social equality would degrade whites and not help blacks.[7]

The Preliminary Emancipation Proclamation promised, first, that Lincoln would again urge Congress to give financial support to voluntary state programs of emancipation, either immediate or gradual. "[T]he effort to colonize persons of African descent, with their consent, upon this continent, or elsewhere . . . will be continued." Then he announced the additional, new direction in policy. On January 1, 1863, slaves in areas whose people "shall then be in rebellion" would become "forever free."

How would Lincoln determine the affected areas? If a state was represented in Congress on January 1 by officials chosen in elections "wherein a majority of the qualified voters of such state shall have participated," that would be "conclusive evidence" that it was not in rebellion. Rebel states had one hundred days, not sixty, to return to the Union and avoid the impact of the proclamation. He then called attention to the Second Confiscation Act and to an earlier law to keep the army from returning fugitive slaves, and he promised to recommend compensation for slave owners who remained loyal.[8]

Interference with slavery in the states had been unthinkable at the beginning of the war. Republicans had denied that the government could do so. Outside Republican ranks, many were sure to be outraged, on constitutional as well as racial grounds. Still, Lincoln had drawn his proclamation thoughtfully and shrewdly. He was still inviting Union sentiment in the South to assert itself, even giving slaveholders a powerful incentive to end their rebellion. If they returned to the Union, they could keep their slaves. Lincoln even sent agents into Union-held areas of Louisiana, Tennessee, and Arkansas to encourage a return to the Union.[9] But if white Southerners continued to fight, despite Lincoln's offer, Republicans could say that the responsibility for ending slavery lay with the rebels.

At first, public reaction seemed mild. Secretary of the Navy Welles found it less extreme, in either direction, than he had anticipated, while Charles Sumner rejoiced that "skies are brighter and the air is purer now." But racist attacks soon developed. Democratic newspapers called the preliminary proclamation a "monstrous usurpation" and an "act of national suicide." The *New York Express* claimed that never before had anyone *"conceived a policy so well fitted, utterly to degrade and destroy white labor, and to reduce the white man to the level of the negro."* A Louisville newspaper declared that "Kentucky cannot and will not acquiesce in this measure. Never!" In Ohio an editor deplored "another step in the nigger business" and an advance toward "tyranny and anarchy." Others warned of a dreaded "Negro Influx." An Iowa paper condemned Lincoln's "insolent fanaticism," and some spoke of assassination as the only way to stop a tyrant. Others charged that the president was encouraging slave revolts, a judgment that Jefferson Davis angrily endorsed. Even in England a newspaper close to the prime minister described the proclamation as "one of the *bloodiest manifestoes*" ever issued by a "civilized government." In Missouri some supporters of the president bemoaned his "negro-ology," and Frank Blair felt compelled to stress the fact that "I am against the social and political equality of the emancipated negro."[10]

Montgomery Blair's worries about the fall elections proved correct. By mid-October John Nicolay, a presidential secretary, was writing, "We are all blue here today on account of the election news. We have lost almost everything in Pennsylvania, Ohio and Indiana." The Democratic Party in those states and in Illinois benefited from campaigning against Lincoln's action, while the failures of the army made the country "groan." Democrats won the governorships in New York and New Jersey and gained thirty-four seats in the House of Representatives. Even though Republicans remained in the majority, Lincoln feared that "he had put himself into a minority with the people."[11]

Nevertheless, he was committed to action, and on December 1 he carried through on the first part of his preliminary proclamation. In the annual address to Congress, Lincoln recommended three constitutional amendments. The first would promise financial compensation to every state that adopted gradual or immediate emancipation by January 1, 1900. The second would give freedom to any slave who had in practice enjoyed freedom "by the chances of the war" but would compensate owners "who shall not have been disloyal." Congress, under the third amendment, could "appropriate money or otherwise provide for colonizing free colored persons with their own consent at any place or places without the United States." Lincoln bolstered these proposals with an extensive argument that the nation could afford the costs involved.[12]

By continuing to advocate for gradual, compensated, state-sponsored emancipation and colonization, Lincoln attracted considerable criticism. Democrats renewed their attacks that all he wanted to do was *"to free negroes."* Republican supporters also were unhappy. Illinois's Orville Browning thought ending the war by compensated emancipation was a "hallucination." Ohio congressman James Ashley was "greatly disappointed." Ashley's colleague, Congressman Henry Dawes, deplored Lincoln's idea that "measures to be accomplished in 1900" could remedy evils "which have thrust us . . . into the very jaws of death." Maryland's Henry Winter Davis called the proposal "ridiculous in relation to the disloyal states." But Illinois's David Davis, whom Lincoln had just appointed to the Supreme Court, recognized that the president's "whole soul is absorbed in his plan of remunerative emancipation." Charles Sumner questioned whether Lincoln's "olive branch would be accepted," but he was more supportive of the president because he was moving in the right direction.[13]

Abolitionists outside the government were more critical and worried that the president might not declare emancipation on New Year's Day. Many waited anxiously through that afternoon and evening while Lincoln shook hands at the traditional White House reception. Finally, he went to his office, steadied his arm, and signed the document in a bold script. A delighted Charles Sumner asked for, and received, the pen used in the signing. African Americans throughout the North rejoiced. "I never saw enthusiasm before," said Frederick Douglass. "I never saw joy before." Outraged critics predicted the "massacre" of Southern whites, another "St. Domingo" in which "half civilized Africans . . . murder their Masters and Mistresses!"[14]

The proclamation justified emancipation as "a fit and necessary war measure" taken "in time of actual armed rebellion," and Lincoln issued it "by virtue of the power in me vested as Commander-in-Chief." His final text, on the recommendation of Montgomery Blair, responded to earlier criticisms by urging slaves "to abstain from all violence, unless in necessary self-defence." Excluded from emancipation were areas in Virginia and Louisiana that were no longer in rebellion because they were under the control of the Union army. Also excluded was Tennessee. Unionists there, with the support of Lincoln's appointed wartime governor, Andrew Johnson, had urged that step to avoid enraging slaveholders, and Lincoln agreed.[15]

Gideon Welles felt that "passing events are steadily accomplishing what is here proclaimed." Still, he recognized that the proclamation "will be a landmark in history." In fewer than two years a slaveholding nation with a constitution that recognized slavery had moved a great distance. To other cabinet members the pace of progress was positively dizzying. Salmon Chase commented that in the Union slaveholders could have kept slavery "for many years to come." Thanks to their "insanity" as a class, the institution was being destroyed. Chase and other Republicans celebrated at Chase's house, and Lincoln's secretary John Hay, who was present, recorded their wonderment and glee. All there felt "a sort of new and exhilarated life; they breathed freer; the Prest. Procn. had freed them as well as the slaves. They gleefully and merrily called each other and themselves abolitionists, and seemed to enjoy the novel sensation of appropriating the horrible name."[16]

Historic as it was, some were already asking what was the practical significance of the Emancipation Proclamation. For slaves held within the Confederacy, real freedom could not arrive until federal armies conquered. Others noted that the legal validity of a war measure would be questionable once the war ended. In addition to parts of the Confederacy excluded from the proclamation, slavery still existed in Missouri, Kentucky, Maryland, and Delaware.

Thus the Union was not rid of human bondage and had not won the war. What would be the next steps? The war had made slavery a visible target, but racism remained fundamental and nearly ubiquitous.

The president's secretary John Nicolay gave the public a signal that colonization was still presidential policy. He wrote an editorial for the *Washington Daily Morning Chronicle* on January 2 which accurately described Lincoln's proclamation as a "warning" and a "promise." It had warned rebelling states that they would lose their slaves if they did not return to the Union; it had promised to let them retain their slaves if they complied. Nicolay then predicted a steady and alarming increase of the African American population, saying it would reach 16 million by 1910 and 64 million by 1960. Fortunately, January 1 marked "the initial point of the separation of the black from the white race. The two races cannot live together under the contingencies of future growth and expansion." The United States would be "the theater of the white man's achievements," wrote Nicolay, whereas in Central and South America black people might have a "great and useful future." Wise statesmen should now work toward the "colonization within the tropics of this continent of the black nation today liberated by the President's wise and just decree."[17]

In fact, colonization efforts had gained new life. In September, Kansas's senator Samuel Pomeroy had become involved in the Chiriqui project. Pomeroy offered to "hunt up a place" and "himself go out and take with him a cargo of negroes." Hundreds of African Americans applied for a place in the venture, including two sons of Frederick Douglass. Lincoln urged the cabinet to "take it into serious consideration." He "thought it essential to provide an asylum for a race which we had emancipated, but which could never be recognized or admitted to be our equals." Montgomery Blair argued at length in support, and Attorney General Edward Bates favored "compulsory deportation." After Lincoln insisted that emigration had to be voluntary, further debate centered on whether to seek a treaty or a contract with some Central American nation. That proved to be the stumbling block.[18]

The governments in Central America expressed opposition, forcing attention to turn away from Chiriqui. Haiti, however, was another possibility. The government there was favorable toward immigration, and a number of black abolitionists had shown interest. Montgomery Blair and other supporters of colonization could be counted on not to give up. Gideon Welles believed that "on important questions, Blair is as potent with the President as either"

Kansas's **Samuel Pomeroy** offered to play an important role in advancing the idea of colonization, but he was suspected by some of seeking financial gain.

Seward or Chase, "and sometimes I think equal to both." Blair even tried to convince Salmon Chase of the virtues of colonization, but the treasury secretary wasn't drawn to the idea, "except as a means of getting a foothold in Central America." The Haiti possibility gained traction in October, when a promoter named Bernard Kock proposed to colonize an island off the coast of Haiti called Ile à Vache, or Cow Island.[19]

On New Year's Eve Lincoln signed a contract with Kock, who was to take 5,000 African Americans to the island, supported by $250,000 in government funds. Secretaries Welles and Seward soon raised serious questions about Kock's integrity, and their concerns caused the contract to be voided. But then two New York financiers, Paul S. Forbes and Charles K. Tuckerman, stepped in, assuming responsibility for the contract and for Kock. Lincoln approved a revised plan in April that would initially involve 500 emigrants, and a ship carrying 453 African Americans departed for Cow Island. A practical experiment in colonization had begun.[20]

The military and social significance of the Emancipation Proclamation were vital questions that remained to be answered. Congress, of course, had shown its interest in using slaves in the war effort back in July, when it passed the Second Confiscation Act. On more than one occasion Lincoln had expressed negative attitudes about black soldiers. The final text of his proclamation, however, said that freed slaves could be "received into the armed service of the United States to garrison forts, positions, stations, and other places, and to man vessels of all sorts in said service." At first Lincoln thought merely of garrison duty or service on ships, two roles where blacks could be useful and relatively safe from Confederate reprisals. He told Frederick Douglass that black soldiers were "a serious offense to popular prejudice." But the nation needed victories. Some were losing hope. A representative from Maine confessed that "nine tenths of the men in Washington, in Congress & out, said it was no use to try any further." To gain the needed victories the army had to have more men.[21]

The army's need coincided with the aims of black abolitionists such as Frederick Douglass. The great crusader and protest leader had been arguing since the early days of the war that the United States should enroll black troops. For Douglass, this was much more than a way to win the war and save the Union. It was a means to lay claim to the equal rights that black Americans deserved. "Once let the black man get upon his person the brass letters, U.S., let him get an eagle on his button, and a musket on his shoulder and bullets in his pocket, and there is no power on earth which can deny that he has earned the right to citizenship in the United States." Henry Highland Garnet agreed: "We must fight! fight! fight!" The *Weekly Anglo-African* of New York City also asked, "What better field to claim our rights than the field of battle?"[22]

In the spring of 1863 the government sent Adjutant General Lorenzo Thomas into occupied rebel territory to recruit black soldiers. Thomas had never been an abolitionist. In fact, the *Chicago Tribune* reported that he "was a southern man, and his prejudices had been opposed to black enlistments." But Thomas followed his orders with alacrity. One of Lincoln's secretaries, John Hay, observed that General Thomas's new attitude "is a straw which shows whither the wind is blowing. The tendency of the country is to universal freedom."[23]

Thomas arrived in the Mississippi Valley and gave "special orders that all negroes coming within the lines of the army should be 'kindly treated.'" To ensure that "every officer and soldier should hear it from my own lips," he addressed units in groups of 4,000 to 7,000 men. To back up his initiative, he made it plain that he would "dismiss from the army any man, be his rank what it may, whom I find maltreating the freedmen." Thomas's recruiting progressed smoothly toward great success. Soldiers, from the common private to men like General Frank Blair, accepted the change as ordered. Many had themselves decided that black troops were needed to help them win the war.[24]

Little had been said, officially, about the social significance of emancipation. Here racism—in its virulent and its commonplace forms—loomed as the greatest problem, and few except the abolitionists were concerned about the rights of freed people. General Lorenzo Thomas certainly was correct when he told soldiers that emancipated slaves would not be sent north. "You all know," he said, "the prejudices of the Northern people against receiving large numbers of the colored race." Many Republican newspapers, such as the *New York Times,* also had been arguing that former slaves needed to stay in the South, where their labor was essential to that region and the national economy.[25]

In his annual message of December 1, 1862, Lincoln had argued that freed slaves would not "swarm forth and cover the whole land." Once slavery was ended, they would have no reason to escape from the South, and he predicted that they would "gladly" labor for wages "till new homes can be found for them in congenial climes and with people of their own blood and race." Besides, he had said, "can not the North decide for itself whether to receive them?" This argument accepted the reality, even the legitimacy, of prejudice. It ignored the question of rights for African Americans.[26]

Lincoln's constitutional duty, his number one priority, was to preserve the Union. How far would he go to conciliate the rebel states and ease the process of reunion? By lagging behind more warlike views, he had repeatedly shown concern for slaveholders' rights and feelings. But the interests of slaveholders and African Americans were opposed. Conciliating rebels probably meant sacrificing the interests of blacks. Striking evidence that Lincoln might make that kind of sacrifice came only one week after the Emancipation Proclamation.

General John McClernand, an Illinois Democrat whom Lincoln knew well, contacted the president to argue the case for some rebels who felt the Emancipation Proclamation had gone too far. Lincoln pointed out that he had been patient with the rebellion and, in words that are often quoted, said that "broken eggs can not be mended. I have issued the emancipation proclamation, and I can not retract it." Yet, at the end of his letter Lincoln offered to make an exception. "If the friends you mention really wish to have peace upon the old terms, they should act at once." The "old terms" meant reunion and retention of slavery. "Every day makes the case more difficult," Lincoln advised, but he promised that they could act "with entire safety, so far as I am concerned."[27]

Lincoln also showed McClernand what his thoughts were about the future status of the freed slaves. The states affected by his proclamation "need not be hurt by it," he wrote. "Let them adopt systems of apprenticeship for the colored people, conforming substantially to the most approved plans of gradual emancipation; and, with the aid they can have from the general government, they may be nearly as well off, in this respect, as if the present trouble had not occurred." By July 1863 the president's thoughts on apprenticeship were unchanged. He then hoped that a former U.S. senator from Arkansas would try to return to Congress, since planned to "bring in his state with a system of apprenticeship" for the former slaves. That system would be "substantially" the same as "gradual emancipation."[28]

Apprenticeship was far less than the citizenship and equal rights that men like Charles Sumner and Frederick Douglass desired. It was far more than most racist Southerners wanted and objectionable even to some Northerners. What might replace slavery? What would postwar society be like, if the Union prevailed? It remained to be seen whether the war could change racial prejudice as it had changed ideas about slavery. Clearly, that would be far more difficult.

14

Traitors or Brothers?

"RECONSTRUCTION . . . should now be employing the best meditations of the statesmen of the country."[1] Salmon Chase, the cabinet's Radical, made this statement to John Hay in July 1863. In doing so, he identified a subject that would unleash vigorous conflict over values and policies.

Before that month discussion of Reconstruction would have seemed premature and impractical. But finally the dark clouds over the Union's military fortunes had begun to lift. Important victories at Gettysburg, Pennsylvania, and Vicksburg, Mississippi, came within a day of each other at the beginning of the month. A relieved President Lincoln "beam[ed] with joy, threw his arm around Gideon Welles, and exclaimed, 'I cannot, in words, tell you my joy over this event. It is great, Mr. Welles, it is great!'" These battles marked a turning point. Lincoln's secretary John Nicolay rightly called them "the turning point of the whole war."[2] The triumph of the Union cause was still far off, but the future finally looked brighter. Politicians began to consider the challenges victory might bring.

The issue of Reconstruction was vitally important. It encompassed a series of interrelated questions. How should the rebels be treated? What should be the status of former slaves? How would seceded states come back into the Union? The answers to these questions would determine whose interests deserved priority—those of the slaveholders or of the African Americans.

CHARLES SUMNER and Salmon Chase, along with the Radicals in their party, believed that great changes were necessary. The task was to reconstruct the Union, not merely to restore it. The rebels were "enemies" and "criminals," said Sumner. "In appealing to war" they had "voluntarily renounced all

Ambitious, vain, and often critical of Lincoln, **Salmon Chase** argued for the rights and interests of the freedmen.

the safeguards of the Constitution." Under the "Rights of War" the Northern Congress could punish them with "extremist rigor" and use "every prerogative of confiscation, requisition or liberation known in war." As for the old rebel states, they had ceased to exist, said Sumner, "call it suicide . . . or suspended animation, or abeyance."[3]

Salmon Chase had taken this position as early as 1861. In that year he met with Senator Benjamin Wade and Congressman James Ashley, who chaired Congress's territorial committees. When a rebel state seceded, said Chase, its "State organization was forfeited and it lapsed into the condition of a Territory with which we could do what we pleased." No longer could it be considered as "in the Union." Instead it "must be readmitted" on such terms "as Congress should provide."[4] For Chase the essential precondition was that "the people of the state should in convention remodel their existing laws on the basis of emancipation." Wade and Ashley agreed. The feelings of rebellious slaveholders were of little importance compared to the future good of the nation.[5]

Those feelings also were far less important than rights for the freed people, argued Sumner and Chase. Sumner challenged Congress to "elevate a race and change this national calamity into a sacred triumph." Chase maintained that "the blacks were really the only loyal population worth counting" in the rebel states. They deserved the support and attention of the government rather than their masters, who were trying to destroy the Union.[6]

Black leaders and abolitionists joined the Radicals in calling for equal rights and strong measures. "Save the Negro and you save the nation," argued Frederick Douglass. Wendell Phillips said that in states like South Carolina "we are not sure there is a white man in it who is on our side," whereas "four million of blacks" were "instinctively on our side." The war, declared Theodore Tilton, was a fight "for social equality, for rights, for justice." Frederick Douglass agreed that "right and justice" required "the full and complete enjoyment of civil and political Equality." The Massachusetts Anti-Slavery Society resolved that every African American deserved "an equal share with the white race in the management of the political institutions for which he is required to fight and bleed."[7]

But the Radicals were only one part of the Republican Party, and few shared their commitment to racial equality. The far more conservative Gideon Welles objected that Sumner "would not only free the slaves but elevate them above their former masters." Welles's priority, and the priority for many Republicans, was reconciliation with white Southerners. By August 1863 many in the cabinet agreed with Seward that "[s]lavery is dead"; Gideon Welles considered "slavery, as it heretofore existed, has terminated in all the States." But for conservatives that made it totally unnecessary to supervise any defeated Confederate state.[8]

In the eyes of Montgomery Blair and his family, the problem was a slave-holding aristocracy that had gained power over the loyal white citizens of the South. Once its power was broken, loyalty would reemerge. Gideon Welles likewise felt that there was no need to make "a war upon the States instead of rebellious individuals." "Forbearance and forgiveness" were needed. Among Republican newspapers, the *New York Times* was key. Its editor, Henry Raymond, would soon become chairman of the party's national committee, and Lincoln called him "my lieutenant general in politics." The *Times* agreed that restoring national unity required "the assent and cooperation of the great body of people in the rebel States."[9]

If Republicans were divided, the Democratic Party of the North was not. It went much further in defending slaveholders and opposing change. Democrats continued their prewar policy of assailing the Republicans and defending the rights of the South. Attacking Lincoln's actions as unconstitutional and tyrannical, they rallied behind the slogan "The Union as it was and the Constitution as it is." The chief barrier to reunion, said the Democrats, was the tyranny of King Abraham and his deplorable abolitionist stands.

How to treat the South was more than a policy question for Abraham Lincoln. It was also a personal one. Lincoln felt he knew and understood Southerners. To a high degree he possessed the politician's special gene for sociability. For years he had relished visiting with ordinary people as he rode the legal circuit, sitting in general stores, conversing and telling stories. In southern Illinois he encountered racial attitudes that were not very different from opinions in any slave state. Lincoln also had deep personal connections with one of those states. Kentucky was part of his history. He had spent his earliest years there. His closest friend, Joshua Speed, had returned to Kentucky to live. Even more important, Lincoln's marriage to Mary Todd linked him to Kentucky, to slaveholders, and to the human tragedies of the Civil War. Like tens of thousands of white families, he experienced the conflict as a "brothers' war."

Mary Todd Lincoln had brothers and sisters in the Confederacy. Emilie Todd was one of Mary's five half sisters and probably her closest connection in the large Todd family. Much younger than Mary, Emilie came to Springfield in 1855 and for six months lived with the Lincolns and with Ninian and Elizabeth Todd Edwards. Abraham and Mary called her "Little Sister," and after she married, Lincoln became close to her husband, Benjamin Hardin Helm. His father had been governor of Kentucky, and Ben Helm, who owned no slaves, discussed slavery in a fairly moderate way that pleased Lincoln. When the war began, President Lincoln used the privileges of his position to try to keep Ben safe from battlefield dangers and political divisions. He wrote out and gave to Helm an envelope containing an appointment as a major in the Union paymaster's corps. This position carried an attractive salary of $3,000 and would keep Helm out of harm's way. Lincoln also promised a posting to the West, where Helm could remain rather neutral.[10]

This was "the highest appointment Lincoln could make without congressional approval." Had the press learned about it, there would surely have been criticism about favoritism for the Todds. In the end, however, Ben Helm declined Lincoln's generous offer and decided to fight for the Confederacy. His decision proved a fatal one. He rose to the rank of brigadier general before dying in 1863 in the Battle of Chickamauga. The news of Ben Helm's death shattered the Lincolns. Illinois judge David Davis said, "I never saw Mr. Lincoln more moved than when he heard of the death of his young brother-in-law . . . only thirty-two years old . . . I found him in the greatest grief. 'Davis,' said he, 'I feel as David of old did when he was told of the death of Absalom. Would to God I had died for thee, oh Absalom, my son, my son!'"[11]

Lincoln tried to help the widowed Emilie. Since Kentucky remained in the Union, he issued passes so that she could return to the Todd family home. He also invited her to come to the White House to visit Mary, who was still distracted by grief over Willie's death. However, Emilie needed to swear allegiance to the United States in order to enter Union territory. When she refused to do so, Lincoln simply directed, "Bring her to me." When she arrived in December 1863, "Mr. Lincoln and my sister met me with the warmest affection. We were all too grief-stricken at first for speech. . . . We could only embrace each other in silence and tears." Emilie and Mary tried to comfort each other. Lincoln reminded her that he had wanted to help Ben and then said, "I hope you do not feel any bitterness or that I am in any way to blame for all this sorrow." He also confessed, "I feel worried about Mary, her nerves have gone to pieces. . . . What do you think?"[12]

Emilie found her half sister "very nervous and excitable." Desperate in her grief, Mary had turned to spiritualists and séances for comfort. She told Charles Sumner, whose status and company she valued, that "a very slight veil separates us from the loved and lost, and to me there is comfort in the thought that though unseen by us, they are very near." She startled Emilie by telling her of dreams in which she saw Alexander Humphreys Todd, the youngest of the five Todd boys and a favorite of his sisters. He, too, had died fighting for the Confederacy. Emilie's visit lasted two weeks and attracted critical attention. General Dan Sickles even confronted Lincoln and chided him for entertaining the wife of a Confederate general in the executive mansion. "My wife and I are in the habit of choosing our own guests," Lincoln firmly replied. "We do not need from our friends either advice or assistance in the matter."[13]

"The Lincolns would have given Emilie Helm and her three children a permanent home," but she left after two weeks. Lincoln invited her to return and offered a special pardon, but this too would require her to swear allegiance to the United States. A year later she again visited Washington and asked to be allowed to sell six hundred bales of cotton. This was too great a request in Lincoln's eyes, since she still refused to take the oath. He denied her plea, and the once-close family ties soured. Back in Kentucky Emilie wrote an angry letter to "Mr. Lincoln." She described another deceased brother as one more "sad victim of more favored relatives" and closed her letter by telling the president that "your minié bullets have made us what we are." This troubled relationship alone could explain Lincoln's feeling that "I have not suffered by the South . . . [but] with the South."[14]

In fact, Lincoln's trials with the Todds were not over. Another of Mary's half sisters, Martha Todd White of Alabama, later showed up at the White House. She and Mary had not been on speaking terms, and the Lincolns refused to meet with her. In a spirit of generosity, however, Lincoln sent her a pass to return to the South. Soon word spread that Martha White had demanded that her baggage not be searched as she passed through Union lines. She appealed to Lincoln, who refused to support her. Nevertheless, a newspaper claimed that she had gotten through the lines with valuable supplies for the Confederacy. Lincoln had one of his secretaries, John Nicolay, write a denial. General Ben Butler, who in fact had not inspected her thirteen trunks, also wrote a cleverly worded statement to try to help Lincoln. But some damage was already done.[15]

A political problem also arose concerning Ninian Edwards Jr., the husband of Mary's sister Elizabeth. Lincoln appointed his brother-in-law as a commissary of subsistence for the army in the summer of 1861. Edwards seemed well qualified for the post, but as time went on the suspicion grew that he was profiting handsomely from his work. Lincoln, subject to criticism that he was favoring various relatives with government jobs, eventually had to act. "Bowing to pressure, the president removed his brother-in-law from the office on 22 June 1863." Another family connection had proved emotionally painful.[16]

In all, Mary Todd Lincoln had one full brother and three half brothers who served in the Confederate army. Four brothers-in-law also fought for the rebellion, and two of her relations were charged with abusing federal prisoners. The quick-tempered Mary cut herself off from most members of her family when they aided the South. She felt that since they were fighting against her husband, they were enemies to her as well. But the many Confederates in her family generated talk that she was disloyal, or that the enemy gained information through her. One morning, as the Senate Committee on the Conduct of the War assembled in secret session to discuss such rumors, President Lincoln suddenly appeared. "Without explanation, he formally stated that he positively knew it to be untrue that any member of his family was holding treasonable communication with the enemy." That ended the Senate's inquiry.[17]

The complications of family in a "brothers' war" afflicted Montgomery Blair as well. His niece, Louisa Buckner, appealed to him for a large loan, saying that she needed to enter the District of Columbia to buy groceries for her family. Despite reports that she might be disloyal, Blair trusted her and granted her request. She entered the District with passes and even a note of recommendation from the president. But instead of buying groceries, she visited drugstores and purchased six hundred ounces of quinine (so important in the malarial South), and then hid them in her skirt. She was discovered and imprisoned for a short time, much to the Blairs' embarrassment. Perhaps this common problem merely deepened the ties between the Lincolns and the Blairs. They agreed on many areas of policy, and Elizabeth Blair Lee, Montgomery's sister, did all she could to support Mary socially in Washington. Mary had deep appreciation for the constant loyalty of Postmaster General Blair toward her husband.[18]

The generosity and compassion that Lincoln showed toward Southern relatives was a characteristic part of his personality. He was not a hater, did not hold grudges, and opted for forbearance instead of settling scores. Once he remarked to John Hay, "It is a little singular that I, who am not a vindictive man, should have always been before the people for election in canvasses marked for their bitterness." As for "personal resentment," he "never thought it paid. A man has not time to spend half his life in quarrels. If any man ceases to attack me, I never remember the past against him." This attitude influenced Lincoln's personal policy of "short statutes of limitation in politics." In 1863, as he began to turn his thoughts toward Reconstruction, it would influence his policies. He directed this compassionate approach mainly toward Southern whites, rather than toward the slaves. The whites, of course, were better known to him and politically far more powerful.

Widespread assumptions about the nature of the American government bolstered a mild approach to the issues of Reconstruction. In Lincoln's own cabinet, the mental habits and constitutional arrangements of the past fostered thinking that followed traditional lines, rather than embracing the changes brought by war. Gideon Welles was a perfect example of this phenomenon.

The secretary of the navy supported the Emancipation Proclamation as a necessary measure. He could not help observing, however, that it was "an arbitrary and despotic measure in the cause of freedom." Welles resisted Salmon Chase's argument that slavery must end, immediately, in every rebel state when the war ended. Replacing slavery with new social arrangements was more than a "delicate" problem. It was also important "not to destroy the great framework of our political governmental system. The States had rights which must be respected, the General Government limitations beyond which it must not pass." Welles admitted that the South had "abuse[d] the doctrine of States' rights." But he believed the doctrine was "sound and wholesome in our federal system when rightly exercised." Despite his recognition that "in the insurgent States . . . the flag and country are hated," Welles clung to these beliefs. Thinking of the South, he said, "The States must have equal political rights or the government cannot stand on the basis of 1789." "No one state can be restricted or . . . have burdens or conditions imposed from which its co-States are exempt."[19]

In these views Welles had an ally in Montgomery Blair and among a portion of the Republican Party. In the fall of 1863 Blair and Charles Sumner crossed swords on the question of how to approach Reconstruction. Sumner developed his views first, in an article published in the *Atlantic Monthly*. Blair responded a few weeks later with a speech in Rockville, Maryland, which created no little sensation.

Sumner began his article, subtitled "How to Treat the Rebel States," with an attack on states' rights. "The dogma and delusion of State Rights," he said, "which did so much for the Rebellion, must not be allowed to neutralize all that our arms have gained." He then developed an argument that "the powers of congress . . . will be important, if not essential, in fixing the conditions of perpetual peace." The natural and wise course was for Congress to establish "provisional governments" or to make the "recognition of [formerly rebellious] States depend upon the action of Congress." The only alternative was to form military governments with governors appointed by the president. That, however, could create a "military empire" of extraordinary "'one man power.'" Besides, presidentially appointed governors had proved unsatisfactory.[20]

Sumner had direct experience with Edward Stanly, a former North Carolinian whom Lincoln had appointed to be the military governor in occupied portions of that state. The president hoped that Stanly would stimulate loyalty among Tar Heels, but instead his decisions faithfully reflected the intractable attitudes of a slaveholding state. After Union forces occupied coastal regions, slaves hungry for freedom poured into towns. In New Bern a religious New Yorker named Vincent Colyer, appointed by General Burnside to be commissioner of the poor, established schools for blacks. Governor Stanly quickly intervened and ordered the schools closed, since North Carolina law forbade

the education of blacks. Sumner, ever the champion of opportunities for African Americans, took up Colyer's protest and went to the White House. Lincoln initially was angry that he was being bothered with a school matter. But
he then countermanded Stanly's order and also told him to stop arresting and
returning runaway slaves.[21]

After arguing that presidential reconstruction was inferior to congressional leadership, Sumner tried to be somewhat diplomatic in his article. He proposed ignoring the already controversial theories described as "state suicide"
or "forfeited rights." Instead he urged a practical recognition of the fact that
"for the time being" there was *the absence of a loyal government* in each rebel
state. Therefore, those states *cannot be recognized by the National Govern-*
ment. It was folly to think of their retaining old laws and constitutions until
"quickened into life by returning loyalty." There were too few loyal citizens
to establish majority rule and loyal governments. He insisted that "the whole
Rebel region, deprived of all local government, lapses under the exclusive jurisdiction of Congress." Since legitimate government "has disappeared in the
Rebel States," Sumner concluded that "the whole broad Rebel region is a *ta-*
bula rasa, or 'a clean slate,' where Congress . . . may write the laws."[22]

Such views were becoming common among Radicals. They received timely
support from the legal scholarship of William Whiting, solicitor to the War
Department. In a letter to Philadelphia's Union League, which was published
in various newspapers, Whiting warned that the defeated Southern states
would ask simply to resume their places in the Union. But the nation should
not allow "men who are traitors in heart, men who hate and despise the Union,"
to rule. They would revert to their former practices and try to "make Slavery
perpetual." The North must insist on its "belligerent rights of civil war." In
every area declared to be in rebellion, the inhabitants "have become public
enemies" with "no rights either State or personal" except belligerent rights.
The only path back into the Union for rebel states would be "by adopting
constitutions such as will forever remove all cause of collision with the United
States, by excluding Slavery therefrom, or [by] continu[ing] military government over the conquered district until there shall appear therein a sufficient
number of loyal inhabitants to form a Republican Government."[23]

To the Blairs these ideas were anathema. The plainspoken and combative
Montgomery Blair attacked Sumner in his Rockville speech early in Octo-
ber, and he attacked mainly on racial grounds. The "ambition of the ultra-
Abolitionists," Blair declared, was "despotic." They aimed "to disfranchise

the South on the pretext of making secure the emancipation of the slaves." Their assumption that rebellious states "are extinct—annihilated by the rebellion— ... is abhorrent to every principle on which the Union was founded." Abolitionists like Sumner would "degrade" the United States racially, said Blair. He sounded a racist warning that under a banner of *"amalgamation, equality, and fraternity"* Sumner and the Radicals would amalgamate "the black element with the free white labor of our land" and infuse African "blood into our whole system." That would produce a disastrous "hybrid race" and a "degraded" government in which "the unmixed blood of the conquering race" would establish "serfdom for the inferior caste."[24]

Then, turning to constitutional and procedural issues, Blair identified his views completely with Lincoln's. The abolitionists could not be permitted to disfranchise "one-third of the States at the very moment the Union is working out the salvation of the nation" in a constitutional manner. Lincoln's approach, Blair claimed, was to "rehabilitate the loyal men and their States and Republican Governments." After the rebellion was crushed, loyal citizens and others who would be amnestied could resume a state's functions. Lincoln "saves the States" by "putting the powers of the Government, as soon as they are redeemed, into the hands of loyal men." Then "the State resumes its place in the councils of the nation with all its attributes and rights." Newly elected "Senators and Representatives ... bringing with them an earnest of returning loyalty, will be met as equals and admitted to the councils" of the nation. In closing, Blair reminded his audience that Lincoln had pledged compensation for loyal slaveholders.[25]

The Rockville speech was widely quoted and debated. It shocked Radicals and all those who accepted the idea that the war had replaced old ideas with new and imperious realities. It asserted that Lincoln's approach was far more conservative. Thus, even before the president gave a major address on Reconstruction, the controversy over how it should be structured was growing. In December 1863, in his annual address to Congress, Lincoln would join the debate, outline his ideas, and signal his priorities.

15

Reconstruction or Restoration?

LINCOLN'S VIEWS ON Reconstruction would be crucial to the nation's future. Yet the president seemed reluctant to be very specific. "My policy is to have no policy." Abraham Lincoln used these words on numerous occasions, describing his approach to the difficult decisions he had to make. His statement irritated Secretary of the Treasury Salmon Chase, who called it an "idiotic notion."[1] Chase was not the only one. Lincoln's claim that he had no policy made no sense to many people; to others it seemed frankly irresponsible.

Lincoln may simply have enjoyed keeping his plans from some questioners, but in another sense his words were sincere. What he meant most of all was that he abhorred being locked into a position before he was sure it was necessary. Lincoln was a leader who liked to keep his options open. He was dealing with complex events, and he felt they needed complex policies that were multidimensional, adaptive, and flexible. That was why he moved forward on more than one path at once, waiting for developments to determine the right path to follow. To a Kentucky Unionist he said, "I claim not to have controlled events, but confess plainly that events have controlled me."[2] Those words were only partially an expression of humility—they were also an honest description of a key part of his decision-making process.

In 1863 the possible paths toward reunion were numerous. Should the Union be reconstructed, with significant changes? Or should there merely be reconciliation with the erring brothers who were in rebellion and a restoration of the Union that had been? Statesmen (and lesser lights) were giving much thought to this important question, and Lincoln came under pressure from many sides.

He had been deeply worried about hostile reactions to the Emancipation Proclamation in the North and in the army. As he later admitted, "hope, and fear, and doubt" had accompanied that decision, and positive and negative reactions had "contended in uncertain conflict." Democrats everywhere denounced emancipation. That was especially true in the West, where Charles Sumner knew that Lincoln feared the Democracy "more than our military chances." John Hay felt that the Democrats showed a "treasonable attitude," and he suspected that by "opposing the Emancipation Proclamation they are really organizing to oppose the war." In Lincoln's own state of Illinois, the Democratic-controlled legislature denounced his action as "a gigantic usurpation" that "invites servile insurrection" and whose consequences provoked "the most dismal foreboding of horror and dismay." General Halleck reported that measures of emancipation were "very distasteful to the Army of the West" as well as to the Army of the Potomac.[3] Only after several months had passed did Lincoln feel that he would weather this crisis.

As he looked to the future and Reconstruction, Lincoln came under frequent pressure from Radical Republicans. Charles Sumner was active as always. In the spring he "persistently demanded the enrolling of Negro troops" and urged land for the freedmen. Then in August he wrote to the president from Boston. He urged Lincoln to stand firm on the Emancipation Proclamation and enclosed letters from England. The respected British statesmen and reformers Richard Cobden and John Bright shared with Lincoln their advice to advance freedom. The next month Sumner brought their letters to the attention of Secretary of State Seward.[4]

About the same time Chase was using his position in the cabinet to lobby Lincoln. The treasury secretary told Gideon Welles that "he makes it a point to see the President daily and converse on this subject [Reconstruction]." Chase was optimistic that "the President is becoming firm and more decided in his opinions," and he urged Welles, unsuccessfully, to second his arguments. Chase was in close contact with Radical Republicans in the Congress, who joined in with similar counsels. Senator Zachariah Chandler of Michigan, for example, wrote to Lincoln and argued that he must resist the conservative advice of the Blairs and Thurlow Weed, the New York publisher and politician who worked closely with Seward.[5]

Events on the battlefield that summer supported the idea that Reconstruction should empower African Americans. In May black troops of the Louisiana Native Guard bravely followed orders and repeatedly charged a formidably strong Confederate position at Port Hudson. General Nathaniel Banks reported that "their conduct was heroic. No troops could be more determined or more daring." Newspapers like the *New York Times* and the *Chicago Tribune* declared that this battle "settled the question" about the bravery of "the negro race." The Republican *Cincinnati Gazette* reported that "they fought with the desperation of tigers." Even a Democratic newspaper in Cincinnati admitted that the troops had displayed "undaunted bravery." In short order other black units distinguished themselves at Milliken's Bend and in an attack at Charleston, South Carolina. The black man "has proved himself," judged the *Chicago Tribune*. The *New York Times* said such bravery showed that African American troops were "entitled to assert their right to manhood."[6]

But change in racial norms was very slight. This evidence of black courage and patriotism also brought out, even stimulated, a virulent racist reaction. Many in Northern society, almost as thoroughly as in the South, rejected any idea of black equality. Shortly after the Union victory at Gettysburg, vicious antiblack riots broke out in New York City. An enraged mob, primarily working class and composed of many Irish immigrants who resented the draft and its inequities, vented special hatred on black people. Racism combined with economic fears that freedom for African Americans might limit others' opportunity. Rioters lynched and killed indiscriminately, even attacking a black orphanage and its helpless children. "The papers are filled with accounts of mobs, riots, burnings, and murders in New York," wrote Gideon Welles. "There have been outbreaks to resist the draft in several other places," he noted, and he commented that these were also a "consequence of the Conscription Act." The prospect was frightening. Welles labeled it "anarchy—the fruit of the seed sown" by hostile Democrats.[7]

Those Democrats relied heavily on racism in the fall elections, trying to win statewide contests. In Ohio they called the Republican candidate for governor a "nigger-lover," the "fat Knight of the crops d'Afrique," and a member of the "nigger-worshiping Republican Party." Young women stood beneath banners proclaiming, "Father, save us from Negro Equality." Republicans, the Democrats charged, would "place negro children in your schools, negro jurors in your jury boxes, and negro votes in your ballot boxes!" In Pennsylvania the Democratic candidate for governor labeled slavery an "incalculable blessing" and hoped his state would favor the South over New England. In both states the Democrats may have lost votes because their candidates were identified with opposition to the war, which now was progressing better. But Lincoln was greatly relieved when his party won the contests there and in four other states.[8]

Conservatives still counseled Lincoln against any strong measures of Reconstruction. Reverdy Johnson, a Democratic senator from Maryland, insisted to the president in October that the South would return to the Union if Lincoln would withdraw his Emancipation Proclamation. Lincoln himself was not entirely dissuaded of such views. He told John Hay in August that Jefferson Davis relied on the Confederate army "against his own people. If that were crushed the people would be ready to swing back to their old bearings." Cheered by progress toward emancipation in Missouri, Lincoln reaffirmed his support for "gradual emancipation" and promised "that the power of the general government would not be used against the slaveowners for the time being," if they adopted an emancipation ordinance. He was also pleased that his military governor in Tennessee, Andrew Johnson, came out for emancipation, and he urged Johnson to arrange elections for loyal voters. There was no doubt, however, about Johnson's general approach to Reconstruction. He sent a telegram to Montgomery Blair in November 1863 urging that the president oppose any idea "of states relapsing into Territories. . . . The institution of slavery is gone & there is no good reason now for destroying the states to bring about the destruction of slavery."[9]

As Johnson's telegram and Blair's Rockville speech showed, a battle over Reconstruction policy was shaping up between the Blairs and the Radicals. Charles Sumner tried to soften the collision. He wrote to Montgomery Blair, "I have never taken any personal exception to your speech [at Rockville]." Hoping to avoid "controversies among friends," he suggested that he and Blair wanted the same things. "Of course you desire to get the *rebel regime* back under the national government. So do I. Of course you desire that it shall be loyal and true. So do I. . . . Where then is the difference?" In an exchange of letters, Blair then argued that loyalists were the suppressed majority in the South; their states must not be treated as if they had committed suicide. Sumner replied that he did not see how Reconstruction could be accomplished "completely *and constitutionally* without the agency of Congress."[10] But there they disagreed. To Blair the only constitutional route that protected states' rights was through the president. He trusted Lincoln to be conciliatory to Southern whites. He knew Congress would be far more stringent.

Lincoln's close cooperation with the Blairs was continuing. As Republicans in Missouri divided bitterly over gradual or immediate emancipation, Lincoln staunchly supported Frank Blair's more conservative course. He also followed Frank's advice on appointments in the state. When "seventy delegates from

Missouri" came to the White House to protest and pressure him, Lincoln met with them but refused to make any changes. Militarily, Frank Blair was proving to be a capable general, but after the fall of Vicksburg Lincoln asked him to return to Congress, "where he could aid the administration politically. He especially desired of Blair the defense of his plan of reconstruction." Frank did come back to Washington, where Lincoln helped him resume his seat in the House, and in increasingly bitter speeches Frank assailed the Radicals. Before Blair returned to Sherman's army, he and his sister Elizabeth Blair Lee "spent the evening with the Lincolns talking military events and politics."[11]

As 1863 drew to a close, many wondered about Lincoln's position on Reconstruction. Apparently he felt that he was steering a sound course between the extremes of opinion in the country. He answered Senator Zachariah Chandler's Radical urgings by saying, "I hope to stand firm enough to not go backward, and yet not go forward fast enough to wreck the country's cause." Similarly, he "thought very excellent" an admiring article by James Russell Lowell in the *North American Review*. Lowell said Lincoln's "policy was a tentative one, and rightly so." He "waited, as a wise man should, till the right moment"—until "the sentiment of the people is so far advanced toward his own point of view, that what he does shall find support in it, instead of merely confusing it with new elements of division." In this way Lincoln has been "firmly uniting public opinion." Lowell marveled that, only one or two years before, "Abolitionism ... was the despised heresy of a few earnest persons, without political weight." Now the war had made "Abolitionists by the thousands." Lowell said nothing about rights for blacks, however, and he predicted that once slavery was dead, "our wounds will not be long in healing."[12]

In December 1863 Lincoln spelled out his policy before the public. He used his annual address to Congress to present his plan for putting the Union back together. In a Proclamation of Amnesty and Pardon he promised to recognize any state returning from rebellion when 10 percent of the former voters had taken a loyalty oath and had "re-establish[ed]" a government. That oath required a person to be loyal "henceforth" and to accept the emancipating actions of Congress and the president, unless they should be "repealed, modified or held void by Congress, or by decision of the Supreme Court." Those who took the oath would receive "a full pardon ... with restoration of all rights of property, except as to slaves." High-ranking Confederates were excluded from taking the oath, and Lincoln noted that Congress had the power to decide whether representatives sent to Congress would be admitted. The state's boundaries, its "constitution, and the general code of laws" could be maintained, subject only to the conditions in his proclamation.[13]

Lincoln added that he would not object to any policies toward the freed people that would "recognize and declare their permanent freedom, provide for their education, and . . . yet be consistent, as a temporary arrangement, with their present condition as a laboring, landless, and homeless class." In his accompanying message to Congress Lincoln explained himself further. He wanted to minimize any "confusion and destitution" that might follow "a total revolution of labor," and he hoped to make acceptance of black freedom easier. He hoped "that the already deeply afflicted people in those States may be somewhat more ready to give up the cause of their affliction"—slavery—if "this vital matter be left to themselves." His requirement of a loyalty oath was designed to identify the loyal, and Lincoln declared that "that test is a sufficiently liberal one, which accepts as sound whoever will make a sworn recantation of his former unsoundness."[14]

Lincoln's readiness to accept "any reasonable temporary State arrangement for the freed people" came less than three weeks after his Gettysburg Address. His famous words uttered on the Gettysburg battlefield resonate in historical memory. There Lincoln had resolved "that this nation, under God, shall have a new birth of freedom." But the nation's "new birth of freedom" clearly had to do with ending slavery, rather than establishing equality. As Lincoln had told Horace Greeley, his priority was "to save the Union," and the Union had been a white man's government. As a measure of reunion, he was planning to leave to the "already deeply afflicted" Southern whites major decisions about the status of emancipated slaves.[15]

At first the president's "ten percent plan" met with approval. "Whatever may be the results or the verdict of history," wrote John Hay, "the immediate effect of this paper is something wonderful. . . . Men acted as if the Millennium had come. Chandler was delighted, Sumner was beaming, while at the other political pole [Kentucky senator Archibald] Dixon and Reverdy Johnson said it was highly satisfactory."[16] How had Lincoln managed to solve a complicated problem in a way that satisfied Radicals, conservatives, and all shades of opinion in between?

In fact, he had not. The various groups initially read into his proclamation what they hoped to find there. Charles Sumner and the Radicals were relieved that Lincoln had stood firm on requiring emancipation. It reassured them that he had even made a personal statement, pledging that he would not "retract or modify" the Emancipation Proclamation "while I remain in my present position" or return to slavery anyone free under it. His reliance on pardons seemed, to the Radicals, to acknowledge the fact that Southerners had compromised their status in the nation. Sumner believed that Lincoln viewed the rebel states as "hav[ing] lost their original character as States of the Union." After all, Sumner reasoned, "We do not *reestablish* a government which continues to exist."[17]

Montgomery Blair and conservatives, on the other hand, felt reassured on racial and states' rights grounds. They rejoiced that Lincoln had treated the war as a rebellion of individuals, not of states. He had spoken of respecting state boundaries and state constitutions and laws, and his program would allow a swift return to the Union. Treatment of the freed people would be left largely up to the states. His "temporary arrangements" sounded a lot like the apprenticeships he had championed in his proposals for gradual emancipation. The proclamation had even mentioned that the Emancipation Proclamation might be subject to modification by Congress or the courts.[18]

"The art of riding two horses," said the *New York Herald* in a wry comment, "is not confined to the circus."[19] Thus, the positive reaction of Radicals and conservatives was deceptive. They differed fundamentally on what should be the status of the former slaves as well as on states' rights and how the rebels should be treated. The path toward a commonly accepted Reconstruction policy was not going to be easy.

Lincoln was hopeful and enthusiastic about his plan. In fact, he was impatient to see it implemented. With his own hand he drew up "record books" in which the government could "receive subscriptions to the oath" of amnesty. "He also prepared a placard himself giving notice of the opening of the books and the nature of the oath required." John Hay noted that Lincoln sent the first set of books to Francis Pierpont, the Unionist governor of certain parts of Virginia under federal control. He planned to send other books to Arkansas. On January 2 he had John Hay travel to a prison camp in Maryland to convince captured Confederate soldiers to take the oath. A couple of months later Lincoln would send Hay to Florida on another amnesty oath mission. But Hay had already found "little of what might be called loyalty" among the oath takers, and in Florida too he had scant success. "I am very sure," he soon concluded, "that we cannot get the President's 10th [the 10 percent] & that to alter the suffrage law for a bare tithe would not give us the moral force we want."[20]

Long before Hay ran into these problems, however, Radical discontent had begun to appear. The *Chicago Tribune* noted that only one day after Lincoln's address to Congress, some Radicals "began to scan it more closely." Frank Blair believed that Radical Republicans who preferred Chase as their candidate for 1864 began to organize on the same day. The focus of their discontent was substantive: the future of African Americans. Ben Butler, whom the war had changed from a Democrat into a Radical Republican, worried that the "Administration has put the negro, his liberty, his future, into the hands of the Supreme Court." Others agreed with Frederick Douglass that Lincoln's plan would "hand the Negro back to the political power of his master," where he was sure to encounter a "vindictive spirit." Missouri's congressman B. Gratz Brown, a relative but rival of Frank Blair, advocated confiscation of land and other steps to change the whole social structure of the South. Charles Sumner remained determined to advance black freedom, and he soon proposed a constitutional amendment to guarantee freedom and establish equality before the law. "All persons," in Sumner's preferred language, "are equal before the law, so that no person can hold another as a slave." Other Republican senators were demanding equal pay for black troops, or an attack on "that wicked pro-slavery prejudice that has ruled in the Congress . . . for more than thirty years."[21]

The Blairs struck back, defending Lincoln's approach. Their focus was on states' rights rather than black rights. Like other former Democrats, the family had formed its political ideology in the days of Jacksonian democracy, with its belief in limited government. That ideology and their racist convictions about the necessity of colonization and white supremacy, began to dictate the Blair family's approach to Reconstruction. As the Blairs spoke out, the gap between conservative and Radical Republicans widened and became more visible.

Montgomery addressed the legislature of slaveholding Maryland on January 22, 1864, and emphasized Lincoln's "continued solicitude for your interests." The president's policy extended pardons, restoration of property, and compensation to loyal slaveholders, and an "invitation" to rebels "to participate again as brethren in the Government." States' rights would have a "perfect restoration." This was very important to Blair, because it meant that "the people and the States most affected" would be able to shape any "changes in State constitutions relating to Slavery." He argued that this was necessary to preserve the principle of a limited central government, but it also meant that Southern states could define their "new relations" with the "freedmen."[22]

Frank Blair spoke up in Congress on February 5 and 27. He attacked the Radicals and supported Lincoln in an aggressive manner that led to greater controversy. He denounced "the Jacobins of Missouri and Maryland" for wanting stronger policies. He criticized Thaddeus Stevens for the "unconstitutional and inhuman" idea of treating the South as "conquered provinces," and attacked others for favoring confiscation. But many of his objections focused on race. Confiscation would sacrifice "our whole kindred in the South to the blacks." The president's policy, instead, meant "amnesty, reconstruction of the States, and the segregation of the white and black races." Rather than black "equality with the white people," Lincoln would "remit the control of the freedmen to the restored States." Frank also directed his hottest anger at Salmon Chase, whose "understrappers" had charged Blair with profiteering, and who was trying to supplant Lincoln. Before Frank left Congress in April to return to Sherman's army, he had used language so intemperate that many turned against him.[23]

The divisions over Reconstruction policy deepened Radicals' belief that their party must have a different presidential candidate in 1864. Salmon Chase clearly wanted the job and was pursuing it. Radical senators, including Charles Sumner, favored a change. Lincoln had recognized, and decided to tolerate, Chase's maneuverings as early as October 1863. But Lincoln did not want to be beaten. He turned to the Blair family for help, and they spearheaded a strategy of getting various state party conventions to endorse the president.[24] Their efforts began to make progress, but the discontent of Radicals only grew. On Reconstruction policy they gained the support of other Republicans who felt that Lincoln had been too generous toward the rebels. By the summer of 1864, before Congress adjourned, the majority had decided that a different Reconstruction policy was needed. Their thoughts crystalized in the Wade-Davis bill.

This legislation was much more demanding than Lincoln's plan. It required a majority of former voters in a rebel state to take the much stronger oath specified in the Second Confiscation Act. According to its language, a person had to declare that he had never voluntarily borne arms against the United States or aided the rebellion. The Wade-Davis bill also looked beyond initial reentry into the Union to ensure that the readmitted states would have a loyal character. It required that delegates be elected to write a new state constitution. That document had to bar high-ranking Confederates, prohibit slavery forever, guarantee all persons' freedom, and repudiate state and Confederate war debts. Once drawn up, the new constitution would have to be approved by the voters and by Congress. If any of these conditions were not met, the rebel state would remain without a "republican form of government" while the provisional governor protected the freedom of the slaves.[25]

Congress sent the bill to the president, only to be surprised when he gave it a pocket veto. Lincoln explained in a proclamation that he was unwilling to see his 10 percent governments in Arkansas and Louisiana "set aside and held for nought." Nor was he willing to "declare a constitutional competency in Congress to abolish slavery in States." He favored a constitutional amendment "abolishing slavery throughout the nation," but he told Senator Chandler, "I do not see how any of us now can deny or contradict all we have always said, that congress has no constitutional power over slavery in the states." Lincoln expected a strong reaction on this point, but "I must keep some standard of principle fixed within myself." Hoping to allay some of the concern, he called the Wade-Davis bill "one very proper plan" but explained that he was not ready "to be inflexibly committed to any single plan of restoration."[26]

The reaction was hostile. Charles Sumner reported to Chase "that there was intense indignation against the President" as a result of the veto. Much of the response concerned the difference between "reconstruction" and "restoration" as well. Congress was worried that Lincoln did not require sufficient guarantees of freedom from a reentering state. Chase and others feared a "possible reconstitution with Slavery." The ambitious secretary of the treasury even believed that "neither the President nor his chief advisers have . . . abandoned" that possibility.[27]

As a result, Lincoln and his party in Congress were on "different paths" toward Reconstruction policy and winning the important elections of 1864. Congressional Republicans had become more stringent and demanding in their approach toward the rebels. Lincoln remained more lenient. The president worried about his chances of reelection, while many members of his party prepared to "publicly repudiate" his plan "in order to reaffirm their own anti-southern credentials with the northern electorate."[28] With the war still not won, 1864 was proving to be a difficult year. It would become even more difficult for Lincoln's attempt to win reelection.

16

Violence and Racism

HEAT AND HUMIDITY are oppressive in Washington, D.C., during the summer months. To gain some relief from the sultry weather, President Lincoln began staying in an isolated cottage at the Soldiers' Home three miles outside town. One night in 1864 he was riding his horse, alone, through the dark toward the Soldiers' Home. Without warning, a shot rang out. A rifle bullet whizzed by at close range, startling Lincoln's horse. The animal bounded forward so rapidly that Lincoln lost his hat. The next day, to minimize the incident, Lincoln told his story to Ward Lamon as a great joke—that hat had cost him eight dollars. But assassination attempts were no joke. When soldiers found his hat, they discovered a bullet hole through the crown.[1] This was one of many signs that an ugly violence was spreading from military battlefields to civilian society.

Racial hatred fed that violence. As the war freed slaves, it threatened all of society's deeply engrained racial arrangements. With change many individuals—including the actor John Wilkes Booth—feared loss of their unquestioned, superior status as whites or competition with black laborers. Resentment at loss of status could easily become acts of hatred toward blacks. In some of the nation's cities, riots targeted African Americans in 1863. In newspapers and political campaigns, racist rhetoric turned ugly. On several battlefields Confederate soldiers demonstrated that their contempt for any sign of racial equality remained strong. Thus, as paths to freedom opened for the slaves, any doorway to equality seemed to be blocked by menacing whites.

URBAN VIOLENCE in the North began in March in Detroit. Rumors spread that a black man had raped a young white orphan girl. In other versions of the rumor the rapist owned a saloon that was an "amalgamation den" (a house of interracial sex). Supposedly he had raped two nine-year-old girls. Both accounts were erroneous, but that made no difference. The desire to punish blacks was contagious. A mob formed and began smashing windows, "hammering against doors, with dreadful curses of 'Kill the Nigger.'" One black man named Joshua Boyd died at the hands of a mob shouting, "Kill him . . . Hang him." Another black man managed to escape with his wife and child, but "[w]e wandered all the night in the woods, with nothing to eat, nor covering from the cold." By morning they had "frosted feet" and found "all our property destroyed." Others noted that the draft angered some whites in Detroit, who blamed the war on African Americans. "If we are got to be killed up for niggers," yelled one man, "then we will kill every nigger in this town."[2]

It was the draft that lit the fuse of violence in New York City. Poorer working men and many Irish immigrants resisted conscription and believed that the rich were escaping their fair share of military duty. The Union's draft law allowed men to avoid service by paying a "commutation" fee of three hundred dollars—far too much for any unskilled laborer to afford. On Monday, July 13, protests began that soon turned violent. Demonstrators started the day carrying placards demanding "No Draft," but by that afternoon attacks were being made on black men. By three in the afternoon a nine-year-old black boy was beaten by a mob. "Kill every 'Black-Republican-nigger-worshiping son of a bitch,'" someone shouted. Emboldened, four hundred rioters descended on the Colored Orphan Asylum. "Burn the niggers' nest," they yelled. Some stole desirable furniture, while others broke up the rest and set fire to it. Alert staff members evacuated over two hundred children, but "one frightened little colored girl, somehow overlooked in the exodus, had hidden under a bed. They found her and they killed her." A few hours later they hanged a black man and burned his body.[3]

"After Monday the crowds increasingly turned their attention toward the local black community." By the middle of the week the rioters were "more predictably Irish and Catholic," and it "became a regular hunt for [African Americans]." The riots were "more murderous and destructive." An unlucky man named William Jones bought a loaf of bread for breakfast and was returning to his home when the mob saw him. Rioters grabbed him, hung him from a tree, lit a fire beneath him, and "capered around it, shrieking as they pelted the body with stones and sticks and clods. . . . When police cut down the body, 'It was said that they found his charred loaf of bread still clutched under one arm.'"[4]

Black victims of the mob were beaten, stripped of their clothes, stomped under foot, knifed, drowned, and frequently hanged. "Old men, seventy years of age, and young children, too young to comprehend what it all meant, were cruelly beaten and killed." Enraged rioters shouted, "Kill the black son of a bitch" or swore "vengeance on every nigger in New-York." Led by young boys, the mob began to mutilate and sexually violate its victims. One dead man was dragged through the streets by his genitals. Another victim of hanging had his fingers and toes cut off. In other places the mob cut "out pieces of flesh and otherwise mutilate[d]" the bodies of its victims. A report by New York merchants later confirmed that "atrocities" committed on the body of one Jeremiah Robinson "are so indecent, they are unfit for publication."[5]

Terrified African Americans fled their homes. Many sought shelter and safety in police stations and in the city arsenal. "Here the poor creatures were gathered by hundreds, and slept on the floor." Only the dispatch of "five Union Army regiments ordered back from Gettysburg" put an end to the violence. The New York City riots left five thousand homeless. More than a week later nearly three thousand black people gathered to receive relief that city merchants had organized. An accurate death toll from the violence is unknown but believed to be at least 105. Rioters had begun by challenging "the authority of the new Republican government in Washington and the future of the post-Emancipation Proclamation war effort." But they soon did their best "to erase the post-emancipation presence of the black community."[6]

There was painful irony in the timing and meaning of the New York City riots. *Harper's Weekly* commented, "It was at the very hour when negroes were pouring out their blood for the stars and stripes on the slopes of Fort Wagner [in Charleston] that naturalized foreigners, who hauled down the Stars and Stripes whenever they saw them, tried to exterminate the negro race in New York." But the sacrifices of African Americans brought out Northern racism on Southern battlefields as well. Black troops at Port Hudson on the Mississippi River "fought & acted superbly." General Nathaniel Banks praised their "heroic" conduct. Yet many white Union officers maintained a "deep instinctive prejudice against serving with them and recognizing them as soldiers in equal standing." By praising their conduct, "Banks not only hurt his popularity with the white troops but also increased their prejudice toward the African Americans."[7]

From Confederates, black troops could expect much worse. At Milliken's Bend in June of 1863, Confederates attacked Union forces atop a levee, and an intense period of hand-to-hand combat—rare in the Civil War—took place.

Black Union troops and rebels fought each other with bayonets and swung their rifles as clubs. When Confederates saw Jack Jackson of the U.S. Ninth Louisiana "smashing in every head he could reach" with the barrel of his musket, they took up the cry, "Shoot that big nigger, shoot that big nigger." Angry Texans yelled, "No quarter." Others shouted, "No quarters for white officers, kill the damned Abolitionists." Several captured black troops reportedly were murdered. The Confederate commander, General Richard Taylor, admitted as much when he wrote that many Negroes were killed and wounded and "unfortunately, some 50 . . . [were] captured."[8]

In April 1864 the Union garrison at Fort Pillow was overrun by troops under General Nathan Bedford Forrest, who later would head the Ku Klux Klan. Federal troops, surrounded, found that few Southern soldiers would give them quarter. "Many, especially among the blacks, died before the massacre ended." Some "massacring Confederates" cursed blacks for "fighting against your master" and rebuked white Unionists for fighting "side by side with niggers." Southern officers shouted, "Kill the God damned nigger" when they caught sight of Duncan Hardin Winslow, who had escaped slavery in Alabama to join the federal army. He was shot through the arm and thigh but survived. Not so lucky were many black Union troops who fought at the Battle of the Crater. Confederates mercilessly shot down black troops who were mired in the loose soil created by a massive federal detonation beneath the Confederate line. Amid the confusion that doomed this Union attack, "racial hatred turned an already brutal struggle into heinous atrocities."[9]

In principle, Abraham Lincoln and his cabinet felt an obligation to defend the black soldiers who were risking their lives to preserve the Union. Before the end of 1863 Lincoln challenged those who criticized the use of black troops. He predicted that when the war was won and democratic government vindicated, "there will be some black men who can remember that, with silent tongue, and clenched teeth, and steady eye, and well-poised bayonet, they have helped mankind on to this great consummation; while, I fear, there will be some white ones, unable to forget that, with malignant heart, and deceitful speech, they have strove to hinder it." In July 1863 he had issued an order of "retaliation upon the enemy's prisoners" for every execution or sale into slavery of black U.S. troops. But in the end, the government did nothing in response to these massacres of captured black troops on the battlefield. A resigned and wary Lincoln told Frederick Douglass, "[I]f once begun, there is no telling where [retaliation] would end."[10]

The acceptance of black troops in the North also left much to be desired. It was equivocal—shot through with racism. True, some soldiers who witnessed black valor at close range shed their prejudice. "The negroes foug[h]t like tigers," wrote one white infantryman who had been at Milliken's Bend. "Not many white regiments would stand the attack of Sunday," wrote another, who concluded, "Their gallant conduct illicited [*sic*] the praise of the whites, who say the nigger will fight and no mistake." But there remained many soldiers who rejected any idea of fighting beside a black man. "We are a too superior race for that," declared one white New Yorker. He and others like him, if they tolerated black troops at all, did so only because African Americans could do heavy labor and "stop Bullets as well as white people." The racist views of Sherman's soldiers—drawn from the western states—were especially well known.[11]

The *Chicago Tribune,* a Republican paper, urged "put[ting] every negro in the ranks at once." But its reasoning was frankly racist: "[W]e should spare as much white blood as possible during the rest of the war." By keeping blacks out of the fight until 1863, "we have paid dearly . . . for our white pride." Similarly, a Northern minister and author who praised blacks' capacity for military service explained that "we need our boys at home." Several Northern states sent recruiters into the occupied South so that black men could fill their states' enlistment quotas. A popular song celebrated "Sambo's Right to be Kilt."[12]

Meanwhile, Democratic newspapers stubbornly questioned the contributions of black soldiers or objected that they received too much praise while "the white soldiers must stand back." The Democratic *New York World* charged that whites have "done all the fighting." The vast majority of black troops did nothing but "swell the pay-rolls and consume" provisions. Even a key Republican paper, the *New York Times,* declared that it was unconvinced that "the ignorant African can fight with the same effectiveness as the intelligent white man." Although almost 500,000 slaves seized the chance to escape bondage, work in Union-occupied territory, and contribute 147,000 troops to the U.S. army, the *Times* denied that they deserved equal rights. The use of black troops was "a purely military question." It was untrue "that any portion of the Republican party or any but a very small and insignificant portion of the people of the North believe the negro race to be the equal of the white race."[13]

Racist stereotypes colored the thinking even of advanced Republicans. John Hay visited Salmon Chase's home at the beginning of 1864 and came upon an arresting scene. Secretary Chase and some "reverend old fellows" from the "Society of Arts & Sciences" were playing with "a most amusing toy, 'the Plantation Breakdown.'" The gyrations of a wooden puppet, imitating black dancing, provoked condescending laughter from this well-educated, cultured group. Hay's diary also recorded such recreation as "Ethiopian entertainment at Sayer's until bedtime." While on assignments from Lincoln in South Carolina and Florida, Hay was impressed to encounter "an intelligent contraband." And when he saw a "dirty swarm" of rebels "escorted by a negro guard," he felt that "Fate had done its worst for the poor devils." They endured "a nigger guard" without, he sensed, feeling resentment.[14]

Racist anger focused on Abraham Lincoln throughout his presidency. "Soon after I was nominated at Chicago," Lincoln told an artist who was memorializing the Emancipation Proclamation, "I began to receive letters threatening my life. The first one or two made me a little uncomfortable . . . but they have ceased to give me apprehension." As his words imply, Lincoln developed a fatalistic attitude about the possibility of assassination. "I long ago made up my mind that if anybody wants to kill me, he will do it. If I wore a shirt of mail, and kept myself surrounded by a body-guard, it would be all the same. There are a thousand ways of getting at a man if it is desirable that he should be killed." In addition, Lincoln objected to the idea of highly visible military guards, standing "with drawn sabres at his door." It might appear that he was "trying to be, or assuming to be, an emperor."[15] The president's attitude duplicated that of others. "Assassination is not an American practice or habit," believed William Seward. Only once had any president been a target—a "crazed Briton" had tried unsuccessfully to shoot Andrew Jackson. Seward wrongly believed that "so vicious" a practice "cannot be engrafted into our political system." Others agreed with Lincoln that perfect security was impossible.[16]

Security measures to protect the president remained rather casual. After appointing Ward Hill Lamon as marshal for the District of Columbia, Lincoln "used him as a bodyguard and troubleshooter." Lamon was a devoted friend and sometimes slept outside the president's bedroom "with a small arsenal of pistols & Bowie knives." But Lamon had other duties that claimed his time and attention. After the assassination attempt in 1864, military escorts began to accompany Lincoln and his wife when they rode to the Soldiers' Home. The Lincolns, however, disliked the noise made by the cavalrymen's spurs and sabers, and rotation of the units assigned meant that the men were not well trained. Throughout the war it was rather easy to gain access to the White House. In February 1864 a "fair, plump lady pressed forward" just as the cabinet was about to meet. No one knew who she was or how she had gotten there, but it turned out she simply wanted to see Lincoln and get his autograph. Laughing, the president told her, "Well, in the matter of looking at one another, I have altogether the advantage."[17]

Less amusing and more frightening was an incident that occurred one night outside the theater. Both Abraham and Mary Lincoln loved to go to plays. It was a favorite relaxation for the busy president, who had an "intimate knowledge" of some of Shakespeare's plays and frequently occupied an upper box at Ford's Theatre or a lower box at Grover's. "The cavalry escort seldom accompanied the President's carriage" on these excursions. One evening the Lincolns were leaving Grover's Theatre with Congressman Schuyler Colfax when they saw a hostile crowd of "secessionist roughs" approaching the president's carriage. The Emancipation Proclamation had heightened the Southern sympathies of this crowd, which surrounded the carriage and began to jeer. At that point the coachman, who was drunk, "fell sprawling on the sidewalk. The crowd gave a threatening shout. There was only a one-armed drummer boy on the box, and Grover was frightened. He sprang to the box himself, took up the reins, and drove to Colfax's residence and then to the White House. Both the President and Mrs. Lincoln warmly thanked him for a very great service."[18]

It was the theater that brought Lincoln and John Wilkes Booth together. Booth made his first professional appearance in Washington in April 1863, when he played a week's engagement at Grover's Theatre. His billing declared him "The Youngest 'Star' in the World." His performance in *Richard III* "was greeted with unbounded applause by a fashionable audience. . . . Business was sufficiently good to warrant Booth in prolonging his stay, for at the end of his brief engagement at Grover's he leased the inconvenient old Washington Theatre and starred, under his own management, for two weeks more." Lincoln might have watched Booth then, or later in November, when he performed for two weeks at Ford's Theatre. In addition to Shakespearean dramas, Booth appeared in productions of *The Marble Heart, The Apostate,* and other popular plays.[19]

Lincoln saw *The Marble Heart* and was enthusiastic about Booth's talent. Another actor, Frank Mordaunt, noted the irony of the fact that "Lincoln was an admirer of the man who assassinated him. I know that, for he said to me one day that there was a young actor over in Ford's Theatre whom he desired to meet, but that actor had on one pretext or another avoided any invitations to visit the White House. That actor was John Wilkes Booth." The journalist George Alfred Townsend also noted that "Lincoln 'applauded the actor [Booth] rapturously, and with all the genial heartiness for which he was distinguished.'" Lincoln then "sent word back stage that he would like to make the actor's acquaintance." Booth, hearing this news, flared in anger. He "said to his informant that he would rather have the applause of a Nigger."[20]

Emancipation had intensified Booth's racism and his passion for the slave-holding South. Increasingly, he could not keep his violent emotions under control. Early in the war, after federal troops were stationed in Annapolis, Maryland, Booth attracted attention with his angry ranting. In taverns and theater dressing rooms he loudly denounced Abraham Lincoln. The president's "despotism," he warned "anyone who would listen ... meant dreaded Negro equality and the end of states' rights." That anger bubbled over in 1862, when Booth was playing at Ben DeBar's theater in St. Louis. He was arrested "for saying that he wished the 'whole damn government would go to hell.'" Early in 1864 he defied federal soldiers while he was on an engagement in occupied New Orleans. Booth loudly sang "The Bonnie Blue Flag," an unofficial national anthem for the Confederacy. He was "quickly surrounded by angry soldiers" but managed to talk his way out of trouble.[21]

Impatient and angry about events he could not control, Booth yearned to turn his emotions into action. He pulled a pistol on a railroad conductor at the beginning of 1864, merely because he wanted the train to continue through some deep snowdrifts in Missouri. Later that year he almost shot a black man who did not behave subserviently on entering a barbershop. Booth went for his gun, but other patrons managed to stop him before he could use it. Even Booth's brother-in-law, John Sleeper Clarke, experienced shockingly violent treatment. Although the two men, in addition to their family tie, were close professional associates, they differed in politics. When Clarke disparaged Jefferson Davis,

> Booth sprang up and hurled himself at Clarke in a wild tempest of fury, catching him by the throat. Other [train] passengers tried to interfere, but Booth held his hold, to all appearances bent on strangling his brother-in-law. He swung Clarke from side to side with maniac strength while his grip tightened. His face was drawn and twisted with rage. Slowly his anger left him, none to[o] soon for Clarke. . . . Booth stood over him with a dramatic gesture.
>
> "Never, if you value your life," he said tensely, "never speak that way to me again of a man and a cause I hold sacred."

By the fall of 1864 Booth's brother Edwin, a Unionist, had broken with John Wilkes because he would not tolerate the latter's frequent calls for a Confederate victory.[22]

John Wilkes Booth dramatized his commitment to the South with claims of violence. In April 1863, while he was in Washington, he had to have a large fibroid tumor cut out of the left side of his neck. An eminent surgeon performed the operation, which was entirely successful. But Booth chose to describe his scar as the result of a bullet wound. He wrote to his agent, "[I] have a hole in my neck you could run your fist in. [T]he doctor had to hunt for my bullet." Such exaggeration sprang from his regret and guilt that he was not a Confederate soldier. "I promised mother I would keep out of the quarrel," Booth admitted, "and I am sorry that I said so."[23]

By this time Booth had entered into clandestine activities for the Confederacy. He began to work as a smuggler and aspired to be a spy. Justifying his nonmilitary role to his sister, he explained, "I have only an arm to give; [but] my brains are worth twenty men, my money worth a hundred. I have free pass everywhere. My profession, my name, is my passport." He "confessed to 'nights of rowing'" when he would carry quinine or other goods across the Potomac into the Confederacy. "Strange men called at late hours" at his sister's house in Philadelphia when Booth visited there. In July 1864 he apparently met with Confederate agents "at the Parker House Hotel in Boston." Later that fall he stayed at a hotel in Montreal that was known to be a headquarters for Confederate agents. He began to develop a plan to kidnap President Lincoln and take him to Richmond. Like John Brown he would use violence, but for the purpose of preventing "nigger citizenship."[24]

The Democratic Party of the North was also determined to block citizenship or equality for African Americans. To achieve this goal Democrats made effective use of a clever hoax that inflamed racist feelings. In December 1863 an inexpensive, seventy-two-page pamphlet appeared titled *Miscegenation: The Theory of the Blending of the Races, Applied to the American White Man and Negro.* Frankly and enthusiastically, this pamphlet advocated the most advanced abolitionist doctrines, and more. It praised unpopular ideas in an earnest, straightforward tone, and its politics were vigorously egalitarian.[25]

"Miscegenation," a newly coined term for race mixing, hinted at the creation of a new and superior mixed race. The pamphlet's text advanced this argument explicitly and celebrated its consequences. Interracial sex and marriage would be the means to strengthen the United States and perfect its society. The racial mixture of whites and blacks would "make us the finest race on earth." "[W]e must let the negro remain with us, recognizing him as one of the great elements of our strength and prosperity." The vigor and health of African Americans would benefit whites and make all Americans more attractive, since the most beautiful human beings were a mix of racial types. Through miscegenation, society could achieve the ideal of "Universal Brotherhood."[26]

On political issues, the pamphlet rejoiced that the war was "a war for the negro." All should be glad that it would end by recognizing at last the "political, civil, and social rights" of African Americans. The Republican Party should headline its platform with the words "Freedom, Political and Social Equality; Universal Brotherhood." Colonization should be abandoned for the good of the nation and posterity. In the future blacks "are to compete with the white man in all spheres of labor." Race mixing would benefit all and prove "of infinite service to the Irish" especially, because "they are a more brutal race and lower in civilization than the negro."[27]

This pamphlet appeared to be the work either of abolitionists or well-educated and advanced advocates of equality. Certainly many of its arguments were matters of principle for abolitionists and Radical Republicans. But in fact *Miscegenation* was a piece of political propaganda written by D. G. Croly and George Wakeman, two journalists who worked for the fervently Democratic *New York World*.[28] The content and tone of their anonymous publication would damage Lincoln and his party by arousing the anger of racists, poor whites, and immigrants. This constituted the first level of the Democrats' hoax.

But there was a second, and equally damaging, part of the *Miscegenation* strategy. Croly and Wakeman sent their pamphlet to several leading abolitionists and sought their endorsement. Charles Sumner was perceptive enough to recognize the publication as a satire or trap. But others either were taken in by the pamphlet or decided to offer encouragement and generally positive comments. Most abolitionists did not, in fact, promote intermarriage; they merely believed that such decisions should be left to individuals. Now, however, Croly and Wakeman had damaging "endorsements" that they shared with Democratic congressman Samuel S. Cox of Ohio.[29]

With this information, Cox flayed Republicans in a speech on the floor of the House. He quoted approving or incautious remarks by Wendell Phillips and Theodore Tilton. Phillips had said that miscegenation could be "God's own method of crushing out the hatred of race." Tilton foresaw that "the negro will lose his typical blackness." Going further, Cox named more than seven others who had "indorsed" the pamphlet. These abolitionists, Cox charged, "are in the van of the Republican movement." It was the Republican Party that had been advancing the status of African Americans step by step throughout the war. "Progressive intermingling" was the "Republican solution." Evidently its goal was to submerge the country in "debt, tyranny, and fanaticism." To repeated laughter from House members, Cox read the pamphlet's predictions that race mixing would produce "the highest type of manhood." A statement that colored people "are our brothers, our sisters" brought guffaws from the audience in the House.[30]

Thus, at the beginning of 1864, Croly, Wakeman, and Cox had laid the foundation for a racist attack on Lincoln and the Republicans. As the crucial 1864 elections approached, Democratic organizations would be able to make good use of all the propaganda spawned by *Miscegenation*. The scholar who has studied the *Miscegenation* pamphlet and its consequences most closely concludes that "in the welter of leaflets, brochures, cards, tracts, and cartoons struck off by all parties during the Civil War, it stands out as centrally significant."[31]

For Abraham Lincoln, the road to renomination and reelection would be rocky. It also would have significant impact on his policies toward freedom and black rights and on his relationship with the Blairs and Charles Sumner.

17

Political Dangers, Ambiguous Policies

LATE IN AUGUST 1864 a depressed but realistic Abraham Lincoln sat down at his desk. Taking up his pen, he wrote a private memorandum, not to be published. "This morning, as for some days past," the president admitted, "it seems exceedingly probable that this Administration will not be re-elected." In that event, Lincoln told himself, "my duty" would be "to so co-operate with the President elect, as to save the Union between the election and the inauguration." Saving the Union afterward, he believed, would be impossible, because pressure on a Democratic president would lead to an armistice and Confederate independence. To steel his resolve, Lincoln folded this memo and had the members of his cabinet sign its back. At a later time, the document could remind a defeated administration of its chief duty.[1]

Saving the Union had always been Lincoln's priority, and Secretary of State Seward regarded it as far more historic than emancipation. Francis Carpenter, a respected artist, was busy painting a large and celebratory canvas depicting Lincoln and his cabinet during the reading of the proclamation. Critical, Seward insisted that the "central and crowning act of the Administration" was not emancipation but "the preservation of the Union." He argued that the "formation of the Republican Party destroyed slavery." Saving the Union, however, would save "popular government for the world."[2] Now, in the most turbulent, dark days of Lincoln's presidency, the future of the Union was in doubt. In fact, everything seemed to be in doubt.

The war was again going badly. Enormous, shocking casualties fueled a war weariness that was overtaking the North. Racist fears and resentments fed anger over strong federal measures and the personal sacrifices involved in war. Democrats and Radical Republicans both sought to unseat the president. All of Lincoln's political advisers despaired of his reelection and feared that the

William Henry Seward was the most prominent Republican of the 1850s, whose radical-sounding rhetoric disguised a political temperament that was actually quite moderate.

influence of the Peace Democrats might lead to Southern independence. In an incendiary political atmosphere, emancipation itself came into question. The idea of racial equality, always scorned and unpopular, became almost invisible.

In addition, a split was opening up in the Republican Party, which from its founding had been an amalgam of very different elements. Lincoln found his relationships with Charles Sumner and the Blairs changing. The shifting fortunes of this electoral year at first distanced him from Charles Sumner. But before the year was over, their ties would again grow closer. The opposite trajectory described his relationship with the Blairs. Close supporters, as they always had been, the Blairs gave critical aid to Lincoln before his nomination and after. But their racism and conservative, states' rights principles put them at odds with the Radical Republicans, who were gaining strength in Washington. For political reasons Lincoln needed to put space between himself and the Blairs.

Lincoln tried to keep a foot in both camps, but practical facts as well as politics forced him to avoid the ideological consistency that guided the Blairs. With Lincoln's support, members of his administration continued to pursue possibilities of colonization. But these efforts failed to achieve any success. Colonization was going nowhere, while sentiments in Congress moved steadily in the opposite direction from the Blairs' views. Lincoln's own conservative impulses hurt him with his party and gained him little with Democrats. As a politician Lincoln would have to use all his ingenuity and cleverness to stay afloat in 1864. Ambiguity and lack of clarity proved necessary to survival. That ambiguity characterized both his rhetoric and his policies.

LINCOLN'S FIRST CHALLENGE in 1864 was simply to secure renomination from his party. It had long been obvious that Salmon Chase wanted his job. An able and intelligent man, Chase was also self-serving and famously ambitious. Senator Ben Wade cleverly remarked that "Chase is a good man, but his theology is unsound. He thinks there is a fourth Person in the Trinity," namely Samuel Chase. As early as 1863 Lincoln's secretaries had remarked on Chase's "Presidential aspirations." John Hay recorded that Lincoln compared them "to a horsefly on the neck of a plough horse" — they "kept him lively about his work." Chase's maneuverings sometimes struck the president as in "bad taste," but he resolved to be "indifferent" to them "so long as [Chase] does his duty as the head of the Treasury Department."[3]

While Lincoln focused on his job, the Blairs early on launched efforts to fend off rivals and secure support for the president. In the summer of 1863 Montgomery Blair had tried to convince Massachusetts's Radical senator Henry Wilson that Lincoln was the best candidate to unite the party's divergent elements, but Wilson "afterward went back on him." Early in 1864 Lincoln asked Frank Blair to check on the plans of General Grant, and Frank soon brought back good news. The popular general assured Frank and the president that he had "no political aspirations."[4] A few months later Montgomery and his father, Francis Preston Blair, both approached George McClellan. Their object was to convince the likely Democratic nominee not to run. In exchange they suggested that McClellan could replace Henry Halleck as chief of staff or return to a field command. This effort did not succeed, but the Blairs were also busy speaking for Lincoln and working with other Lincoln loyalists in state party organizations.[5]

These efforts brought the challenge from Secretary of the Treasury Chase to a halt in February 1864. Lincoln's supporters in New Hampshire, Pennsylvania, and several other states pushed pro-Lincoln resolutions through their state parties. Chase's backers then issued circulars arguing the need for a stronger candidate — Chase. This caused other state parties and the Republican

National Committee, most of whose members were appointed by Lincoln, to endorse the president. Frank Blair, on leave from the army and back in Congress with Lincoln's help, delivered a blistering attack on Chase for corruption in Treasury affairs. Then the Republican convention in Chase's home state of Ohio urged Lincoln's renomination, and a somewhat embarrassed Chase announced that he would not be a candidate.[6]

Republicans who believed in stronger antislavery and war policies were not deterred, however. They had many supporters in Congress. In fact, "the chairmen of the most important Senate committees"—Henry Wilson, Ben Wade, Zachariah Chandler, and James Grimes—were all "openly opposed to a second term."[7] The party's "best men" felt that the president had been "in the way" and that any success had been achieved "in spite of him." Senator William Fessenden judged him "weak as water." Outside Washington, support for Lincoln was "only apparent," admitted Lyman Trumbull. A Minnesota official felt "we need a great leader and not one who must be pushed," and abolitionists damned him for "conciliat[ing] the Democratic party" and being "not up to the office."[8]

Charles Sumner had not yet broken with the president. He did not want to lose his influence in the White House, but his views on policy were in line with the opposition. Sumner "was at one of the lowest points in his long public career." He had made a bellicose speech against Great Britain for allowing the construction of warships, the so-called Laird rams, for the Confederacy, only to look silly when it was learned that Britain had already seized them. His quarrel with Montgomery Blair over Reconstruction ended in nothing better than a draw. Worst of all, his influence in the Senate seemed slight, and he had only a minor role in the framing of an amendment to abolish slavery.[9]

Sumner tried to be Congress's liberating abolitionist in 1864. He spoke repeatedly in favor of equal pay for black soldiers, the repeal of the old fugitive slave acts, and the need to end discrimination on Washington's streetcars. He offered lengthy resolutions on Reconstruction, which he believed must be designed by Congress. Using ceremony to promote universal emancipation, he had two African Americans carry a huge petition, the "Prayer of the Hundred Thousand," into the Senate chamber and deposit it on his desk. But although he gained approval to head the Special Committee on Slavery and the Freedmen, the Judiciary Committee controlled discussion of a Thirteenth Amendment. Frustrated and losing prominence, Sumner felt he had received little help from Lincoln.[10]

Before long, Sumner joined the Radicals and abolitionists in wishing for a different presidential candidate. He even said that any member of Massachusetts's congressional delegation was better qualified than Lincoln. But he refused to back a rival candidate unless Lincoln chose to withdraw.[11] Leading abolitionists went much further. Elizabeth Cady Stanton declared that Lincoln had "proved his incapacity," and Wendell Phillips accurately pointed out that Lincoln "wishes to save slaveholders as much loss & trouble as he can." Frederick Douglass voiced the discontent of the most radical when he insisted on "perfect equality for the black man in every State before the law, in the jury box, at the ballot-box and on the battle-field." In May a "people's provisional committee" called for a national convention, to meet in Cleveland and nominate a third-party candidate.[12]

The Blairs monitored this development closely. A couple hundred abolitionists and activists met in Cleveland, announced the formation of a new "Radical Democratic Party," and nominated John C. Frémont for president. Their platform avoided specifics such as black suffrage or land redistribution but spoke of "equality before the law." It also endorsed amending the constitution to abolish slavery, a measure that had now passed the Senate but not the House. An ally of the Blairs reported, "Convention tremendous fizzle. Less than two hundred . . . disappointed contractors, soreheads, Garrisonians and Copperheads."[13]

A week later the Republican Convention met in Baltimore. Lincoln urged the party's chairman to endorse an amendment outlawing slavery, thus matching Frémont's platform plank. It was done, amid tumultuous enthusiasm. Nothing was said, however, about equal rights or equality before the law. The admission of some delegates from the South "in effect endorsed Lincoln's approach" to Reconstruction, but another resolution was understood as a demand for the resignation of conservative members of the cabinet, Montgomery Blair foremost among them. As Lincoln's running mate, the convention nominated the Unionist but former Democrat from Tennessee Andrew Johnson.[14] That move accompanied a re-titling of the party as the "Union Party," in a bid to capture the votes of all who stood for preservation of the Union.

A long and difficult summer was only beginning, however, and Lincoln's chances of reelection soon plummeted. The military news was ghastly and depressing. For many weeks nothing definitive was heard from Sherman's army in Tennessee and Georgia. But from Virginia came news that was appalling.

Grant had decided to "fight it out on this line if it takes all summer." With twice as many men as Lee and the ability to replenish his ranks, Grant pushed forward relentlessly. He was ready to accept "very severe" losses, and his attacks had precisely that result. There were 28,000 casualties at the Battle of the Wilderness, 14,000 at Spotsylvania, and nearly 9,000 at Cold Harbor, with most in the first half hour. Union soldiers pinned their names and hometowns to the back of their uniforms so that their bodies could be identified after the battle. By the battle of Petersburg, Grant had lost three times as many men as Lee. During that summer Grant's casualties were as great as all the men Lee had in his army.[15]

In time such carnage would fatally weaken the Confederacy, but first it produced a powerful revulsion in the North, intensifying "the peace movement and the opposition to Lincoln." Every day Northern newspapers published long lists of the killed and wounded. What people called "the butcher's bill" was unprecedented. At one point "there were three days and nights in which the procession of ambulances" to Washington "never ceased." To people in the capital, "staring at the jolting caravans, it seemed that Grant's whole army was being carried back to the city." Every day, lamented Gideon Welles, soldiers' bodies, "slain or mutilated," arrived in Washington "by the hundreds. . . . The immense slaughter of our brave men chills and sickens us all." It created "a feeling of despondency" shared by men in high places and ordinary citizens. Lincoln understood that this bloody arithmetic favored the Union. "Every great battle, even if it is a drawn one, is a defeat to the rebels," he said. But the political costs were enormous.[16]

"The Plain Truth," declared the Democratic *New York World,* was that "months of the most terrific fighting and bloodshed the world ever saw" had produced results "worse than nugatory." The great losses without visible gains showed that Lincoln's plans were "wrong from the beginning." His Republican administration was responsible for "an army shattered in strength, and wounded to the heart by many failures and sore abuse; a campaign spoiled and overturned; ground already gained already lost." On military grounds alone, the paper asked, "Are these the men in whom we have longer a right to put one atom of a patriot's trust?"[17]

But Democratic attacks went well beyond the military situation. Racism was a central tool of the Democrats. It fueled and intensified the opposition's campaign. The *Cincinnati Enquirer* charged that Lincoln's actions, as well as his long limbs and "buffoonery," showed "that he is the outcrop of a remote

African in his ancestry." Other Democratic journals published racist doggerel, such as

> Hurrah for the nigger
> The sweet-scented nigger,
> And the paradise for the undertaker!
> Hurrah for Old Abe.

Only people "crazy with 'negro on the brain,'" charged the Democrats, would support such an abolitionist president. The "whole Republican party has followed its blind leaders, the abolitionists," said the *New York World*. The progress of Republican legislation showed that Lincoln's goal was "political equality for slaves—social, civil, political equality of the white and black race North and South."[18]

Intermarriage was, supposedly, a Republican goal. Democrats in Illinois campaigned under banners reading "Ours is a White Man's Government, Defile it not with Miscegenation." White nurses in occupied Port Royal, South Carolina, claimed the *New York World*, "had given birth to mulatto infants," and for abolitionists "Negro equality is no longer the doctrine; it is now negro superiority." Democratic campaign documents, distributed as guides to party orators, highlighted the *Miscegenation* pamphlet and seized on any Republican comment favorable to racial equality. Greeley's *New York Tribune*, noted the Democrats, had said "that blacks and whites should intermarry if they wish." Lincoln's 10 percent government in Louisiana was "compelling white and black children to mingle together at public school." The Central Lincoln Club in New York supposedly hosted a "negro ball," where "love-sick" Republicans danced with voluptuous, "wriggling" black belles, some of whom were "of the pure Congo or Bozoo character, black as the ace of spades." Another Democratic publication, "What Miscegenation Is!," featured a drawing of a black man with grotesquely large lips kissing a fair white maiden.[19] Republicans knew that such charges were highly damaging. An Ohio Republican judged that "hatred to rebels has made thousands eager to abolish slavery, but no one is the less prejudiced against negro social equality." In fact, he warned Senator John Sherman, "the prejudice against social equality is just as strong now as ever."[20]

There were additional weapons in the Democratic arsenal. All through the war Democrats had been assailing Lincoln as a tyrant. King Abraham, they said, was violating the Constitution, destroying liberty, and ruining the

country. In May two New York papers printed a bogus presidential proclamation that Lincoln was calling for 400,000 more troops. Other common
charges were that his use of military force was supplanting civil authority and
"rob[bing] the people of their personal rights." Lincoln was "guilty of executive usurpations which ought to subject him to impeachment." The huge cost
of the war threatened the nation with "ruin" at the hands of a party that "has
taken the first step toward a repudiation of the national debt." And after three
years, Democrats argued, the South "is in a better condition to fight than it
has been at any preceding period."[21]

For all these reasons Lincoln's campaign for reelection was sure to be difficult. Then, in July, a crisis arose that seemed to guarantee defeat. Jefferson
Davis had sent commissioners to Canada, just across from Niagara Falls, to
promote peace sentiment and pro-Confederate activities. These agents attracted the attention of the *New York Tribune*'s Horace Greeley. This influential editor enjoyed "the largest national circulation of any newspaper." Now
he wrote to Lincoln, urging the president to send someone to negotiate with
the Confederates. "[O]ur bleeding, bankrupt, almost dying country," Greeley
argued, "longs for peace—shudders at the prospect of fresh conscriptions,
of further wholesale devastations, and of new rivers of human blood." In a
subtle warning that he might go public with his pressure, Greeley added that
any suspicion that Lincoln shunned peace would do "great harm . . . in the
approaching Elections."[22]

Lincoln had to respond. He sent an unwilling Greeley to sound out
the commissioners, and on July 18 he issued a public statement headed "To
Whom it may concern": "Any proposition which embraces the restoration of
peace, the integrity of the whole Union, and the abandonment of slavery, and
which comes by and with an authority that can control the armies now at war
against the United States will be received and considered by the Executive
government of the United States, and will be met by liberal terms on other
substantial and collateral points." In the war-weary North, this statement ig-
nited a firestorm of criticism and political outrage. The problem lay in five
words: "and the abandonment of slavery." Despite the fact that a constitutional amendment was being discussed to make Lincoln's war measure permanent, Democrats were livid and even some Republicans were troubled.[23]

Lincoln and his supporters had always maintained that their purpose was
to restore the Union. The Preliminary Emancipation Proclamation began
with the assertion that "as heretofore" the "object" of the war was to "practi-

cally restor[e]" the Union. Lincoln justified his final proclamation on January 1, 1863, as a "military necessity" and a "fit and necessary war measure for suppressing" the rebellion. Major Republican papers such as the *New York Times* steadily declared that emancipation was "secondary in importance to the salvation of the Union, and not to be sought at its expense." Again in the spring of 1864 the *Times* had explained that Lincoln had "but one fixed aim, and that was the salvation of the Republic," rather than emancipation. Now it seemed to all parties that Lincoln had elevated emancipation to the status of a nonnegotiable war aim, equal with reunion. Democrats leapt to the attack as Republicans quailed.

Lincoln's "peace ultimatum," said the *New York Herald*, revealed that "the abolition of slavery" was now a *"sine qua non"* to ending the war. "Why has he now taken this extreme ground, when he has always, heretofore . . . insisted that the Union is the paramount, while slavery is but a secondary question?" The *Cincinnati Daily Enquirer* charged that Lincoln favored "depopulating and impoverishing the country" to achieve abolition. He had admitted what critics long suspected, that "the war is waged . . . not to restore the Union, but for the abolition of slavery as the main object." White men were to give their lives "for the negro." The *New York World* claimed that the Confederates were ready to make peace on reasonable terms, but Lincoln "insists on the complete abolition of slavery as an indispensable condition of peace." The president had "abandoned, finally all pretense or appearance of waging a constitutional war." "[H]e has no more right to continue a war for the abolition of slavery than he would have had to commence a war for that purpose." Voters would teach Lincoln a lesson: "They will not supply men and treasure to prosecute a war in the interest of the black race."[24]

This bombshell was too much for Republicans to withstand. Loyal party men throughout the North lamented that Lincoln had "blunder[ed]." A Buffalo newspaper that had supported the president now asked, "What are we fighting for?" and speculated that peace might have been possible except for Lincoln's surprising statement. "I am in active correspondence with your staunchest friends in every state," wrote the incoming chairman of the Republican National Committee, Henry Raymond. "[F]rom them I hear but one report. The tide is setting strongly against us." The "lack of military success" had been bad enough, but now the public believed "that we are not to have peace *in any event* under this administration until Slavery is abandoned." Raymond urged Lincoln to counter this impression through an "authoritative act." The

New London Chronicle summed up the reaction to Lincoln's new propositions on the abandonment of slavery. They "*are an effectual bar against peace.* HE MUST MODIFY THEM SOMEWHAT, OR HE WILL NEVER BE REELECTED PRESIDENT."[25]

Lincoln reacted to this crisis in the customary manner of politicians. He and his allies tried to escape from a tight spot by applying the lubricant of slippery language. A loyal War Democrat, an editor from Wisconsin, had written to Lincoln, complaining that his words left "us no ground to stand upon." In response, Lincoln drafted a letter containing this argument: "To me it seems plain that saying re-union and abandonment of slavery would be considered, if offered, is not saying that nothing *else* or *less* would be considered if offered." Lincoln then claimed that his statement to Horace Greeley in 1862—which began, "If I could save the Union without freeing any slave I would do it"— was as true "now, as when I first said it." He closed this letter with the words, "If Jefferson Davis wishes, for himself, or for the benefit of his friends at the North, to know what I would do if he were to offer peace and re-union, saying nothing about slavery, let him try me."[26]

Lincoln consulted various people on whether to send this letter. He met with Frederick Douglass to discuss how more slaves could be encouraged to escape into Union lines, and Douglass—not surprisingly—objected strongly to the letter's backsliding on emancipation.[27] Ultimately, Lincoln decided not to send the letter, but his allies made its arguments for him. The *New York Times* answered Democratic criticisms in unqualified language. The *Times* insisted that Lincoln had "*never* 'refused' to receive or consider any proposition looking to peace or Union unless accompanied with the abandonment of slavery.' He has *never* 'prescribed' that abandonment as a '*sine qua non*' of receiving or considering such propositions." The paper then repeated, just as Lincoln had, the president's words in 1862 to Horace Greeley and emphasized that Lincoln used language carefully. Returning to the idea of "let Davis try me," the *Times* concluded: "Mr. Lincoln did say that he *would* receive and consider propositions for peace, coming with proper authority, *if* they embraced the integrity of the Union *and* the abandonment of slavery. But he did not say that he would *not* receive them even if they embraced neither."[28]

The *Albany Evening Journal* published a similar article, Interior Secretary John Usher made the same argument in a public address, and Secretary of State Seward gave a supportive speech in Auburn, New York. Seward's words were important because they later found their way into Lincoln's policy statements. Seward answered criticism that Lincoln was insisting on abolition by declaring that once rebels "laid down their arms, the war will instantly cease." Thereafter, "all the moral, economical, and political questions, as well questions affecting slavery as others which shall then be existing, . . . will, by force of the Constitution, pass over to the arbitrament of courts of law and to the councils of legislation."[29]

What, exactly, did that mean? A role for courts and "councils of legislation" suggested that Lincoln's emancipation might not be the final word. Since "councils" was plural, it implied future actions by state legislatures as well as Congress. Could Southern states gain a voice on the Thirteenth Amendment "by force of the Constitution"? The National Convention of Colored Men drew that conclusion and protested that "in returning to the Union, slavery has a fair chance to live." Angrily the convention criticized the administration as "not only ready to make peace with the Rebels, but to make peace with slavery also."[30]

Charles Sumner was able to suggest a helpful, practical step. Sumner was present when the journalist James Gilmore reported to Lincoln on a conversation that he and Colonel James Jacquess had arranged with Jefferson Davis. The Confederate president had insisted to these Northern visitors that the Confederacy would never accept reunion. Only independence would be considered. Immediately Sumner suggested that Gilmore publish this information in newspapers and the *Atlantic Monthly*. This magazine as well as a Boston newspaper carried appropriate stories, which would help to demonstrate that Lincoln's conditions were not preventing reunion.[31]

But what saved Lincoln from defeat was the fall of Atlanta. General Sherman captured the city on September 2, 1864, and a wave of joyous relief swept over the Republican Party. At last a victorious conclusion to the war seemed almost inevitable. John Nicolay judged that the "Atlanta victory alone ought to win the Presidential contest for us." A few days later he noted, "There is a perfect revolution in feeling. Three weeks ago our friends everywhere were despondent, almost to the point of giving up the contest in despair. Now they are hopeful, jubilant, hard at work and confident of success." Charles Sumner rallied to Lincoln's support and gave speeches in New York, Connecticut, and Massachusetts. Southerners, too, sensed with Mary Boykin Chesnut that "[o]ur all depends on that army at Atlanta. If that fails us, the game is up."[32]

A few political adjustments remained before Lincoln could be safely reelected. At the end of June the president had disposed of his ambitious secretary of the treasury. When Chase, miffed over some patronage appointments, offered one of his periodic resignations, Lincoln promptly accepted it. Lincoln then virtually had to require an unwilling Senator Fessenden to accept responsibility for the Treasury Department. But with a leading Radical like Chase out of the cabinet, Radicals and other Republicans demanded the ouster of the conservative Montgomery Blair.[33]

Personal relations between the president and all the Blair family were still close and warm. Lincoln had sympathized with his postmaster general when Confederate raiders invaded Maryland and destroyed his Silver Spring home that summer. When an angry Blair denounced the army's failure to protect his property, General Halleck and Secretary of War Stanton demanded Blair's dismissal. But Lincoln defended Blair's understandable "vexation at so severe a loss" and lectured the cabinet: "I must myself be the judge, how long to retain in, and when to remove any of you from his position." Still, Lincoln could no longer ignore the direction of Republican sentiment inside Congress and out. Backers of Frémont indicated that he might quit the race if Blair were gone. Even the Republican Party's Executive Committee urged Blair's removal.[34]

For their part, the Blairs remained ready to help the president in whatever way they could. On September 23 Montgomery Blair surprised Gideon Welles by announcing that he was "decapitated . . . no longer a member of the Cabinet." Lincoln's had explained his decision to Blair in a letter: "You have generously said to me more than once, that whenever your resignation could be a relief to me, it was at my disposal. The time has come. You very well know that this proceeds from no dissatisfaction of mine with you personally or officially. Your uniform kindness has been unsurpassed by that of any friend." The president added that he could remember "no single complaint" about Blair's work in the Post Office. Welles and Blair both recognized that the resignation was "a peace-offering to Frémont and his friends."[35]

The Blair family promptly began making speeches in support of Lincoln. Montgomery explained, "I retired on the recommendation of my father" who "would not permit a son of his to stand in the way of the glorious and patriotic President who leads us on to success." At this point Lincoln *was* on the road to success. A last-minute tour of New England by the ever-hopeful Salmon Chase had aroused no enthusiasm. With Blair gone from the cabinet, John C. Frémont soon ended his campaign, which had failed in any case to build much momentum. Most of Frémont's die-hard backers swallowed hard or held their noses and gave their support to Lincoln. Maryland's Radical Henry Winter

After he became secretary of the interior, **John Usher** assisted Lincoln with ideas for colonization, but he was not always effective.

Davis was "so disgusted that he cannot talk." But Senators Ben Wade and Zachariah Chandler campaigned hard for Lincoln's reelection. "To save the nation," said Wade, "I am doing all for him that I possibly could for a better man."[36]

Thus, Lincoln survived a politically dangerous time and won reelection. A close observer would be hard pressed to tell whether Lincoln's policies were going to become more Radical or continue to be significantly conciliatory. His endorsement of the Thirteenth Amendment suggested one thing. His backtracking after the "To Whom It May Concern" letter, and the words of allies like Seward and Henry Raymond, pointed in the opposite direction. The next significant indication of Lincoln's direction would come in his annual address to Congress in December.

Meanwhile, the future of colonization was becoming clearer. Events were determining Lincoln's future policy on colonization, for no workable plan had emerged. As a practical matter, colonization remained merely an idea rather than a policy that could be implemented and turned into action. The administration's experiment on Haiti's Ile à Vache had failed miserably. The emigrants had received little support from Bernard Kock and had been stricken with serious illnesses. Many died, and in February 1864 the government brought back 368 survivors of the original 453 colonists. What might have become a promising blueprint for future emigration instead tended to discredit the whole idea.

Even at that point, however, Lincoln did not banish colonization from his mind. He had continued in 1863 and 1864 actively to support various plans. After the draft riots, Lincoln commented that colonization could avert "such scenes as those in New York the other day, where negroes were hanged to lamp posts." With Montgomery Blair and his secretary of the interior, he investigated possibilities in British Honduras and even in Surinam. At one point the British Honduras Company was allowed to proclaim Boston, New York, and Philadelphia as ports for emigration, and a number of black leaders showed real interest in British Honduras. On at least two occasions, Lincoln personally urged members of his administration to aid colonization efforts.

But for a number of reasons, no breakthrough or meaningful agreement came to pass. Within the administration, Secretary of War Stanton refused to cooperate and Interior Secretary John Usher was not always helpful. Secretary of State Seward also moved slowly or purposely frustrated Lincoln's plans. In Britain, the Colonial Office and the Foreign Office could not agree on whether to encourage emigration to Honduras. A treaty with the Dutch, who controlled Surinam, was drawn up in December 1863 and was still being discussed early in 1864. But both the U.S. Senate and Secretary Seward seem to have concluded that the Union needed the military service and agricultural labor of ex-slaves. In January 1865 the Dutch streamlined their rules, by royal decree, in order to encourage emigration to Surinam, but few African Americans were interested. They believed their future lay in the United States.[37]

The events of war produced challenges and problems at a rapid pace. They often proved more powerful than policy makers, and they changed attitudes and forced decisions. Such events had favored emancipation but had overtaken the slowly developing affairs of colonization. It would not figure in Lincoln's annual address to Congress at the end of 1864.

18

They Can Have Peace

As LINCOLN WAS preparing his address to Congress, John Wilkes Booth was penning a justification of his plans for revenge. The president's "To Whom It May Concern" letter in July, which listed "the abandonment of slavery" as a condition for peace, had enraged Booth. Unmoved by Lincoln's later backtracking, he now appropriated "To Whom It May Concern" as his own title and began, "Right or wrong, God judge me, not man."

Booth hated all of Lincoln's policies, but race was his central obsession. "This country was formed for the *white* not for the black man," he wrote. Slavery was "one of the greatest blessings (both for themselves and us) that God ever bestowed upon a favored nation." Abolitionists were "*the only traitors* in the land." They deserved hanging, "the fate of poor old [John] Brown." "My love," said Booth, "is for the South alone," which was suffering under the North's "*cruelty and injustice.*" Booth resolved to aid the South by kidnapping Lincoln—making "for her a prisoner of this man, to whom she owes so much of misery."[1]

Blinded by racist anger, Booth could not see that there was a great distance between Lincoln and the Radical Republicans or abolitionists. The latter believed in equal rights for blacks and congressional control of Reconstruction. Only if Congress directed Reconstruction, they believed, would it be possible to protect the freed people and ensure loyalty. Lincoln's 10 percent governments were neither fair to African Americans nor representative of the white population. Yet the president was pushing forward with his conciliatory plans. He wanted the Union's erring brothers, the "deeply afflicted" Southern slaveholders, to return to the Union willingly. To that end he had outlined prompt reestablishment of governments, minimal changes in state constitutions, and "temporary arrangements" for the freedmen to avoid "a total revolution of labor." He also pledged liberality in pardons for rebels.[2]

As his previous policies had shown, Lincoln's views on emancipation and race were very similar to those of the Blairs, although more empathetic toward blacks. Now events and politics were forcing him to move away from the Blairs and toward the more reformist, Radical wing of his party. But as he always did, Lincoln moved slowly, incrementally, and even in different directions at the same time. He believed in keeping his options open, and he avoided committing himself to any one course of action before developments showed that it had become necessary. This approach suited his temperament. It also had proved useful in meeting the challenges that faced a politically and racially divided North and in holding together the divergent elements of the new Republican Party. By their nature, such policies were never totally popular, but neither were they obnoxious to all.

In the latter months of the war, Lincoln's personal experiences would make him more sympathetic to the interests of African Americans. But his first concern—as a politician and as a western man with personal ties to Kentucky slaveholders—remained the interests of whites. Victorious in reelection, his problems did not diminish. The issues of Reconstruction were complex in both the Northern and the national contexts. He seized the opportunity to solidify emancipation, but his desire to gain Southern cooperation would alarm and offend part of his party. Equal rights and Southern interests were incompatible, just as conciliation toward the South and cooperation with the Radicals were inconsistent. Despite these problems, Lincoln tried to combine the irreconcilable. Yet he also gave clear signals of the approach he preferred— one that continued priority for re-union over equal rights.

THERE WAS NO shortage of advice for the president, just conflicting counsels. Charles Sumner carefully maintained his ties with the White House. It was to his advantage that Mary Lincoln sought his company; Sumner's reputation as an intellectual (even a pedantic, showy one) made him an ornament for her social circle. Capitalizing on his popularity with Mary, he missed no chance to advise or urge ideas on her husband.

Writing to Lincoln on November 20, 1864, Sumner insisted that freedom, once given, could never be taken back. As diplomatically as possible, he argued against Lincoln's path toward Reconstruction. It was most compatible with the Constitution and laws, Sumner said, to have Congress set the terms for Reconstruction. I "most dread," he wrote, "a premature State Government in a rebel state," one that would endanger peace and liberty. The rebels, Sumner believed, were intransigent. He urged Lincoln to reread parts of his speech "Slavery and the Rebellion, One and Inseparable," where Sumner had maintained that human bondage must be extinguished forever. *"Slavery cannot exist in any country which it does not govern,"* he wrote. Letting rebel states regain their rights without strict safeguards for African Americans would mean "Slavery and nothing else." The nation needed a radically changed South, with roads and schools, "emigrants from the North and from Europe ... new values ... new commerce ... 'poor whites' reinstated in their rights ... [and] a whole race ... lifted to manhood and womanhood."[3]

In Congress Sumner was devoting his efforts to the principle that "all persons shall be equal before the law." That meant "no denial of the electoral franchise or of any other rights, on account of color or race." He fought, too, for the Freedmen's Bureau, not to give African Americans privileged treatment but to protect them from white hostility. He also believed it was essential *"to establish the jurisdiction of Congress over"* the region in rebellion. Defeated slaveholders would "never again be loyal to the Union." The "only Unionists of the South are black." Sumner joined with Benjamin Wade and Zachariah Chandler in pressing the Radical agenda. To advance its aims, he repeatedly urged Lincoln to appoint Salmon Chase to replace the deceased Roger Taney as chief justice of the Supreme Court.[4]

Francis Preston Blair Sr. recommended a different man for that job. If the president "would make one of his Ex-Cabinet men a Judge," the most qualified candidate was Montgomery Blair. Mary Lincoln agreed fully. She had approached the older Blair to complain that men like Sumner "are besieging my Husband for [Chase] for the Chief-Justiceship. I wish you could prevent them."[5] Francis Blair pointed out that Montgomery had extensive experience before the Supreme Court, had been a judge, and was well versed in "our land law, Spanish law, as well as the common and civil law." But political forces were running against the Blairs and in favor of the Radicals. Although Lincoln heartily disliked Chase and said he would rather "eat flat irons" than elevate the Ohioan, he named Chase chief justice on December 6.[6]

That same day Montgomery Blair gave Lincoln advice on Reconstruction that was very different from Sumner's. Though out of the cabinet, the former postmaster general continued to support Lincoln and to meet and advise with him. "In compliance with your request," Blair put in "writing the views to which I referred in a recent conversation." Blair wanted defeated Southerners to regain control of their affairs without delay. Rather than equal rights for all, he wanted a postwar settlement that protected white supremacy. Therefore he praised Lincoln's amnesty proclamation and the progress of his 10 percent governments in Tennessee, Arkansas, and Louisiana. He argued that "the rising up" of state governments "just as soon as . . . the Rebellion is driven out" was "the reign of the constitution." He praised Lincoln for restoring the states "without the intervention of Congress" and for supporting a Thirteenth Amendment. With slavery dead, "What then is the motive for annihilating State rights?"[7]

"Mr. Sumner's 'doctrine of State suicide,'" or forfeiture of states' rights, said Blair, was dangerous on constitutional and racial grounds. He warned that Radicals planned to control Reconstruction, "reduc[e] the States to territories," and "disfranchise" them. In "depriving the States of their hitherto unquestioned right of regulating suffrage," the Radicals' goal was "undoubtedly to disfranchise the white race" and require "conditions on [re]admission which shall put the blacks and whites on equality." Under such a "revolutionary" scheme "it may turn out that those who have been held in servitude may become themselves the masters of the Government." Blair used legal reasoning in an effort to convince Lincoln that he had committed himself to the right policy, and he deplored the possibility that "loyal citizens" in the South might suffer the "humiliation of receiving their law and constitution . . . from a Congress of northern members without a representative of their own among them."[8]

As these comments showed, Montgomery Blair's concern was for the rights of Southern whites rather than the future of former slaves. His feelings went beyond mere willingness to pardon rebels. To him white Southerners were not just erring brothers but "a great and courageous people." Pride of race, which Blair praised, had caused ordinary Southerners to support the aristocrats' rebellion, and then Jefferson Davis had become a "military dictator" who controlled otherwise right-thinking Americans. With the end of the war "another class of usurpers" — the Radicals — must not be allowed to dominate and to "deprive the white people of their right of municipal legislation."[9]

Now that victory was in sight, Lincoln had to address these issues. In his annual message to Congress in December he tried to encourage unity among Northerners and offer something to both Radicals and conservatives. The 1864 elections, he argued, had proved that nearly all were committed to seeing the war through and maintaining "the integrity of the Union." That goal would be reached, because the "national resources" were "inexhaustible." Although Jefferson Davis "would accept nothing short of severance of the Union," "we have *more* men now than we had when the war *began*." Negotiations were impossible, but victory was sure.[10]

For Radicals he offered something tangible and important as well as reassuring rhetoric. To remove all legal doubts about emancipation, Lincoln threw his support behind passage of the proposed Thirteenth Amendment, which had narrowly failed in the House. The recent election showed that the new Congress, soon to be seated, would approve this amendment. Therefore Lincoln argued that by reconsidering and approving the amendment, this Congress could contribute to the "unanimity" that was so important "in a great national crisis." His words signaled that he and his administration would be working to convince congressmen and win a positive vote. Lincoln declared that would take back none of his statements against slavery. Nor would he "return to slavery any person" who had become free through the Emancipation Proclamation. And for those jealous of Congress's role in Reconstruction, he noted that "the Executive power itself would be greatly diminished" by the end of the war.[11]

For conservatives Lincoln offered different words that were reassuring to them and their vision of Reconstruction. He asserted that among the rebellious Southerners there were some who "already desire peace and reunion." There was only "a single condition of peace." "They can, at any moment, have peace simply by laying down their arms and submitting to the national authority under the Constitution." Lincoln said nothing about the abandonment of slavery as a condition for re-union. Instead, he recycled the vague but encouraging formula that Secretary of State Seward had invented during the summer's political crisis. "If questions should remain," Lincoln said, "we would adjust them by the peaceful means of legislation, conference, courts, and votes, operating only in constitutional and lawful channels."[12]

Did this mean that the South, constitutionally, could have a voice in the postwar settlement? Could rebel states vote on the Thirteenth Amendment? In this address Lincoln made no clarifying comments. But he emphasized that he had shown "clemency" and granted "special pardons" even to rebels in the "excepted classes" of his Proclamation of Amnesty and Reconstruction. Indeed, "no voluntary application has been denied." He urged Southerners not to delay but to take advantage of his liberality.[13]

In the weeks that followed, Lincoln pushed ahead to gain Congress's

approval of both the Thirteenth Amendment and his 10 percent governments. Lincoln personally lobbied some members of the House to vote for
the amendment. Patronage appointments were suggested or promised. Agents
working for Secretary of State Seward "evidently offered cash for votes." Montgomery Blair was convinced that Seward wanted Lincoln to believe that "he
[Seward] had carried that Amendment by Corruption." Blair insisted, to the
contrary, that the Democrats who voted for the amendment were motived
by "patriotic and party considerations." In any case, the amendment won the
necessary two-thirds approval of those voting on January 31, 1865. The constitutional prohibition of slavery now lacked only ratification by three-quarters
of the states.[14]

Equally important to Lincoln was the legitimation of his 10 percent governments. Charles Sumner and other Radicals wanted Reconstruction to
guarantee rights for African Americans and therefore had opposed the white-
dominated 10 percent governments. They also objected that governments
elected by so few voters were hardly representative and could become a tool
of despotic presidential power, manipulated under military influence in close
elections. Democrats readily joined in that argument. Previously Congress
had refused to seat representatives from Arkansas. Now Lincoln focused his
efforts on seating representatives from Louisiana, where a larger (but still
small) vote had chosen supposedly loyal congressmen. The president sent
General Nathaniel Banks from Louisiana to Washington to lobby for Louisiana's admission. Banks, formerly a Speaker of the House, spent months at
this task.[15]

Charles Sumner "had repeated talks with Lincoln" and with Congressman James Ashley and other leaders to try to structure a compromise. After
Lincoln's reelection, the tide had shifted momentarily against the Radicals,
and Sumner knew that a majority was ready to admit the Louisiana congressmen. But the 10 percent government in that state had done little for blacks,
and Sumner was against its "premature recognition." Nevertheless, he decided
to "hold my peace, *if I can secure a rule for the other States.*" The formula that
developed was to admit Louisiana but also "adopt for all the other Southern
states a reconstruction act 'giving the electoral franchise to "all citizens," without distinction of color.'"[16]

Such an idea was anathema to conservatives and racists like Montgomery
Blair. Lincoln met with Blair and Banks to discuss the bill that was being
written. Blair was undoubtedly pleased that Lincoln saw reasons to object.

According to John Hay, the president opposed wording that seemed to suggest that Congress was declaring emancipation. He also felt the bill's language was "rather calculated to conceal" an "objectionable" feature: "negroes would be made jurors & voters under the temporary governments." Blair hotly condemned the motives of the Radicals, but Lincoln characteristically counseled avoiding an angry confrontation. Banks got Ashley to limit black suffrage only to those serving in the military.[17]

Sumner was ready to accept Louisiana in order to gain ground on the principle of black suffrage. But over the Christmas recess this compromise "unraveled" as both conservatives and Radicals turned against it. Disappointed but undaunted, Sumner used delaying tactics to block Lincoln's 10 percent representatives. That and Sumner's refusal to help Ashley with some horse-trading in support of the Thirteenth Amendment angered the president. When Ashley asked Lincoln to try to influence Sumner, Lincoln told one of his secretaries, "I can do nothing with Mr. Sumner." He felt that Sumner hoped "to succeed in beating the President so as to change this government from its original form, and making it a strong centralized power." But Lincoln curbed his anger and kept his lines of communication with Sumner open.[18]

Personal experiences as well as political trends were pushing Lincoln toward greater, though limited, support for African Americans. Mary Lincoln and Elizabeth Keckley had become involved in efforts to help the "contrabands" and escaped slaves who had flooded into Washington. Along with hospital visits, this was an activity that Mary, so often criticized for her extravagance and temper, could pursue with public approval. Her concern for the suffering refugees was deep and genuine, however. She, Elizabeth Keckley, and the president became acquainted with "Aunt" Mary Dines, a runaway slave who was the cook at the Soldiers' Home. Aunt Mary lived in a contraband camp nearby, and she reported that Lincoln often stopped at the camp "to visit and talk," or to sing spirituals and hymns with the former slaves. On a number of occasions Mary Lincoln asked her husband for money to aid the freedmen, and he always complied.[19]

The president himself had been touched by the death of William Johnson, a black servant who had accompanied the Lincolns from Illinois, only to contract smallpox after traveling with the president to Gettysburg in 1863. Lincoln bought Johnson's coffin and paid much of a debt owed by the deceased man. Lincoln then became acquainted with William Slade, an African American messenger for the Treasury Department. Slade became Lincoln's valet and "confidential messenger," and according to his daughter "was treated by Lincoln with the greatest intimacy." In the last two years of the war Lincoln met with black leaders like Frederick Douglass, Abraham Galloway from North Carolina, and leaders of free blacks in New Orleans. He was especially impressed by the bearing and eloquence of the latter group, who declared in 1864, "We are men; treat us as such." Their visit caused Lincoln to express "regret" that they could not "secure" all their rights.[20]

These contacts led to increased public recognition of African Americans as part of the American community. In July well-dressed blacks in Washington enjoyed a Sunday-school picnic near the White House, as white observers hooted or cursed. At Lincoln's traditional New Year's Day reception in 1865 "a crowd of colored folk" waited outside the White House in hopes of being admitted. At the end of the day a "weary president" noticed them and "rallied his forces to welcome" the crowd. "For a little time, the trampled reception room knew laughter and tears and cries of 'God bless Abraham Lincoln.'" After Congress sent the Thirteenth Amendment to the states for ratification, Lincoln invited Henry Highland Garnet, an important black leader and minister, to give a sermon in the House chamber.[21]

Still, racism constrained the thinking even of Republicans deeply involved in the war effort. Secretary of the Navy Gideon Welles, for example, would soon write, "I would not enslave the negro, but his enfranchisement is another question." Welles did not "want him at my table, nor do I care to have him in the jury-box, or in the legislative hall, or on the bench." To him, Sumner and the abolitionists were examples of "fanaticism, zeal without discretion," men who would "not only free the slaves but elevate them above their former masters." Although Welles occasionally recognized the South's hatred toward the North, he always believed that, despite rebellion, "the rights of the States are unimpaired."[22] Democrats and other Northerners remained more vociferously racist.

In this fractured racial environment, Lincoln began the war's endgame, a period of continued fighting punctuated by talk of peacemaking. Several individuals were trying to arrange peace talks. Colonel James Jacquess and the journalist James R. Gilmore had earlier gained permission from Lincoln to pass through the lines and travel to Richmond, where they wanted to meet with Jefferson Davis. Although they were not empowered to negotiate for the Union, they hoped to further some settlement. In this they were disappointed, as Jefferson Davis insisted that the South would accept nothing but independence.[23]

The next traveler to Richmond was Illinois's James Singleton, a Peace Democrat who had the backing of Orville Browning. Lincoln had told Singleton that he was "misunderstood on the subject of slavery—that it shall not stand in the way of peace." The summer's "To Whom It May Concern" letter, Lincoln explained, had "put him in a false position—that he did not mean to make the abolition of slavery a condition." Lincoln said the same thing to Orville Browning on Christmas Eve, and to Singleton he added that he would not retract the Emancipation Proclamation, but the courts might rule it invalid. With this encouragement, Singleton went to see Davis early in January 1865. He returned saying that the Confederates desired peace on "liberal terms"—particularly that there be "the clearest recognition of the rights of States respectively to determine each for itself all questions of local and domestic government." They wanted *"fair compensation"* and control over African Americans.[24]

Francis Preston Blair reinforced Singleton's efforts. The Blairs were nothing if not consistent in their beliefs and aims. Drawing on his prewar ties to Jefferson Davis, the elder Blair revived the idea of extending American power into Central America. He argued that the war was undermining republicanism. The way to avoid monarchical power, in both North and South, was to have the rival armies combine and launch a joint military expedition to drive the French out of Mexico. This would end the war, bring the country together, and "extend its dominion to the Isthmus." Blair reported to Lincoln that the Confederate president was ready to cooperate, and Davis sent a letter promising to appoint commissioners who could discuss peace for "the two countries." That phrase almost scuttled Blair's efforts, but when Alexander Stephens, John A. Campbell, and R. M. T. Hunter arrived at the Union's lines, General Grant convinced Lincoln to meet with them.[25]

The Hampton Roads Conference demonstrated Lincoln's desire to engage the Confederates and win their cooperation in restoring the Union. But its outcome showed that neither Lincoln's cabinet, nor still less the Republicans in Congress, were prepared to be as conciliatory as the president.

The cabinet, in fact, reacted "unfavorably" to the news that Lincoln and Seward had gone to Hampton Roads. Even a conservative Republican such as Gideon Welles worried that Lincoln would "undertake to arrange terms of peace without consulting any one." The president had "much shrewdness and much good sense," but Welles also felt that Lincoln "takes sometimes singular and unaccountable freaks." He might go overboard. And in fact, after the conference was over, Welles commented that Lincoln's desire "to conciliate

Although **Gideon Welles,** secretary of the navy, saw that the war was bringing immense changes, he remained conservative in temperament and policy.

and effect peace was manifest," but there was "such a thing as so overdoing as to cause a distrust or adverse feeling," especially in Congress.[26]

At Hampton Roads, Lincoln barred any consideration of Confederate independence. He insisted that to have peace, Southerners must lay down their arms. When Alexander Stephens advocated joint military action in Mexico, Lincoln rejected that notion, saying the "only basis" for a settlement was the reestablishment of national authority. But Lincoln and Seward emphasized the December address to Congress, which named "abandonment of armed resistance" as "the only indispensable condition to ending the war." In answer to Stephens's questions, Lincoln described the Emancipation Proclamation as a "*war measure*" that would become "inoperative" in peace. Ultimately, he said, the courts might decide how many slaves it had affected, and Lincoln and Seward inaccurately suggested that "only about two hundred thousand slaves" had actually begun to enjoy freedom under its terms.[27]

Then Seward informed the Southerners that Congress had proposed the Thirteenth Amendment. He added that it would "probably not be adopted," since only ten states needed to object to ratification. Stephens understood

Seward to be saying that "if the Confederate States would then abandon the war, they could of themselves, defeat this amendment, by voting it down as members of the Union." The Confederate vice president therefore asked if Southern states would be readmitted to the Union once they ceased to fight. Lincoln "promptly" said that they "ought to be." It was his "own opinion" that "when resistance ceased and the National Authority was recognized, the States would be immediately restored to their practical relations to the Union." Stephens also understood Lincoln to advise that Southerners delay the ratification of the Thirteenth Amendment for "say . . . five years" so as to "avoid, as far as possible, the evils of immediate emancipation."[28]

R. M. T. Hunter objected to any emancipation and declared that it would cause starvation among the slaves, once they no longer received food from their masters. In response, Lincoln told a story about an Illinois farmer who avoided caring for his hogs by planting potatoes, which they could dig up. When asked what the hogs would do when the ground was frozen, the farmer replied, "Well, let 'em root!" This story may have shown that Lincoln was not to be dissuaded by Hunter's paternalistic prediction, but it also indicated that he contemplated no special measures to help the freed people. They would have to fend for themselves. Lincoln also promised the Southerners that he would exercise his pardoning powers "very liberally" and brought up the subject of "an indemnity for the loss to owners." He told the commissioners that they would be surprised how many Northerners were willing to be taxed to provide such an indemnity.[29]

The Hampton Roads Conference ended without any specific agreement. But immediately on his return to Washington, Lincoln tried to make his efforts at conciliation tangible. He drafted a proposed joint resolution of Congress that would cover all the slaveholding states. The resolution would establish a fund of $400 million in government bonds, the same amount Lincoln had mentioned as an "indemnity." If the states in rebellion ended "all resistance to national authority" by April 1, 1865, half of that amount would be paid to the states, in proportion to their slave populations. To gain the remaining $200 million dollars, the Thirteenth Amendment would have to be ratified by July 1. Clearly Lincoln considered this a wise measure of conciliation and reunification. It would recruit Southerners' participation in ending both the war and slavery and give them an incentive to accept a postwar Union. It was "overdoing" it, however, in the eyes of the cabinet, which opposed it unanimously. Saddened, Lincoln filed the measure away and never sent it to Congress, where it would have encountered a more hostile reception.[30]

Thus, Hampton Roads produced no result that affected the North. Ironically, its impact was in the dying Confederacy, where it gave some small hope to the slaveholding elite. The Confederate Congress was considering Jefferson Davis's proposal that, as a desperate measure, slaves be put in the army and rewarded for fighting with their freedom. There was much discussion among influential Confederate congressmen after they heard from Stephens, Campbell, and Hunter. Leading figures became more determined to oppose Davis's plan, given what Lincoln had said. Blinded by Southern racism in a nationally racist era, they decided not to surrender to Davis something that they just might be able to prolong under Lincoln.[31]

Thus, as Lincoln's second inauguration approached, a destructive war was still under way and successful reunion was still a goal. The inaugural address gave Lincoln another opportunity to advocate the kind of reunion that he felt was optimal. In his remaining weeks of life he steered a course between racists and Radicals, continuing a complex approach to Reconstruction policy.

19

With Malice toward None; with Charity for All

INAUGURATION DAY, March 4, 1865, dawned rainy and windy. The city was "quite full of people," and General Henry Halleck, fearing "mischief," urged precautions and the closing of the Navy Yard. Well-dressed spectators waded through Washington's unpaved streets, ankle-deep in mud, and dark clouds rolled across the sky. The day's ceremonies also began on a dark note, since Vice President Andrew Johnson was drunk. In the Senate chamber where he was sworn in, Johnson "made a rambling and strange harangue, which was listened to with pain and mortification" by the cabinet and Republican notables. As this preliminary ceremony concluded, Lincoln ordered a marshal, "Do not permit Johnson to speak a word" during the remaining events.[1]

As dignitaries moved to the east front of the Capitol for the presidential oath of office, John Wilkes Booth took his place on the reviewing stand. Booth, ironically, had just become engaged to Lucy Hale, the daughter of an abolitionist senator from New Hampshire. From her, Booth had gained a ticket to the stands, where he prepared to watch the most important political ceremony of a country he hated. He now spoke of the South as his country. The North was guilty of "vile and savage acts committed on my countrymen, their wives & helpless children." Booth would later exclaim, "What an excellent chance I had to kill the President on inauguration day if I wished."[2]

Suddenly, as members of the presidential party took their places, the sun came out. The crowd grew quiet, straining to hear Lincoln's address. It was uncommonly short and less a political speech than a sermon calling on Americans to rise above wartime hatreds. Its content and tone reflected Lincoln's troubled and humane musings over the nation's costly confrontation with slavery. His words, tracing the partial evolution in the nation's values, were generous and expansive in regard to the tragedies brought by slavery but silent on the larger cancer of prejudice.

Slavery, said Lincoln, was "somehow, the cause of the war." A religious people, who read the same Bible and prayed to the same God, had gone to war over slavery's perpetuation or restriction. Both sides were astounded by the scope of the conflict and by the end of slavery. Although the North had not *made* war but merely *accepted* it, Lincoln refused to fix blame. "Let us judge not that we be not judged." Perhaps the Almighty had decreed that "every drop of blood drawn with the lash" was to "be paid by another drawn with the sword," and that all the wealth produced by slavery was to be sacrificed in the destruction of "this terrible war." The task ahead—Reconstruction—required an attitude of "malice toward none" and a policy of "charity toward all." In that spirit Americans might achieve "a just, and a lasting peace."[3]

These attitudes made sense to conservatives like Gideon Welles, who believed that "a large portion" of the rebels "are not enemies of the Union; they sincerely desire its restoration and the benefits that would flow from it." The best way to restore the Union was to "promote friendly intercourse" whenever possible. Welles worried, however, about the "wild, radical element" in Congress. He recognized the gulf between his belief in states' rights and the views of Republicans, like Charles Sumner, who believed that it was necessary to treat the South as "territories without rights" and to supervise closely their return to the Union.[4]

An optimistic Lincoln was still hoping to bridge these divisions, to gain Southerners' cooperation, and to return the rebel states promptly to their proper practical relation with the Union. As he tried to conciliate Southern rebels, he reached out to Radicals as well as conservatives in his party. Charles Sumner, despite his recent opposition to the Louisiana government, remained a key player in the Congress. Lincoln cultivated, rather than restricted, his ties to him. To bring Sumner closer and to please Mary, Lincoln involved him in the first family's inaugural celebration. He sent a note to the Massachusetts senator: "I should be pleased for you to accompany us to-morrow evening . . . to the Inaugeral-ball [*sic*]. I inclose a ticket. Our carriage will call for you at half past nine."[5]

Mary Lincoln gloried in her importance at such events. For receptions and formal affairs within the White House, she insisted that the president always be her escort. Guests, she said, had to "recognize the position of the President as first of all," and "if they recognize his position, they should also recognize mine." She knew, however, that protocol for the Inaugural Ball was different. It required that Lincoln arrive with the Speaker of the House. Therefore she contented herself to follow immediately behind and to circle the "huge 280-foot floor of the Patent Office" on Charles Sumner's arm. He was, after all, a senator whom even conservatives viewed as "a scholar and critic, a statesman," and a man of "culture."[6]

But balls were one thing, and policy another. The gap between Lincoln's views on Reconstruction and Sumner's was wide. The president wanted to shun theoretical issues and concentrate on practical solutions. "Whether certain states have been in or out of the Union during the war" was, he felt, "a merely metaphysical question and one unnecessary to be forced into discussion." It was "much better," Lincoln thought, "to restore the Union without the necessity of a violent quarrel among its friends" over such issues.[7] But Lincoln was overly optimistic. He was misjudging both his Republican friends and the Southerners. Behind differing theories lay very different assessments of the loyalty and disposition of the soon-to-be-defeated rebels.

That defeat now seemed imminent, and Lincoln decided to view the war's closing drama. A visit to the front would also allow the president to see his son. Robert had repeatedly and impatiently pressed to leave Harvard, where he was a student. But for many months his bereaved mother had insisted, despite public criticism of the Lincolns, that he remain out of harm's way, safe in Boston. Finally, after Robert graduated and as victory approached, Lincoln wrote to General Grant and asked a favor. Could Robert "go into your Military family with some nominal rank, I, and not the public, furnishing his necessary means?" Robert joined the general's staff, and Lincoln now prepared to visit the army as it neared Richmond.[8] On March 23 he boarded a ship with Tad and Mary. His visit would produce touching encounters with Union troops and Southern slaves but also acutely embarrassing behavior from the First Lady.

Mary Lincoln's irrational, self-centered, and jealous tirades began at once. When the Lincolns' boat arrived at City Point, General and Mrs. Grant arrived to greet them. No sooner had Julia Grant sat down beside the First Lady than Mary demanded, "How dare you be seated until I invite you!" She then demanded repeatedly that the president's boat have a preferred position at the dock, over General Grant's. During the next few days, as Lincoln visited the troops, a journalist observed that Mary "seemed insanely jealous of every person, and everything, which drew him [Lincoln] away from her and monopolized his attention for an hour." When Mrs. Grant tried to smooth one of these outbursts, Mary turned on her and snapped, "I suppose you think you'll

She had aided her husband's ascent in politics, but **Mary Todd Lincoln's** behavior and emotional state deteriorated during the White House years, a fact that tested the president's patience.

get to the White House yourself, don't you?" Angrily Mary complained when she heard that Lincoln had spoken with some officer's wife or encountered a pretty woman during a military review. She lectured officers that "I never allow the President to see any woman alone." In front of various people she demanded explanations from the president. These were never satisfactory, and a startled major reported that "she turned on him like a tigress."[9]

Lincoln was nearly exhausted and had lost a great deal of weight. Mary's behavior was a strain on him, and at one point he exclaimed, "My God, will that woman never understand me?" In conversation he was relaxed and amusing but also withdrawn and introspective. One observer noticed these alterations when "all of a sudden he would retire within himself; then he would close his eyes, and all his features would at once bespeak a kind of sadness as indescribable as it was deep. . . . In one evening I happened to count over twenty of these alternations and contrasts." Nevertheless, Lincoln seemed buoyed by his visits with the troops. He often shook their hands, one by one, and he visited wounded men—both Union and Confederate—in the hospitals.[10]

Mary Lincoln returned briefly to Washington on April 1, and on April 4 the president and Tad had the remarkable and moving experience of entering Richmond. Lincoln walked through the streets and sat in Jefferson Davis's chair. African Americans surrounded him as he walked through the city, "shouting, clapping, dancing, throwing hats into the air, waving bonnets and handkerchiefs, and applauding loudly." They shouted their blessings to him, and some knelt down to show their reverence and gratitude. "Don't kneel to me," Lincoln told them, suggesting that they thank God "for the liberty you will hereafter enjoy." At Richmond's Capitol Square he briefly addressed a crowd of freed people. Congratulating them on being free, "free as air," he added: "Liberty is your birthright. God gave it to you as he gave it to others, and it is a sin that you have been deprived of it for so many years. But you must try to deserve this priceless boon. Let the world see that you merit it, and are able to maintain it by your good works."[11]

On April 6 Mary Lincoln returned to Virginia with Elizabeth Keckley, Charles Sumner, and three or four others from the government. She visited Richmond without incident, but after arranging a tour of Petersburg, she "exploded in anger at Admiral Porter for inviting his wife" and other women to join the excursion. She wanted no women present to draw any of the president's attention away from her. Beside herself in rage, Mary threw herself to the ground, rolled about, and "tore her hair." A couple of days later, in front of others, she "struck her husband in the face, damned him, and cursed him." When told that women in Richmond had welcomed and admired the president, her eyes flashed, she took offense, and created another scene. The president told others, when possible, that Mary was unwell.[12]

Meanwhile, Lincoln was looking for ways to close hostilities in the lenient, generous spirit of his Second Inaugural Address. Repeatedly during his visit to the front he spoke of his intention to be conciliatory toward the rebels. Secretary of the Navy Welles believed that Lincoln extended his visit to the front because he "has been apprehensive that the military men . . . will exact severe terms." He "wishes the War terminated, and, to this end, that severe terms shall not be exacted of the Rebels."[13] In that spirit, Lincoln allowed himself to be tempted into an unwise experiment by John A. Campbell, the former Supreme Court justice who was the Confederacy's assistant secretary of war.

After talking with Campbell, the president directed that "the gentlemen who have acted as the Legislature of Virginia, in support of the rebellion," would be allowed to assemble in order "to withdraw the Virginia troops" and pledge their support for the Union. However, this was a dangerous move that would embroil Lincoln in the legal theories he wished to avoid. It would give a rebel state legislature the opportunity to assume the role of the legitimate government of Virginia. As Lincoln's military governor of Virginia noted, a Confederate legislature might "creep into the Union with all its rebel legislation in force." The cabinet objected vehemently, and in fact Campbell and the legislators did try to assume wider powers. As had been the case with many of Lincoln's earlier overtures to rebellious Southerners, the Virginians refused to respond in a cooperative manner. Embarrassed, he had to revoke his order, admitting that "he had perhaps made a mistake."[14]

On the voyage back to Washington, Lincoln was in the mood to reminisce. Rather than discussing Reconstruction policy, he talked with Charles Sumner about the events of the war. Showing a continued openness to the senator, Lincoln remarked that he could not understand why so many people believed that Seward had been his chief adviser. "I have counseled with you," he said, "twice as much as I ever did with him."[15] The same could have been said about Montgomery Blair. In fact, by background and political temperament, Lincoln had been naturally much closer to the Blairs than to Sumner. But he kept his mind open to a variety of ideas beyond those he favored at any given moment, and he was capable of moving with events.

Lincoln returned to a Washington that was celebrating the fall of Richmond and Lee's surrender on April 9. After four years of war, there was abundant reason to celebrate. But soon the hard problems of reconstructing the Union had to be faced and solved. Lincoln gathered his thoughts for what turned out to be his last public address. On April 10 a "multitude" of citizens assembled in front of the White House. Lincoln was not ready to speak that night, but he promised to do so the next evening. As a member of the cabinet noted, Lincoln then gave "a prepared address disclosing his views on the subject of resumption of friendly national relations." That last address was an optimistic combination of different approaches. It featured his lenient impulses toward the South, a willingness to consider measures favored by the Radicals, and his hope that good feelings might prevail.[16]

After praising General Grant and the men of the army, Lincoln devoted most of his words to defending his 10 percent government for Louisiana. Disclaiming any purpose to dictate to Congress, he nevertheless praised what had been accomplished there. Louisiana had written a new constitution "declaring emancipation for the whole State" and not even requiring "apprenticeship for the freed-people." That constitution allowed the legislature to give the ballot to black men, if it wished, and the 10 percent government had established public schools for blacks and whites. Lincoln granted that it would have been better if more than 12,000 whites in Louisiana had participated in this effort. But he argued that if the state's government was now only as the egg is to the fowl, wouldn't "we . . . sooner have the fowl by hatching the egg than by smashing it?" Wouldn't it be wise not to discourage the loyal whites or the aspiring blacks in Louisiana?[17]

Holding out an olive branch to his party's Radicals, Lincoln said that he was not irrevocably wedded to his plan. He would change "whenever I shall be convinced" that it was "adverse to the public interest," and he admitted that conditions differed so much from state to state that "no exclusive, and inflexible plan" was possible. Again he urged that "all join in . . . restoring the proper practical relations between these states and the Union," without considering theories as to whether they "have even been out of the Union." Then he made his first public declaration supportive of black suffrage. Noting that some believed that the "colored man" should have the ballot, Lincoln said, "I would myself prefer that it were now conferred on the very intelligent, and on those who serve our cause as soldiers." This was, of course, only a statement of his preference and not a requirement, but it put the president on record.[18]

With continuing hope that white Southerners would cooperate, Lincoln added a final comment on the Thirteenth Amendment. How this measure was to be ratified was under discussion. Charles Sumner was arguing that only the loyal states should be permitted to vote on ratification. Like many Radicals, he judged that white Confederates remained defiant. Black Southerners, though loyal, had no political voice. Therefore, putting the decision in the hands of former Confederates would imperil the end of slavery. But this president, who had been born in Kentucky and had close ties with many slaveholders, still believed that he could gain white Southerners' cooperation.

Limiting ratification to the loyal states only, said Lincoln, "would be questionable, and sure to be persistently questioned." A ratification that permitted the former rebel states to vote, however, "would be unquestioned and unquestionable." Probably Lincoln agreed with many of his advisers who believed that "slavery is dead," or at least fatally wounded by the war.[19] Clearly he hoped, in his last public address, that he would be able to gain enough support from the rebel states to pass the amendment. He wanted them to participate willingly in the process of Reconstruction, and he offered a "kindly feeling toward the vanquished." But he had admitted at the beginning of his speech that all the questions of Reconstruction were "fraught with great difficulty." No clear path lay ahead, only "disorganized and discordant elements." Even "the loyal people" disagreed on what to do. The work of Reconstruction was only beginning.[20]

20

Assassination

As LINCOLN SPOKE, one person in the crowd outside the White House listened with anxious attention. By now John Wilkes Booth was obsessed with the idea that he had a "sacred duty" to help the South. Regretting that he had "promised mother I would keep out" of the Confederate army, he had started "to deem myself a coward and to despise my own existence." For months he had virtually suspended his acting career; his last performance had been on March 18. He was drinking heavily, "putting away brandy by the quart." After the fall of Richmond he talked "recklessly of riding through the streets of Washington and waving a rebel flag." His clandestine activities had accomplished nothing of great importance for the Confederacy, and he longed to act.[1]

When Lincoln announced his preference that some black men could vote, Booth "was enraged. 'That means nigger citizenship,' he said. 'Now, by God! I'll put him through. That is the last speech he will ever make.'" Either then or on April 14 Booth discarded his plan to kidnap the president and resolved to kill him. That violent act would satisfy Booth's desire to "do something which the world would remember for all time." Meeting with three men from his kidnapping team, he laid plans to murder Secretary of State Seward and Vice President Johnson, as well.[2]

Fear of the possibility of assassination was in the air. It had haunted Washington for months. Back in the spring of 1864 Senator James Lane visited the president's secretary John Hay. Lane "said the President must now chiefly guard against assassination. I pooh-poohed him," wrote Hay, "& said that while every prominent man was more or less exposed to the attacks of maniacs, no foresight could guard against them." Mary Todd Lincoln was never free from worry for her husband's safety. "Mister Lincoln's life is always exposed," she lamented. During the president's visit to Virginia, General Edward Ripley had felt compelled to warn Lincoln about a plot against his life. Critical newspapers, North and South, had alluded to or even called for assassination.[3]

Lincoln dismissed all these concerns. "Letters threatening my life," he claimed, arrived "in every week's mail" and "have ceased to give me apprehension." He had tucked eighty of them into a pigeonhole of his desk. In 1863 he had told Senator Lane during a meeting that it was impossible to guard against all assassination attempts. "If I make up my mind to kill you for instance, I can do it and these hundred gentlemen could not prevent it. They could avenge but could not save you." Responding to General Ripley's warning, Lincoln said, "I must go on as I have begun in the course marked out for me; for I cannot bring myself to believe that any human being lives who would do me any harm." Soon after, perhaps to convince those who worried, Lincoln observed, "I walked alone on the street [in Richmond], and anyone could have shot me from a second-story window."[4]

But Lincoln was not optimistic about his future. By this time he had, in fact, developed a fatalistic sense of his deteriorating health. The stress of war and governing had taken its toll. Observers at the second inauguration, noted the *Chicago Tribune,* "were painfully impressed with his gaunt, skeleton-like appearance." Henry Villard described him as "almost cadaverous." Secretary of the Navy Welles recorded that Lincoln was "much worn down" and kept too demanding a schedule. The president was aware of his physical decline but felt he could do nothing about it. "The springs of life are wearing away," he told one person. To a sympathizer who urged him to get more sleep, he replied, "The tired part of me is *inside* and out of reach."[5]

As early as July 1864 Lincoln had said, "I feel a presentiment that I shall not outlast the rebellion. When it is over, my work will be done." He told Harriet Beecher Stowe that "*I* shan't last long after it's over," and he shared with Owen Lovejoy his worry that he might die even before peace was won. "This war is eating my life out," Lincoln told Lovejoy. "I have a strong impression that I shall not live to see the end." To his wife he mentioned a chilling dream—one in which he heard the sound of weeping in the White House and found a coffin and catafalque in the East Room. When he asked soldiers who had died, they answered, "The President." Mary Lincoln also feared a dream he had had at the time of his first election. Lying down on his bed in Springfield, Lincoln saw his face reflected in a mirror on the dresser. But the reflection was unnatural; he saw two images of his face, one being separate and paler. No matter how he moved, the dual image persisted. Mary was convinced that it meant her husband would win a second term but would not live to complete it.[6]

On April 14 Mary Lincoln issued several invitations to the theater. First she approached General and Mrs. Grant, but her rudeness and hostility toward Julia Grant in Virginia had soured the possibility of friendship in that quarter. Julia Grant decided on the spot to leave town that night, rather than be subjected to Mary's unstable temper. Mrs. Edwin Stanton refused for the same reason, and Speaker of the House Colfax and one of Secretary Stanton's assistants also declined. Mary persisted, however, since it had been announced that the president and General Grant would be in attendance. She felt the crowd's disappointment would be great if neither man appeared. Major Henry Rathbone and his fiancée, whom Mary knew, agreed to accompany the president and his wife.[7]

Lincoln was scarcely guarded that night, and not guarded effectively at all. Ward Lamon was away on an assignment. A metropolitan policeman, whose duty was to protect the White House's furnishings rather than its occupant, and a White House messenger provided the only security on the scene. It is likely that Lincoln encouraged the policeman to go off and enjoy himself during the play. The messenger remained nearby, but when Booth approached the hallway to the president's box, he showed his card and was allowed to pass. About that same time one of Booth's confederates was carrying out an attack on Secretary of State Seward and his son. Another ally abandoned the planned attack on Vice President Johnson, however, in favor of a visit to a tavern.[8]

For a few moments Booth stood at the doorway to the president's box. Because he was familiar with the evening's play, he waited until the stage was nearly empty. Then he quickly opened the door, entered, and fired a .44-caliber pocket pistol, a derringer, into the back of Lincoln's head. When Major Rathbone rose to resist him, Booth stabbed Rathbone in the arm with a knife. Then he leaped to the stage, but caught one of his spurs on a flag draping the box and injured his left leg as he landed. Shouting "Sic semper tyrannis," the motto of Virginia, Booth hurried from the stage. Mounting a horse behind the theater, he rode out of town. He was able to give his true name to a sentry guarding a bridge, and was not stopped. But thereafter Booth would be a hunted man, lame, endangered, and painfully surprised not to be acclaimed as a hero. Shortly before he was killed by federal troops, he wrote, "wet cold and starving, with every mans hand against me, I am here in despair."[9]

Three doctors quickly made their way to the president's box. Seeing that

The assassination of
President Lincoln
shocked the North
and unleashed a fren-
zied effort to catch
and punish Booth and
his conspirators.

$30,000 REWARD

DESCRIPTION
OF

JOHN WILKES BOOTH!

**Who Assassinated the PRESIDENT on the Evening
of April 14th, 1865.**

Height 5 feet 8 inches; weight 160 pounds; compact built; hair jet black, inclined to
curl, medium length, parted behind; eyes black, and heavy dark eye-brows; wears a large seal
ring on little finger; when talking inclines his head forward; looks down.

Description of the Person who Attempted to Assassi-
nate Hon. W. H. Seward, Secretary of State.

Height 6 feet 1 inch; hair black, thick, full and straight; no beard, nor appearance of
beard; cheeks red on the jaws; face moderately full; 22 or 23 years of age; eyes, color not
known—large eyes, not prominent; brows not heavy, but dark; face not large, but rather
round; complexion healthy; nose straight and well formed, medium size; mouth small; lips
thin; upper lip protruded when he talked; chin pointed and prominent; head medium size;
neck short, and of medium length; hands soft and small; fingers tapering; shows no signs of
hard labor; broad shoulders; taper waist; straight figure; strong looking man; manner not
gentlemanly, but vulgar; Overcoat double-breasted, color mixed of pink and grey spots, small
—was a sack overcoat, pockets in side and one on the breast, with lappells or flaps; pants
black, common stuff; new heavy boots; voice small and thin, inclined to tenor.

The Common Council of Washington, D. C., have offered a reward of $20,000 for the ar-
rest and conviction of these Assassins, in addition to which I will pay $10,000.

L. C. BAKER,
Colonel and Agent War Department.

Lincoln's condition was hopeless, they rejected the idea of taking him to the White House. Lincoln's unconscious body was carried across the street to a boardinghouse. There they arranged it diagonally across a bed too small to hold such a tall man. "Where is my husband! Where is my husband!" shouted a frantic Mary Lincoln. When she reached his bedside she kissed his damaged head and vainly implored him to speak. Little Tad had been seeing a play at Grover's Theatre. When the news was announced to that audience, Tad shouted hysterically and was taken to the White House. Robert Lincoln heard of the attack with John Hay in the White House, and immediately rushed to his father's bedside.[10]

Charles Sumner was one of the first to arrive. He had been visiting with two other senators when a servant raised the alarm. Hurrying to the White House, he encountered Robert Lincoln and left with him for Ford's Theatre. A doctor told Sumner that Lincoln was across the street but that his wounds were fatal. Although the little bedroom was crowded, Sumner was determined and made his way in. He took Lincoln's hand and tried to speak to him. When doctors told him, "It's no use, Mr. Sumner—he can't hear you. He is dead," Sumner insisted, "No, he isn't dead. Look at his face; he is breathing." Then the physicians explained that Lincoln could never regain consciousness. Still, Sumner remained at his bedside, "from a quarter till eleven until after seven the next morning, holding the President's hand in his own and sobbing with his own head bowed until it almost touched the pillow." As Lincoln's last breaths came, Robert cried aloud and rested "his head on Sumner's tall shoulder for support."[11]

A messenger roused Secretary Welles from bed with news of the attacks on Lincoln and Seward. Welles went first to the Seward home, where he met Secretary of War Stanton and learned that the president was not at the White House but still near Ford's Theatre. Welles insisted on going to the president, and pressured Stanton to accompany him, though others warned that "the streets were full of people" and that it was "unsafe for the Secretary of War to expose himself." Outside the room where Lincoln lay, a Dr. Hall told Welles that "the President was dead to all intents," though he lingered on for several hours. Welles noted that "his slow, full respiration lifted the clothes with each breath that he took." Soon "his right eye began to swell and that part of his face became discolored." About once every hour Mary Lincoln entered the overcrowded room and was overcome with emotion. Other officials came and went. Except for a brief walk, Welles stayed until nearly 7:30 in the morning, when he witnessed the end "of the good and great man who was expiring before me."[12]

Mary Lincoln collapsed and went into seclusion in the White House. Deep in mourning, she saw only some spiritualists and a few friends. Among those few were Montgomery Blair's sister, Elizabeth Blair Lee, and Charles Sumner. All were dismayed by her condition. The mourning was scarcely less intense throughout the capital. When John Nicolay returned a few days later, by boat from the South, he could not describe "the air of gloom which seems to hang over this city. As I drove up here from the Navy yard . . . almost every house was draped and closed. . . . The silence and gloom, and sorrow depicted on every face are as heavy and ominous of terror, as if some great calamity still hung in the air, and was about to crush and overwhelm every one."[13]

"Great crowds" pressed into the East Room, "taking their last look at the President's kind face." "Strong and brave men wept when I met them," wrote

Gideon Welles. But the deepest mourning, he felt, was visible in "several hundred colored people," standing in "a cheerless cold rain . . . in front of the White House." Their numbers did not "diminish through the whole of that cold, wet day." Welles concluded that "[t]here were no truer mourners, when all were sad, than the poor colored people who crowded the streets, joined the procession, and exhibited their woe. . . . Women as well as men, with their little children, thronged the streets, sorrow, trouble, and distress depicted on their countenances and in their bearing." He imagined that they wondered "what was to be their fate since their great benefactor was dead."[14]

Soon others began to wonder what would be the fate of Reconstruction, now that Lincoln was dead. Under his leadership the North had, in war, confronted and taken hold of the problem of slavery. Although the Thirteenth Amendment was not yet ratified, the events of war had deeply undermined the institution. Now the assassination of the president would strengthen Northern determination to see its official, constitutional end. But slavery was only part of the nation's central problem. Race, "the proper *status* of the negro," was equally significant and far-reaching. The problem of race, and the question of equal rights for African Americans, remained.[15]

21

Unfinished Business

THE WAR YEARS had been immensely stressful for Abraham Lincoln. Had he lived, the years of Reconstruction might well have been worse. It cannot be said that a man as intelligent and experienced as Lincoln was naive. But as Reconstruction began, he was unrealistically positive. He approached its intractable problems with a desire that the nation might rise above its troubled past and atone for war's suffering and destruction. Ready to forgive and be generous himself, he tried to inspire the same feelings in others. His call for "malice toward none" and "charity for all" revealed a hopefulness and idealism about human nature that were sure to be disappointed.

In his final months of life Lincoln had shown a repeated desire to be lenient, welcoming, and helpful toward Southern rebels. In his last public speech he had also spoken in favor of voting rights for some African Americans. These positions certainly reflected "charity for all" and the absence of malice. Beyond that, they indicated his wish that a better, more humane society could emerge from four ugly years of suffering and bloodshed. Such a result would amount to a transformation.

But Lincoln was trying to reconcile unreconcilable elements. The hatreds generated by a destructive war were too great. The sense of racial superiority produced by almost 250 years of slavery was too engrained. As he himself admitted, Northerners were divided among themselves as to Reconstruction. Some of the sharpest divisions of principle and belief lay within his own party, between men like Charles Sumner and Montgomery Blair. In the South, African Americans wanted freedom, opportunity, and the rights of citizenship that had so long been denied them. Resentful and defeated Southern whites, however, were determined not to lose any more status or power. The war's emotions and the unsolved problem of race made Lincoln's idealistic agenda impractical.

White Southerners simply were not going to welcome black freedom or quietly accept black suffrage. Events after Lincoln's death amply demonstrated that the rebel states were determined to maintain white supremacy and enforce racial subordination. Southern whites resisted black freedom with tenacious determination. Violence quickly became their tool of choice in preserving racial barriers, as the Ku Klux Klan murdered, beat, and threatened thousands of blacks who voted Republican or simply tried to defend their rights. Within a decade the white South had negated political equality, reestablished an oppressive racial domination, and erased the few economic gains that had come with freedom. In little more than a generation the system of disfranchisement and segregation had replaced slavery.

The minority of Radical Republicans, such as Charles Sumner, were more accurate than Lincoln when they argued that white Southerners wanted to retain slavery and that only the freed people were completely loyal. Sumner, Thaddeus Stevens, and a few others in Congress urged strong measures to protect black rights. But most members of the Republican Party either retreated before Southern intransigence or—like the Blairs—deserted their party in order to support discrimination, white supremacy, and states' rights.

Thus, Lincoln misread white Southerners on the eve of Reconstruction, just as he had overestimated the border states' Unionism when he called for troops in 1861.[1] As a native of Kentucky and an admirer of Henry Clay, he thought he recognized a progressivism in Southern thought. Generosity toward former rebels also was part of his nature. As a friend of slaveholders like Joshua Speed and the husband of Mary Todd, he had affectionate ties to Southerners. During his presidency Lincoln had consistently tried to respect their rights. Repeatedly he had offered the rebels chances to avoid unpleasant policies and incentives to cooperate.

Never were these offers accepted. Had he lived longer, the same pattern probably would have emerged, and Lincoln would have had to revise his estimate of Southern cooperation. He would have had to insist that rebel states ratify the Thirteenth Amendment. He would have had to *require*, rather than prefer, voting rights for some blacks. He would have had to stand firm on any degree of fair treatment, for the opposition to change was formidable, even in the North. In 1865 three Northern states with minute African American populations considered black suffrage. In Connecticut blacks were less than 2 percent of the population; in Wisconsin and Minnesota they were less than three-tenths of 1 percent. Yet all three states rejected black suffrage. Racially conservative Republicans, like the Blairs, soon left the party they had helped to create and went into vigorous opposition rather than support racial change in the South.

To secure any progress on race, Lincoln would also have had to abandon, or ignore, his theory that Southern states had not, and could not, leave the Union. Throughout the war he had insisted that if the idea were accepted that "the insurrectionary states are no longer states in the Union ... [then] I am not President, [and] these gentlemen are not Congress." The war was legitimate because secession was illegal. On the other hand, if the Southern states were in the Union and could promptly regain their rights once the war was over, they would block any progress. Even the former Democrat Andrew Johnson had to require them to ratify the Thirteenth Amendment. Perhaps Lincoln was beginning to sense this difficulty when he urged all to avoid the "merely metaphysical question" as to whether rebel states had left the Union.[2]

If the rebel states could simply accept the war's changes and return to loyalty, Reconstruction would be so much easier. This was Lincoln's desire. But he knew there was a price to white Southerners' cooperation. Reconstruction, in fact, presented a choice: compel Southern whites in order to aid the freed people or sacrifice black rights in order to gain Southern cooperation. The evil of racism was an insuperable obstacle to easy solutions and to the fond wishes of Lincoln's Second Inaugural Address.

Perhaps "American Slavery" had been an "offence" that "the Almighty ... will[ed] to remove" through war. It had taken a war before the Union faced the problem of slavery and chose to end it. Still, the nation was not ready to confront the problem of race—what Alexander Stephens called "the proper *status* of the negro." Neither society's patterns of power and influence nor the dominant attitudes toward African Americans had changed. Most Northerners remained strongly opposed to equality. Gideon Welles openly admitted his own prejudice. He felt that even Charles Sumner, despite his "love for the negroes in the abstract ... is unwilling to fellowship with them, though he thinks he is." Black leaders had often criticized white abolitionists for prejudiced behavior. In the South, defeated Confederates were determined that emancipation mean as little as possible. Even if God viewed as just the destruction of all the wealth created by slavery, even if the Almighty decreed the necessity for bloodshed equal to all the blood spilled under slavery, the deeper problem of race remained unsolved.[3]

Eleven years after Lincoln's death Frederick Douglass reflected on both

Frederick Douglass, the great black abolitionist and protest leader, influenced Lincoln and fought for equal rights for freed African Americans.

the nation's progress and its failure. He saw both as bound up and represented in the career of Abraham Lincoln. Praising the president, Douglass gratefully acknowledged, "In his heart of hearts he loathed and hated slavery." He had done much to lift up African Americans. But Douglass also affirmed that "President Lincoln was a white man, and shared the prejudices common to his countrymen towards the colored race." African Americans "were not the special objects of his consideration." In fact, "[h]e was preeminently the white man's President, entirely devoted to the welfare of white men." For that reason he was often "ready and willing" to "sacrifice the rights of humanity in the colored people to promote the welfare of the white people of this country."[4]

With intellectual detachment, Douglass also evaluated Lincoln and his actions in the context of his flawed society. Douglass felt

> compelled to admit that this unfriendly feeling on his [Lincoln's] part may be safely set down as one element of his wonderful success in or-ganizing the loyal American people for the tremendous conflict before

them, and bringing them safely through that conflict. His great mission was to accomplish two things: first, to save his country from dismemberment and ruin; and second, to free his country from the great crime of slavery. To do one or the other, or both, he must have the earnest sympathy and the powerful cooperation of his loyal fellow-countrymen.

Thus in leading the nation it was an advantage for Lincoln that "viewed from the genuine abolition ground," he "seemed tardy, cold, dull, and indifferent." His views were "zealous," however, or even "radical" when measured "by the sentiment of his country, a sentiment he was bound as a statesman to consult."[5]

That racial sentiment was stubbornly hostile to equality. As a result, the civil war did not resolve and correct "the proper *status* of the negro." The ideals of the Declaration of Independence remained challenging and unmet, and the progress made in Reconstruction soon would go backward. New structures of oppression would be created, and more lives would be lost. The struggle for equality would consume many additional decades and continue to the present day.

Though Lincoln is revered, his career is widely misunderstood, and the social context so important to Frederick Douglass's analysis is largely forgotten. To cite just one example, the Associated Press observed the 150th anniversary of Lincoln's Preliminary Emancipation Proclamation with an article distributed to newspapers around the country. That article's summary of the proclamation was entirely mistaken. It described the proclamation as giving the Confederacy one hundred days to "end its 'rebellion' against the United States and voluntarily abolish slavery."[6] In fact, of course, the proclamation gave rebel states one hundred days to return to the Union and *keep* slavery. This reversal of meaning reflected a widespread and comforting ignorance of the unpleasant facts in American history. To recognize those realities is to understand more truly both Lincoln's achievements and the nation's failures.

Acknowledgments

I am grateful to the many scholars who have helped me during my career and particularly to those persons who have assisted me with this book. I thank my wife; my good friend Jeffrey Crow; Professor Gordon McKinney and an anonymous reader for the University of Virginia Press; Richard Holway, Ellen Satrom, and their colleagues at the Press who made valuable suggestions; and Simone Caron, who as chairperson of my department has always supported my work. As always, any deficiencies remain my responsibility.

Notes

Introduction: Two Speeches

1. Welles, *Diary,* 2:280; Booth, *"Right or Wrong, God Judge Me,"* 145.

2. Welles, *Diary,* 2:272–73, 278.

3. Ibid., 2:280; W. E. Smith, *The Francis Preston Blair Family,* 2:326. The residence is known today as Blair House and is the official state guesthouse for the president of the United States.

4. Welles, *Diary,* 2:279; Booth, *"Right or Wrong, God Judge Me,"* 7. On Lincoln's admiration of Booth as an actor, see Hay, *Inside Lincoln's White House,* 325n.

5. Booth, *"Right or Wrong, God Judge Me,"* 15.

6. Key portions of Stephens's speech may be found in Durden, *The Gray and the Black,* 7–9.

7. Lincoln, *This Fiery Trial,* 64.

8. This and subsequent quotations from Lincoln's last speech on April 11, 1865, are taken from Lincoln, *This Fiery Trial,* 223–27.

9. Ibid.

10. The Confederacy also claimed Kentucky and Missouri as member states. But for almost all of the war these states functioned as part of the Union, and their Confederate "officials," though welcome in Richmond, could not go home. Within the wartime Union, slavery had existed in Missouri, Kentucky, Maryland, and Delaware. Missouri and Maryland had decided by this time to end slavery. Kentucky and Delaware had not, and Kentucky would be the last state to ratify the Thirteenth Amendment.

1. Prejudice and Human Sympathy

1. See, e.g., the case of Daniel Worth, an elderly Wesleyan Methodist minister, in 1859 in North Carolina. Lefler and Newsome, *North Carolina,* 446.

2. Litwack, *North of Slavery,* 75, 91.

3. Ibid., 93.

4. Ibid., 70–71; Berwanger, *The Frontier against Slavery,* 140.

5. Litwack, *North of Slavery,* 97.

6. Blight, *Frederick Douglass' Civil War,* 15–16.

7. See Richards, *Gentlemen of Property and Standing.*

8. Gossett, *Uncle Tom's Cabin,* 164; Norton et al., *A People and a Nation,* 4th ed., 406.

9. Stowe, *Uncle Tom's Cabin,* 99.

10. Ibid., 505.

11. Campbell, *The Slave Catchers,* 150–57.

12. Ibid., 124–30; Shapiro, "The Rendition of Anthony Burns," esp. 40 and 44–45.

13. McPherson, *Battle Cry of Freedom,* 120.

14. Campbell, *The Slave Catchers,* 167–68.

2. Founding the Republican Party

1. W. E. Smith, *The Francis Preston Blair Family,* 1:366, 2:189; E. B. Smith, *Francis Preston Blair,* xii.

2. E. B. Smith, *Francis Preston Blair,* chaps. 1–10.

3. Ibid.; W. E. Smith, *The Francis Preston Blair Family,* 2:137.

4. W. E. Smith, *The Francis Preston Blair Family,* 1: chap. 18.

5. Ibid., 1:263.

6. Ibid., 1:210–11, 290–91, 386–87, 514.

7. Ibid., 1:373–75, 455–59, 415–17; Burlingame, *Abraham Lincoln,* 1:435. Frank Blair was well educated. He earned his undergraduate degree at Princeton before studying law at Transylvania University.

8. Burlingame, *Abraham Lincoln,* 1:121.

9. Ibid., 1: chaps. 4 and 5; Lincoln, *This Fiery Trial,* 8.

10. Burlingame, *Abraham Lincoln,* 1: chap. 8, esp. 267, 282–83, and 288–89.

11. See Ripley, ed., *The Black Abolitionist Papers,* 4:196. One of the most insightful analyses of the Kansas-Nebraska bill and its effects is in Potter, *The Impending Crisis,* chap. 7.

12. Congress adopted much of Jefferson's draft but omitted the provisions on slavery. Soon after, however, the Northwest Ordinance of 1787 prohibited slavery north and west of the Ohio River.

13. This and subsequent quotations from the Peoria speech may be found in Lincoln, *Collected Works,* 2:247–83.

14. See chaps. 1–4 in Donald, *Charles Sumner and the Coming of the Civil War.* Sumner's father was a lawyer who in 1826 gained appointment as sheriff of Suffolk County, which included Boston.

15. Ibid., chaps. 1–6, and pp. 96–98, 127–28.

16. Ibid., 139–42.

17. Key excerpts from Sumner's brief in *Sarah C. Roberts v. The City of Boston* (1849), may be found in Martin, ed., *Brown v. Board of Education,* 48, 50, 53–55, 57; Donald, *Charles Sumner and the Coming of the Civil War,* 152.

18. Donald, *Charles Sumner and the Coming of the Civil War,* 156–71.

19. Sumner, *Freedom National; Slavery Sectional,* 8, 9, 13, 19, 15, 22, 29. This argument

was not a new invention of Sumner's. The essence of the argument had been put forward previously by Salmon Chase.

20. Ibid., 51, 50, 42, 65; Donald, *Charles Sumner and the Coming of the Civil War,* 176. Butler took a liking to his young seatmate, and Sumner checked the classical allusions that Butler planned to quote in his speeches. It was ironic, in view of later events, that Sumner considered Louisiana's senator Pierre Soulé his best friend in the Senate in these early years.

21. Sumner, *Landmark of Freedom,* 18, 49, 36, 9–10, 64; Donald, *Charles Sumner and the Coming of the Civil War,* 213.

22. Donald, *Charles Sumner and the Coming of the Civil War,* 219–21.

23. Ibid., 229.

24. Blight, *Frederick Douglass' Civil War,* 47, 16.

3. ATTITUDES TOWARD SLAVERY AND RACE

1. Jefferson, *Works,* 1: entry for February 8, 1821, in Autobiography Draft Fragment.

2. Jefferson, *Notes on the State of Virginia,* quoted in Rose, ed., *A Documentary History of Slavery,* 74, 75, 70, 71, 74.

3. John C. Calhoun, Speech in 1837, quoted in Finkelman, ed., *Defending Slavery,* 59, 58; "Slavery and the Bible," from *De Bow's Review,* September 1850, in ibid., 109, 114; George Fitzhugh, quoted in ibid., 190, 199; James Henry Hammond, Speech on the Admission of Kansas, March 4, 1858 (the Mudsill Speech), in ibid., 80–88, quotation on 87.

4. Editorial in the *Liberator,* January 1, 1831, and "Declaration of the National Anti-Slavery Convention," December 14, 1833, both in Cain, ed., *William Lloyd Garrison,* 70, 90. See also, for important background and analysis of the abolitionists' early crusades, Richards, *Gentlemen of Property and Standing.*

5. Clarke, *John Wilkes Booth,* 48–49.

6. Ibid., 72, 76.

7. Ibid., 53.

8. Ibid., 71–73, 48–49; Booth, *"Right or Wrong, God Judge Me,"* 38–39.

9. Clarke, *John Wilkes Booth,* 77; Booth, *"Right or Wrong, God Judge Me,"* 6.

10. W. E. Smith, *The Francis Preston Blair Family,* 1:201. A good short summary of Jacksonian democratic ideology is in Pfau, *The Political Style of Conspiracy,* 52–54. See also Silbey, *The Transformation of American Politics.*

11. The fact that the Blairs came from the Democratic Party and from a slave state, in addition to their vital role in forming the Republican Party, weighed in favor of Montgomery having a role in the cabinet.

12. W. E. Smith, *The Francis Preston Blair Family,* 1:211.

13. Ibid., 1:210–11.

14. Fehrenbacher, *Slavery, Law, and Politics.*

15. The Articles of Confederation government, in its waning days, passed the Northwest Ordinance, but many of the men who wrote the federal constitution had taken part

in the action by the Articles government. They soon reaffirmed that action as members of the new Congress.

16. M. Blair, Argument of Montgomery Blair. Roswell Field had begun work on the case in Missouri and assisted Blair, as did George Ticknor Curtis.

17. Another valuable analysis of the case may be found in Potter, *The Impending Crisis*, 267–96.

18. Blight, *Frederick Douglass' Civil War*, 27; Ripley, ed., *The Black Abolitionist Papers*, 4:364.

19. W. E. Smith, *The Francis Preston Blair Family*, 1:404–11, 443.

20. Ibid.

21. Frank Blair, Address at the Mercantile Library Association. See also Foner, *Free Soil, Free Labor, Free Men*, 270, 276, 269.

22. Donald, *Charles Sumner and the Coming of the Civil War*, 216–17.

23. Ibid., 217–18; Norton et al., *A People and a Nation*, 4th ed., 408.

24. Donald, *Charles Sumner and the Coming of the Civil War*, 218.

25. Ibid., 225.

26. Sumner, "The Antislavery Enterprise," 10, 11, 4, 6.

27. Pike, *Ida May;* Gage, "A White Slave Girl." See also Joe Lockard, "Ida May."

28. Blight, *Frederick Douglass' Civil War*, 50, 52.

4. Lincoln's Attitudes on Slavery and Race

1. Lincoln to Albert G. Hodges, April 4, 1864, in Lincoln, *This Fiery Trial*, 194.

2. This point is made by David Donald in his biography of Lincoln and in his comments on the PBS series *Abraham and Mary Lincoln*.

3. Burlingame, *Abraham Lincoln*, 1:18.

4. These are the words of Samuel C. Parks, another Illinois lawyer, quoted in ibid., 1:166.

5. Ibid., 1:108–10.

6. Ibid., 1:154–55.

7. Ibid., 1:160. Burlingame judges that Lincoln was "probably" the author of the last letter cited.

8. Ibid., 1:156–57.

9. Ibid., 1:158–59, 190–93.

10. This famous statement was made by Lincoln's Springfield law partner, William Herndon.

11. PBS, *Abraham and Mary Lincoln;* Current, *The Lincoln Nobody Knows*, 1–2, 12; Elodie Todd quoted in Berry, *House of Abraham*, 158.

12. Berry, *House of Abraham*, 21–22.

13. Ibid., 21–22, 24–37; PBS, *Abraham and Mary Lincoln*, for "desolate." Ninian Edward Jr., describing Mary's flirtatiousness, quoted in PBS, *Abraham and Mary Lincoln*.

14. Burlingame, *Abraham Lincoln*, 1:176.

15. Ibid., 1:174–76, 182–83, 187, 195, 197. Burlingame gives credit to Wayne C.

Temple's hypothesis "that she seduced Lincoln the night before and made him feel obliged to wed her immediately in order to preserve her honor" (197).

16. Winkle, *Abraham and Mary Lincoln,* 50–54, 60–64; Burlingame, *Abraham Lincoln,* 1:219.

17. Burlingame, *Abraham Lincoln,* 1:201–2.

18. Ibid., 1:238–41, 247–48.

19. Ibid., 1:257–60.

20. Ibid., 1:260–62.

21. Ibid., 1:260–61, 274–75.

22. Ibid., 1:265–67, 287–89.

23. Ibid., 1:296–307.

24. Ibid., 1:357–60. I follow Professor Burlingame in viewing the years from 1849 to 1854 as ones of personal crisis and growth, but I analyze the causes somewhat differently.

25. Ibid., 1:173, 358–59.

26. Ibid., 1:223–24, 310.

27. Ibid., 1:356–56.

28. Under political pressure, as will be shown in chap. 5, Lincoln on occasion used racist language. But this was rare, and his previous practice of volunteering racist jokes or stories seems to have ceased.

29. Lincoln's Peoria speech, October 6, 1854, in Lincoln, *Collected Works,* 2:255, 265–66.

30. Lincoln, *Collected Works,* 2:398–410.

31. Lincoln, *This Fiery Trial,* 34–37.

32. Ibid.

33. Ibid.

34. Ibid.

5. Warning Whites about Slavery

1. For example, at the end of 1857 Douglas spoke in Chicago and charged that "Black Republicans . . . will allow the blacks to push us from our sidewalk [Oh!] and elbow us out of car seats [Oh? Oh!] *and stink us out of our places of worship.*" Quoted in Lincoln, *Collected Works,* 2:450n.

2. Abraham Lincoln to Elihu Washburne, May 27, 1858, in ibid., 2:455.

3. Lincoln to Charles L. Wilson, June 1, 1858, in ibid., 2:456–57. See also 2:448–49. Lincoln felt no particular animus toward either Greeley or Seward. He believed Greeley was totally sincere in his antislavery views and simply regarded Douglas as more influential and better able than Lincoln to advance them. Seward did not disseminate his views through a newspaper, and Lincoln had no knowledge that Seward was giving private advice against Lincoln.

4. See ibid., 2:452.

5. Ibid., 2:461–62.

6. W. E. Smith, *The Francis Preston Blair Family,* 1:411.

7. Ibid., 1:462–64.

8. Ibid., 1:465–66.

9. Ibid., 1:463, 465.

10. Ibid., 1:467.

11. Ibid., 1:468–69.

12. Parrish, *Frank Blair,* 68, also 74. In addition to campaigning in Illinois, Blair made "an extended tour of Wisconsin, Indiana, and Illinois," preaching "his doctrine of colonization wherever he went."

13. Lincoln, *Collected Works,* 3:296, 112, 178.

14. Ibid., 3:112–13, 296.

15. Ibid., 3:3, 4, 9.

16. Ibid., 3:213–14.

17. Ibid., 3:105, 55–56, 171. Douglas's story about Frederick Douglass and the carriage varied in its details from Freeport to Jonesboro. At Freeport the daughter was outside the carriage and her mother inside. At Jonesboro both women sat inside with Douglass.

18. Ibid., 3:96, 2:405, 3:179.

19. Ibid., 2:406.

20. Ibid., 2:405, 407; 3:145–46.

21. Ibid., 2:521, 3:80.

22. Ibid., 2:409.

23. Ibid., 3:20, 27, 77.

24. Ibid., 2:546.

25. Ibid., 3:254, 87, 181.

26. Ibid., 2:500, 527; 3:312.

27. Ibid., 2:521, 515; 3:233, 29, 27, 30.

28. Blight, *Frederick Douglass' Civil War,* 52, 48, 51.

6. Violence

1. Rice, *The Rise and Fall of Black Slavery,* 307.

2. Booth, *"Right or Wrong, God Judge Me,"* 38–39; Clarke, *John Wilkes Booth,* 48–49.

3. Clarke, *John Wilkes Booth,* 77; Booth, *"Right or Wrong,"* 5.

4. William Shakespeare, *Richard III,* act 1, scene 1.

5. Ibid., act 5, scene 6. These quotations come from the version of the play "Restored and Rearranged from the text of Shakespeare, As Performed at the Theatre Royal, Covent Garden. London: Printed for R. and M. Stodart, 81 Strand. 1821." The company with which Booth performed may have used this version. Modern scholars, however, attribute the second and third quotations given above to other Shakespeare plays.

6. Booth, *"Right or Wrong,"* 46n2.

7. Ibid., 79.

8. Clarke, *John Wilkes Booth,* 43–44.

9. Ibid., 6–7.

10. Booth, *"Right or Wrong,"* 6.

11. Ibid., 49. The exact nature of Booth's gunshot wound is unclear. It was variously described as "in the side," "in the fleshy part of the leg," "in the thigh," or "in the rear."

12. Ibid., 56–64.

13. Ibid.

14. Donald, *Charles Sumner and the Rights of Man,* 251.

15. Sumner, *Landmark of Freedom,* 5, 10–12, 14, 18, 49, 64.

16. Eventually voting in the territory made clear that a sizable majority wanted to bar slavery from Kansas. But an even larger number favored prohibiting the entry of African Americans.

17. Donald, *Charles Sumner and the Coming of the Civil War,* 239.

18. Sumner, "The Crime against Kansas."

19. Ibid.

20. Ibid.; Donald, *Charles Sumner and the Coming of the Civil War,* 239–41.

21. Donald, *Charles Sumner and the Coming of the Civil War,* 241–42.

22. Ibid., 241–49; Hoffer, *The Caning of Charles Sumner,* esp. chap. 1.

23. Donald, *Charles Sumner and the Coming of the Civil War,* 244, 247–48.

24. Ibid., 251; Norton et al., *A People and a Nation,* 4th ed., 414. Quarrels had led to canings and even to fatal duels in earlier years. But in previous Congresses the more violent confrontations had usually taken place outside the legislative chambers.

25. W. E. Smith, *The Francis Preston Blair Family,* 1:348, 186; Donald, *Charles Sumner and the Coming of the Civil War,* chap. 12.

26. Parrish, *Frank Blair,* 87.

27. Ibid., 87.

28. Welles, *Diary,* 2:20; Parrish, *Frank Blair,* 194.

29. Hay, *Inside Lincoln's White House,* 249. Lincoln also said (245) that he harbored little "personal resentment" and "never thought it paid. A man has not time to spend half his life in quarrels. If any man ceases to attack me, I never remember the past against him."

30. Burlingame, *Abraham Lincoln,* 1:190–94.

31. Ibid., 194.

32. Rice, *The Rise and Fall of Black Slavery,* 307.

7. Ambition, Triumph, and Crisis

1. Lincoln, *This Fiery Trial,* 82.

2. W. E. Smith, *The Francis Preston Blair Family,* 1:444–46.

3. Ibid., 1:446–47.

4. Frank Blair, Address at the Mercantile Library Association.

5. Francis Preston Blair Sr. to Abraham Lincoln, May 26, 1860, Abraham Lincoln Papers.

6. Burlingame, *Abraham Lincoln,* 1:564.

7. Ibid., 1:565–66.

8. Ibid., 1:566–67.

9. Ibid., 1:569.

10. Ibid., 1:566, 568–69.

11. Ibid., 1:571–72.

12. Stashower, *The Hour of Peril*, 67.

13. W. E. Smith, *The Francis Preston Blair Family*, 1:451–52.

14. Thoreau, "A Plea for Captain John Brown"; Emerson quoted in the *New York Daily Tribune*, November 8, 1859.

15. Burlingame, *Abraham Lincoln*, 1:575–76.

16. Ibid., 1:576.

17. Ibid., 1:574, 577.

18. Frank Blair, Speech at Cooper Institute.

19. Lincoln, *Collected Works*, 3:522–33, quotations from 534 and 535.

20. Ibid., 3:536–41.

21. Ibid., 3:542–47.

22. Ibid., 3:547–50.

23. Burlingame, *Abraham Lincoln*, 1:593.

24. Lincoln, *This Fiery Trial*, 81.

25. Burlingame, *Abraham Lincoln*, 1:618–24.

26. Ibid., 1:626.

27. Ibid., 1:664–65.

28. Ibid., 1:666.

29. Ibid., 1:636–38; Ripley, ed., *The Black Abolitionist Papers*, 5:71; Blight, *Frederick Douglass' Civil War*, 53 and 91 (where H. Ford Douglas, a black leader in Illinois, is quoted explaining his belief that Republicans "will do nothing for freedom now" yet hoped that the "anti-slavery element" in the party "will increase").

30. Donald, *Charles Sumner and the Coming of the Civil War*, 298.

31. Ibid.; Sumner, "The Barbarism of Slavery," 33; Sumner to Lincoln, June 8, 1860, Abraham Lincoln Papers; Donald, *Charles Sumner and the Coming of the Civil War*, 298.

8. Secession

1. Blight, *Frederick Douglass' Civil War*, 57–58.

2. See Potter, *Lincoln and His Party in the Secession Crisis*.

3. John A. Gilmer to Abraham Lincoln, December 10, 1860, Abraham Lincoln Papers.

4. Nicolay, *With Lincoln in the White House*, 7 (entry for November 5, 1860).

5. Ibid., 10 (November 16, 1860).

6. Lincoln to Gilmer, December 15, 1860, Abraham Lincoln Papers.

7. Ibid.

8. W. E. Smith, *The Francis Preston Blair Family*, 1:514.

9. Potter, *The Impending Crisis*, 549–50.

10. Nicolay, *With Lincoln in the White House*, 15.

11. This is the testimony of Stephen Douglas, quoted in Rhodes, *History of the United States*, 3:151–55. See also Current, *The Lincoln Nobody Knows*, 88–90.

12. Lincoln, *Collected Works,* 4:158–59.

13. Letter to Lyman Trumbull, ibid., 4:158, and Resolutions, 4:156–57, especially the note on 157.

14. Declarations of Causes of Seceding States: Civil War South Carolina.

15. Lincoln, *Collected Works,* 4:160.

16. Stashower, *The Hour of Peril,* 82–85.

17. Francis Preston Blair Sr. to Lincoln, January 12, 1861, and Montgomery Blair to Lincoln, December 8, 1860, both in Abraham Lincoln Papers; Goodwin, *Team of Rivals,* 312.

18. Escott, *"What Shall We Do with the Negro?,"* 3–4.

19. Lincoln to Francis P. Blair Sr., December 21, 1860, in Lincoln, *Collected Works,* 4:157; Burlingame, *Abraham Lincoln,* 1:749, 758.

20. See Burlingame, *Abraham Lincoln,* 1: chaps. 18 and 19; and Goodwin, *Team of Rivals,* 283–319.

21. Benjamin Wade to Preston King, November 20, 1860; Lyman Trumbull to Lincoln, December 18, 1860; William Pinckney Ewing to Lincoln, February 2, 1861; and Francis S. Corkran and John C. Underwood to Lincoln, February 26, 1861, all in Abraham Lincoln Papers.

22. Burlingame, *Abraham Lincoln,* 2:35; Goodwin, *Team of Rivals,* 310.

23. Stashower, *The Hour of Peril,* 157.

24. Goodwin, *Team of Rivals,* 310–11; Burlingame, *Abraham Lincoln,* 2:36.

25. Welles, *Diary,* 1:55, 10; Stashower, *The Hour of Peril,* 15.

26. Welles, *Diary,* 1:39.

27. Burlingame, *Abraham Lincoln,* 2:46; Lincoln, *This Fiery Trial,* 96. It is known that more than one of the three advisers recommended that the seceded states should be and appear the aggressors.

All quotations in the remaining paragraphs of this chapter come from the Inaugural Address, as found in Lincoln, *This Fiery Trial,* 88–97.

9. Making War and Alliances

1. Nicolay, *With Lincoln in the White House,* 46–47.

2. Gienapp, *Abraham Lincoln and Civil War America,* 25; Berry, *House of Abraham,* 51–52; Burlingame, *Abraham Lincoln,* 1:2.

3. See Potter, *Lincoln and His Party in the Secession Crisis.*

4. Welles, *Diary,* 1:33.

5. This was Charles Francis Adams Jr.'s description of Seward's feelings. See Burlingame, *Abraham Lincoln,* 2:98.

6. Ibid., 2:98–99.

7. Ibid., 2:99; Goodwin, *Team of Rivals,* 341.

8. Burlingame, *Abraham Lincoln,* 2:100.

9. Ibid., 2:101.

10. Ibid., 2:102–4.

11. Ibid., 2:105–7, 117–19.

12. Ibid., 2:120–22.

13. Welles, *Diary,* 25.

14. Lincoln, *Collected Works,* 4:331–32; Burlingame, *Abraham Lincoln,* 2:138.

15. Burlingame, *Abraham Lincoln,* 2:138; Leech, *Reveille in Washington,* 57.

16. Nicolay, *With Lincoln in the White House,* 34; Burlingame, *Abraham Lincoln,* 2:139 and 147; Hay, *Inside Lincoln's White House,* 11.

17. Donald, *Charles Sumner and the Rights of Man,* 21.

18. Donald, *Charles Sumner and the Coming of the Civil War,* 323; Donald, *Charles Sumner and the Rights of Man,* 13. Andrew Johnson of Tennessee was coauthor of these resolutions.

19. Hay, *Inside Lincoln's White House,* 19.

20. Ripley, ed., *The Black Abolitionist Papers,* 5:19; McPherson, ed., *The Negro's Civil War,* 79, 81.

21. E. B. Smith, *Francis Preston Blair,* 320.

22. Donald, *Lincoln,* 344.

23. Edwards to Lincoln, August 9 and 10, 1861, Abraham Lincoln Papers. Edwards further advised that officials of New Granada had attested to the authenticity of Ambrose Thompson's claims and that any legal questions about the United States possessing lands within the boundaries of another nation could be avoided by leasing the land for a naval base.

24. Donald, *Lincoln,* 344.

25. Parrish, *Frank Blair,* 95–111; W. E. Smith, *The Francis Preston Blair Family,* 2:113. Parrish criticizes the capture of the military encampment outside St. Louis, arguing that it was unnecessary. There is no doubt, however, that Frank was in the forefront of pro-Union activity in Missouri.

10. Shocking Defeat, Alternate Paths

1. The quotation is from Lincoln's message to the Special Session, July 4, 1861, in Lincoln, *Collected Works,* 6:429.

2. Burlingame, *Abraham Lincoln,* 2:166.

3. Lincoln, *Collected Works,* 6:431–32, 422–31.

4. Ibid., 6:433–34.

5. Ibid., 6:434, 438.

6. Among Sumner's words on October 1, 1861, were these: that "reason, justice, and policy unite, each and all, in declaring that the war must be brought to bear directly on the grand conspirator and omnipresent enemy" of slavery and that "the overthrow of slavery will make an end of the war." Quoted in the Library section of the website of The Lincoln Institute, an American History Project of The Lehrman Institute, accessed April 17, 2012, http: mrlincolnandfreedom.org/inside.asp?ID=74&subjectID=4. See also McPherson, *The Negro's Civil War,* 18.

7. W. E. Smith, *The Francis Preston Blair Family,* 2:244; Pearson, *The Life of John A. Andrew,* 1:249.

8. Burlingame, *Abraham Lincoln,* 2:180–81; Leech, *Reveille in Washington,* 98.

9. Nicolay, *With Lincoln in the White House,* 51–52; Burlingame, *Abraham Lincoln,* 2:182–83; Leech, *Reveille in Washington,* 98, 103.

10. The First Confiscation Act was passed on August 6, 1861, as congressmen recalibrated their understanding of the challenge posed by the rebellion.

11. Donald, *Lincoln,* 314; Leech, *Reveille in Washington,* 242–44.

12. Burlingame, *Abraham Lincoln,* 2:162, 354.

13. There are many accounts of the Trent affair. Burlingame covers the issue in ibid., 2:229 and chap. 24.

14. Freehling, *The South vs. the South,* 18–19, 61–63.

15. W. E. Smith, *The Francis Preston Blair Family,* 2:53, 78–80.

16. Burlingame, *Abraham Lincoln,* 2:202.

17. Quoted in Lincoln, *This Fiery Trial,* 110–11.

18. Burlingame, *Abraham Lincoln,* 2:207. On Montgomery Meigs, see ibid., 164.

19. E. B. Smith, *Francis Preston Blair,* 300; Burlingame, *Abraham Lincoln,* 2:304.

20. We do not know the precise day on which Lincoln wrote out his plan for Delaware, but it is apparent that it coincided closely with the Blairs' initiatives on Chiriqui.

21. Burlingame, *Abraham Lincoln,* 2:229.

22. Lincoln, *Collected Works,* 5:29–31. Burlingame and Ettlinger point out (in Hay, *Inside Lincoln's White House,* 356) that other supporters of colonization included Benjamin Wade, Salmon Chase, Horace Greeley, Thaddeus Stevens, Samuel Pomeroy, Harriet Beecher Stowe, Henry Ward Beecher, James G. Birney, Martin R. Delaney, Lyman Trumbull, Henry Wilson, and Gerrit Smith.

23. Francis P. Blair Sr. to Abraham Lincoln, November 16, 1861, Abraham Lincoln Papers.

24. Ibid.

25. Ibid.

26. Ambrose Thompson to Francis P. Blair Sr., November 17, 1861, and November 18, 1861; orders written by Francis P. Blair Sr.; and Frank Blair to Montgomery Blair, December 1861, all in ibid.

27. Burlingame, *Abraham Lincoln,* 2:229–30, 231.

28. Ibid., 2:231.

29. Ibid., 2:392.

30. Lincoln, *Collected Works,* 5:48. At this same time a black minister from New Jersey, William E. Walker, petitioned Congress to "designate Florida as a territory reserved for blacks." Frederick Douglass supported the idea in the pages of *Douglass' Monthly* with the prediction that Florida would attract 150,000 freedmen from neighboring Georgia and South Carolina over a twelve-month period. Ripley, ed., *The Black Abolitionist Papers,* 5:128.

31. Senator James A. Bayard, quoted in Burlingame, *Abraham Lincoln,* 2:231.

32. Ibid., 2:335.

33. Ibid, 2:238–39.

11. OBSTACLES

1. Welles, *Diary,* 1:55, 67, 127.

In 1855 Lincoln was hired as one counsel in a case concerning infringement of patents for the mechanical reaper. Although Lincoln prepared assiduously, Stanton brusquely took over the case and ignored his co-counsel's work.

2. Lincoln, *This Fiery Trial,* 119–20.

3. Ibid.

4. Chase, *Inside Lincoln's Cabinet,* 65–69. As chap. 14 will show, Chase also approved more-intrusive ideas.

5. Burlingame, *Abraham Lincoln,* 2:335, 338.

6. Ibid.; Lincoln, *This Fiery Trial,* 119–20.

7. Nicolay, *With Lincoln in the White House,* 216; Burlingame, *Abraham Lincoln,* 2:341; W. E. Smith, *The Francis Preston Blair Family,* 2:201.

8. Montgomery Blair, Letter to the Meeting held at the Cooper Institute.

9. Ibid.

10. Ibid.

11. Ibid.

12. W. E. Smith, *The Francis Preston Blair Family,* 2:198; Frank Blair, Speech in the House, April 11, 1862. There is considerable evidence against Blair's interpretation of the origins of secession, but his awareness of racism among Southern non-slaveholders was accurate.

13. Hay, *Inside Lincoln's White House,* 356n. The editors add that at certain times Samuel Chase and Thaddeus Stevens also were supporters.

14. See Escott, *"What Shall We Do with the Negro?,"* 37–38.

15. Burlingame, *Abraham Lincoln,* 2:341.

16. An Act for the Release of certain Persons held to Service or Labor in the District of Columbia, National Archives and Records Administration, http://www.archives .gov/exhibits/featured_documents/dc_emancipation_act/transcription.html; Burlingame, *Abraham Lincoln,* 2:345.

17. Hunter, General Orders No. 11; Escott, *"What Shall We Do with the Negro?,"* 40; Chase, *Inside Lincoln's Cabinet,* 20–21. Secretary of War Stanton also had seen copies of Hunter's order.

18. Lincoln, *This Fiery Trial,* 110, 123–24.

19. Sumner, "Indemnity for the Past and Security for the Future"; Burlingame, *Abraham Lincoln,* 2:398.

20. Lincoln, *This Fiery Trial,* 125–27.

21. Response of the Border State Representatives, July 14, 1862, http://cenantua .wordpress.com/2010/01/04/the-border-state-representatives-respond-to-lincolns -appeal/.

22. Ibid.

23. Welles, *Diary,* 1:70.

24. Burlingame, *Abraham Lincoln,* 1:385.

25. Second Confiscation Act, available from the Freedmen and Southern Society Project, http://www.history.umd.edu/Freedmen/conact2.htm; Beck, "Lincoln and Negro Colonization in Central America," 173; Chase, *Inside Lincoln's Cabinet,* 99, 110.

12. Suffering

1. Burlingame, *Abraham Lincoln,* 2:220.

2. See McClellan's letters to his wife, in McClellan, *The Civil War Papers,* esp. 70, 81–82, 85, 106, 112–13, 114, 116; Burlingame, *Abraham Lincoln,* 2:197.

3. Burlingame, *Abraham Lincoln,* 2:296.

4. Ibid., 2:322. The telegraph operator omitted McClellan's insubordinate final statements.

5. Nicolay, *With Lincoln in the White House,* 84; Burlingame, *Abraham Lincoln,* 2:325, 324.

6. The cigars eventually led to Grant's fatal cancer of the mouth and throat. In regard to Farragut, Gideon Welles wrote at the beginning of 1863 that the admiral "will more willingly take great risks in order to obtain great results than any officer in high position in either Navy or Army, and unlike most of them, prefers that others should tell the story of his well-doing rather than relate it himself." Welles, *Diary,* 1:230. Grant would prove that he was Farragut's equal in these important respects.

7. Burlingame, *Abraham Lincoln,* 2:306–7.

8. Welles, *Diary,* 1:93–94, 100–101, 103, 116, 129; Pope's message of July 14, 1862, to the Army of Virginia, http://www.civilwarhome.com/popesmessage.htm; Leech, *Reveille in Washington,* 193; Escott, *The Confederacy,* 41.

9. Hay, *Inside Lincoln's White House,* 40; Welles, *Diary,* 1:116, 113; David Donald, in Chase, *Inside Lincoln's Cabinet,* 131.

10. Welles, *Diary,* 1:113, 116.

11. Leech, *Reveille in Washington,* 199; Welles, *Diary,* 1:117, 146, 111. Lincoln interviewed and then cashiered Major Key.

12. Burlingame, *Abraham Lincoln,* 2:382–83. The words "opportunity of a lifetime" were McClellan's own words.

13. Leech, *Reveille in Washington,* 205; Burlingame, *Abraham Lincoln,* 2:382–83.

14. Escott, *The Confederacy,* 57; Welles, *Diary,* 193, 209; Burlingame, *Abraham Lincoln,* 2:446.

15. W. E. Smith, *The Francis Preston Blair Family,* 2:137.

16. Burlingame, *Abraham Lincoln,* 2:300.

17. Ibid., 2:299–301.

18. Nicolay, *With Lincoln in the White House,* 69, 71, 217; Burlingame, *Abraham Lincoln,* 2:298–99.

19. Welles, *Diary,* 1:70; Burlingame, *Abraham Lincoln,* 2:264; Montgomery Blair to Abraham Lincoln, September 3, 1862, Abraham Lincoln Papers.

20. Burlingame, *Abraham Lincoln,* 2:300; Leech, *Reveille in Washington,* 298.

21. Burlingame, *Abraham Lincoln,* 2: chap. 25.

13. Military Necessity and a Covenant with God

1. Burlingame, *Abraham Lincoln,* 2:398.

2. Ibid., 2:399.

3. Ibid., 2:333, 398; Chase, *Inside Lincoln's Cabinet,* 95–99.

4. Lincoln, *This Fiery Trial,* 131–32. A record of this meeting was published in the newspapers.

5. Burlingame, *Abraham Lincoln,* 2:390–91.

6. Horace Greeley, "The Prayer of Twenty Millions"; Lincoln, *This Fiery Trial,* 135.

7. Welles, *Diary,* 1:142–43, 158–60; W. E. Smith, *The Francis Preston Blair Family,* 1:203, 208; Chase, *Inside Lincoln's Cabinet,* 152, 181–82, 191–92.

8. Text of the Preliminary Emancipation Proclamation available at http://www .13thmass.org/1862/emancipation.html.

9. Freehling, *The South vs. the South,* 111.

10. Welles, *Diary,* 1:158–60; Burlingame, *Abraham Lincoln,* 2:412, 415–17; Escott, *"What Shall We Do with the Negro?,"* 57; W. E. Smith, *The Francis Preston Blair Family,* 2:216.

11. Nicolay, *With Lincoln in the White House,* 89; Welles, *Diary,* 1:176; Burlingame, *Abraham Lincoln,* 2:420–22.

12. Lincoln, Annual Address to Congress, December 1, 1862, in *Collected Works,* 5:518–37; also available at http://www.presidency.ucsb.edu/ws/index.php?pid=29503.

13. Burlingame, *Abraham Lincoln,* 2:440–41.

14. Ibid., 2:469, 470, 471–72. In the final weeks, as Lincoln worked on the proclamation's text, Charles Sumner shared with him George Livermore's book *An Historical Research Respecting the Opinions of the Founders of the Republic on Negroes as Slaves, as Citizens, and as Soldiers.*

15. The text of the Emancipation Proclamation is available many places, including http://www.historynet.com/emancipation-proclamation-text; Burlingame, *Abraham Lincoln,* 2:463; see also Escott, *"What Shall We Do with the Negro?,"* 63; Harris, *With Charity for All,* 54–56.

16. Welles, *Diary,* 1:212; Hay, *Inside Lincoln's White House,* 41.

17. Nicolay, *With Lincoln in the White House,* 101.

18. Welles, *Diary,* 1:123, 150–54, 162; Burlingame, *Abraham Lincoln,* 2:392–94.

19. Burlingame, *Abraham Lincoln,* 2:395; Welles, *Diary,* 1:205; Chase, *Inside Lincoln's Cabinet,* 103.

20. Burlingame, *Abraham Lincoln,* 2:395–96; W. E. Smith, *The Francis Preston Blair Family,* 2:323.

21. Chase, *Inside Lincoln's Cabinet,* 99; Emancipation Proclamation; Welles, *Diary,* 1:218; transcript of PBS, *Abraham and Mary Lincoln;* Burlingame, *Abraham Lincoln,* 2:474.

22. Escott, *"What Shall We Do with the Negro?,"* 72–73.

23. Ibid., 72; Hay, *Inside Lincoln's White House,* 69.

24. Parrish, *Frank Blair,* 165.

25. Escott, *"What Shall We Do with the Negro?,"* 72, 36–39.

26. Lincoln, Annual Address to Congress, December 1, 1862.

27. Lincoln, *This Fiery Trial,* 153 and 154.

28. Ibid.; Hay, *Inside Lincoln's White House,* 68–69. Lincoln said the same thing to General Stephen Hurlbut in Arkansas. The Emancipation Proclamation applied to Arkansas and those who "have tasted actual freedom I believe can never be slaves." But "for the rest, I believe some plan, substantially being gradual emancipation, would be better for both white and black." Burlingame, *Abraham Lincoln,* 2:591.

14. Traitors or Brothers?

1. Hay, *Inside Lincoln's White House,* 65.

2. Welles, *Diary,* 1:364; Nicolay, *With Lincoln in the White House,* 118.

3. Sumner, "Indemnity for the Past and Security for the Future," esp. 14, 17, 23, 33–34, 44–47.

4. Chase, *Inside Lincoln's Cabinet,* 50–51. Chase was sometimes inconsistent; see p. 117.

5. Ibid.; Hay, *Inside Lincoln's White House,* 65.

6. Hay, *Inside Lincoln's White House,* 52; Chase, *Inside Lincoln's Cabinet,* 105–6.

7. Escott, *"What Shall We Do with the Negro?,"* 112, 115–16.

8. Hay, *Inside Lincoln's White House,* 73; Welles, *Diary,* 1:410. John Hay agreed in October 1863 that the institution of slavery was not only gravely wounded by the war but "as flagrantly dead as was Lazarus." Hay, *Inside Lincoln's White House,* 98.

9. Welles, *Diary,* 1:502, 412; Burlingame, *Abraham Lincoln,* 2:668; *New York Times,* December 28, 1863.

10. Berry, *House of Abraham,* 51, 69, and the table of relatives at the beginning of the volume.

11. Ibid., 69, 147; Burlingame, *Abraham Lincoln,* 2:555.

12. Baker, *Mary Todd Lincoln,* 223; Burlingame, *Abraham Lincoln,* 2:556; PBS, *Abraham and Mary Lincoln;* Berry, *House of Abraham,* 150–56.

13. Berry, *House of Abraham,* 150–56; Baker, *Mary Todd Lincoln,* 220; Burlingame, *Abraham Lincoln,* 2:556.

14. Baker, *Mary Todd Lincoln,* 225; Berry, *House of Abraham,* 181.

15. Baker, *Mary Todd Lincoln,* 226: Burlingame, *Abraham Lincoln,* 2:556; Berry, *House of Abraham,* 157–65.

16. Nicolay, *With Lincoln in the White House,* 211n.

17. Berry, *House of Abraham,* table of relatives; Winkle, *Abraham and Mary Lincoln,* 95; Leech, *Reveille in Washington,* 293.

18. Leech, *Reveille in Washington,* 158; Winkle, *Abraham and Mary Lincoln,* 95; Burlingame, *Abraham Lincoln,* 2:264.

19. Welles, *Diary,* 1:145, 403, 378, 210, 411, 430.

20. Sumner, "Our Domestic Relations," 507–29, quotations on 507–8, 517, 509.

21. Burlingame, *Abraham Lincoln,* 2:581–82.

22. Sumner, "Our Domestic Relations," 519–21, 518, 523, 524.

23. Whiting, "Dangers in the Present Crisis of the War," 2, 3, 5, 6.

24. Montgomery Blair, "Speech . . . on the revolutionary schemes," 3, 19, 4. The occasion for this speech was a meeting of the Unconditional Union Party.

25. Ibid., 6, 16, 17, 19–20.

15. RECONSTRUCTION OR RESTORATION?

1. Donald, *Lincoln*, 15; Chase, *Inside Lincoln's Cabinet*, 226–27.

2. Lincoln to Albert Hodges, April 4, 1864, in Lincoln, *This Fiery Trial*, 195; Burlingame, *Abraham Lincoln*, 2:479.

3. Lincoln, *This Fiery Trial*, 186; Nicolay, *With Lincoln in the White House*, 102; Resolutions of the Illinois Legislature, January 7, 1863; Chase, *Inside Lincoln's Cabinet*, 134.

4. Donald, *Charles Sumner and the Rights of Man*, 119; Sumner to Lincoln, August 21, 1863, Abraham Lincoln Papers.

5. Welles, *Diary*, 1:413; Hay, *Inside Lincoln's White House*, 114.

6. Escott, *"What Shall We Do with the Negro?,"* 81–82. Even with such praise, racist perspectives crept into the newspaper articles, which soon noted that fighting by black soldiers could spare white lives.

7. Bernstein, *The New York City Draft Riots;* Welles, *Diary*, 1:369.

8. Burlingame, *Abraham Lincoln*, 1:564–66.

9. Hay, *Inside Lincoln's White House*, 98, 71, 89, 84; telegram from Johnson to Blair, November 24, 1863, Abraham Lincoln Papers.

10. W. E. Smith, *The Francis Preston Blair Family*, 2:244–45.

11. Hay, *Inside Lincoln's White House*, 89; Nicolay, *With Lincoln in the White House*, 92–93, 235; W. E. Smith, *The Francis Preston Blair Family in Politics*, 2:162; Parrish, *Frank Blair*, 186–87.

Constitutionally, an individual cannot be in the army and in Congress simultaneously. Lincoln withdrew and returned Frank Blair's commission, as needed, to get around this problem. The Senate, angry over this tactic, passed a resolution "condemning Lincoln for violating the Constitution." See Burlingame, *Abraham Lincoln*, 2:621.

12. Hay, *Inside Lincoln's White House*, 114; Welles, *Diary*, 1:504; Lowell, "The President's Message."

13. Lincoln, *This Fiery Trial*, 190–92.

14. Ibid., 192, 188, 187.

15. Ibid., 184, 188.

16. Hay, *Inside Lincoln's White House*, 121–22.

17. Escott, *"What Shall We Do with the Negro?,"* 110; Burlingame, *Abraham Lincoln*, 2:596; Donald, *Lincoln*, 473.

18. Burlingame, *Abraham Lincoln*, 2:598–99.

19. Ibid., 2:596.

20. Hay, *Inside Lincoln's White House*, 133–34, 137–40, 163, 173.

21. Burlingame, *Abraham Lincoln*, 2:600–602; Parrish, *Frank Blair*, 186–87; Escott, *"What Shall We Do with the Negro?,"* 110–12.

22. Montgomery Blair, "Slavery and the War."

23. Parrish, *Frank Blair,* 188; Frank Blair's speeches in the House of Representatives on February 5 and 27, and April 23, 1864, in *Congressional Globe,* 38th Congress, 1st Session, pp. 513, 46–50 (Appendix), 1827–32.

24. Hay, *Inside Lincoln's White House,* 93; Burlingame, *Abraham Lincoln,* 2:610, 617.

25. A transcript of the Wade-Davis bill is available at http://ourdocuments.gov/doc .php?doc=37&page=transcript.

26. Lincoln, *This Fiery Trial,* 200; Hay, *Inside Lincoln's White House,* 218 and 219.

27. Chase, *Inside Lincoln's Cabinet,* 130. Chase's fears were exaggerated. As the 10 percent government being formed in Louisiana prepared to hold a constitutional convention, Lincoln wrote to Governor Michael Hahn. He suggested for Hahn's "private consideration, whether some of the colored people may not be let in" to the suffrage, "as, for instance, the very intelligent, and especially those who have fought gallantly in our ranks." When this idea was rejected, Lincoln made no objection.

Whereas Sumner and others were indignant over Lincoln's veto of the Wade-Davis bill, conservatives such as Gideon Welles viewed Sumner as "a centralist," that is, someone seeking a stronger central government. Welles objected that "[c]onsolidating makes it more a government of the people than of the states." Welles, *Diary,* 2:96.

28. Holt, *Political Parties and American Political Development,* 325, 330, 339–43, 350–51.

16. Violence and Racism

1. Leech, *Reveille in Washington,* 302; Donald, *Lincoln,* 549–50. Leech put this event in 1862, but Donald accepts the finding of 1864 in Tidwell, *Come Retribution.*

2. *Anti-Negro Riots in the North,* iv, 19, 10, 3; Schecter, *The Devil's Own Work,* 106.

3. Bernstein, *The New York City Draft Riots,* 18, 21, 27; McCague, *The Second Rebellion,* 75, 74; *Anti-Negro Riots in the North,* 24; Schecter, *The Devil's Own Work,* 146. Some Republicans defended the $300 commutation fee as a cap that would keep the price of escaping service from soaring higher (as it did in the Confederacy). In time, it proved to be true that many workingmen formed "commutation clubs" in local taverns and, in a kind of insurance scheme, used the contributions from many to pay the commutation for some who were drafted. But class-based resentment of the commutation was strong.

4. Bernstein, *The New York City Draft Riots,* 27, 23, 40; Headley, *The Great Riots of New York,* 181; McCague, *The Second Rebellion,* 103–4.

5. Bernstein, *The New York City Draft Riots,* 28–30; Headley, *The Great Riots of New York,* 208; Schecter, *The Devil's Own Work,* 157, 172; *Anti-Negro Riots in the North,* 14, 15.

6. Headley, *The Great Riots of New York,* 209; *Anti-Negro Riots in the North,* 7–8; Bernstein, *The New York City Draft Riots,* 5, 3.

7. *Harper's Weekly,* July 18, 1863; J. D. Smith, ed., *Black Soldiers in Blue,* 97–98.

8. J. D. Smith, ed., *Black Soldiers in Blue,* 121–22, 125; McPherson, *Battle Cry of Freedom,* 634.

9. J. D. Smith, ed., *Black Soldiers in Blue,* 151, 154, 186; testimony in Report Number

65, Fort Pillow Massacre, 1864, House of Representatives, 38th Congress, 1st Session, 15–16; McPherson, *Battle Cry of Freedom*, 794.

10. Lincoln, *This Fiery Trial*, 179, 169; McPherson, *Battle Cry of Freedom*, 794.

11. J. D. Smith, ed., *Black Soldiers in Blue*, 127; McPherson, *The Negro's Civil War*, 165; Norton et al., *A People and a Nation*, 5th ed., 425.

12. Escott, "*What Shall We Do with the Negro?*," 83, 73; J. D. Smith, ed., *Black Soldiers in Blue*, 25; Norton et al., *A People and a Nation*, 5th ed., 425.

13. *New York World*, February 12, 1864, July 20, 1864, 4; Escott, "*What Shall We Do with the Negro?*," 82, 83, 67, 73; Ripley, *The Black Abolitionist Papers*, 5:273. Ripley estimates that Northern black recruits to the Union army represented 70 percent of the region's black males of military age.

14. Hay, *Inside Lincoln's White House*, 141, 54, 162.

15. Burlingame, *Abraham Lincoln*, 2:808–9.

16. Ibid., 2:809.

17. Burlingame, *Abraham Lincoln*, 1:332, 2:808–9; Welles, *Diary*, 1:528.

18. Leech, *Reveille in Washington*, 309; Hay, *Inside Lincoln's White House*, 127–28.

19. Leech, *Reveille in Washington*, 360–61.

20. Hay, *Inside Lincoln's White House*, 110, 325–26.

21. Steers and Holzer, *The Lincoln Assassination Conspirators*, 4; Booth, "*Right or Wrong, God Judge Me*," 87, 104.

22. Booth, "*Right or Wrong, God Judge Me*," 97–98, 104, 128, 134; Burlingame, *Abraham Lincoln*, 2:811.

23. Booth, "*Right or Wrong, God Judge Me*," 88; Clarke, *John Wilkes Booth*, 116.

24. Clarke, *John Wilkes Booth*, 81–83, 85–87; Booth, "*Right or Wrong, God Judge Me*," 11, 12–13, 15.

25. Kaplan, "The Miscegenation Issue in the Election of 1864."

26. Croly and Wakeman, *Miscegenation*, 11, 53, 18, 63, 53; Kaplan, "The Miscegenation Issue," 284–90.

27. Croly and Wakeman, *Miscegenation*, 53, 34, 19, 30, 50.

28. Kaplan, "The Miscegenation Issue," 277.

29. Ibid., 284–90, 295–321.

30. Speech of Samuel Sullivan Cox, Democrat of Ohio, in the House of Representatives, February 17, 1864, *Congressional Record*, 38th Congress, 1st Session, 708–13, available from American Memory, Library of Congress. See esp. 709, 710–11, and 713.

31. Kaplan, "The Miscegenation Issue," 277.

17. Political Dangers, Ambiguous Policies

1. Lincoln, *This Fiery Trial*, 205; Donald, *Lincoln*, 529–30.

2. Hay, *Inside Lincoln's White House*, 211.

3. Ibid., 77, 78, 93.

4. Ibid., 65; Peter L. Foy to Frank Blair Jr., January 31, 1864, Abraham Lincoln Papers; Burlingame, *Abraham Lincoln*, 2:628.

5. Burlingame, *Abraham Lincoln*, 2:658, 617; W. E. Smith, *The Francis Preston Blair Family*, 2:279.

6. Donald, *Lincoln*, 481–83.

7. Ibid., 477.

8. Burlingame, *Abraham Lincoln*, 2:609–10.

9. Donald, *Charles Sumner and the Rights of Man*, 141, 125–47.

10. *Ibid.*, 119–22, 148, 154–62.

11. Burlingame, *Abraham Lincoln*, 2:620; Donald, *Charles Sumner and the Rights of Man*, 188–89.

12. Burlingame, *Abraham Lincoln*, 2:634–36. John Nicolay, one of Lincoln's secretaries, compiled a list of abolitionists and Radicals who "joined the movement to dump Lincoln. They included Parke Godwin, Theodore Tilton, George Wilkes, John A. Andrew, David Dudley Field, and Horace Greeley." Nicolay, *With Lincoln in the White House*, 249.

13. Burlingame, *Abraham Lincoln*, 2:636; Edwin Cowles to Montgomery Blair, May 31, 1864, Abraham Lincoln Papers.

14. Burlingame, *Abraham Lincoln*, 2:641–42.

15. Escott, *The Confederacy*, 106–7; transcript of PBS program, *Abraham and Mary Lincoln*.

16. Randall and Donald, *The Civil War and Reconstruction*, 419–21, 423; Leech, *Reveille in Washington*, 322; Welles, *Diary*, 2:44, 53, 102–3; Burlingame, *Abraham Lincoln*, 2:650.

17. *New York World*, August 3 and 4, 1864, p. 4 each day.

18. Burlingame, *Abraham Lincoln*, 2:696–98; *New York World*, February 22, 1864. See also, e.g., February 20, March 25 and 30, 1864.

19. *New York World*, March 30 and February 27, 1864; White, *Miscegenation Indorsed by the Republican Party;* Seaman, *What Miscegenation Is!*

20. Burlingame, *Abraham Lincoln*, 2:695, 641, 697.

21. Ibid., 2:650; *New York World*, February 24, 1864, August 6, 1864, March 2, 1864, March 19 and 12, 1864.

22. Donald, *Lincoln*, 521–22; Escott, *"What Shall We Do with the Negro?,"* 129.

23. Lincoln, *This Fiery Trial*, 201; Escott, *"What Shall We Do with the Negro?,"* 130.

24. Escott, *"What Shall We Do with the Negro?,"* 130; Burlingame, *Abraham Lincoln*, 2:671; *New York World*, July 22, 23, and 30, 1864.

25. Escott, *"What Shall We Do with the Negro?,"* 130–31.

26. Lincoln, *This Fiery Trial*, 203–4.

27. Burlingame, *Abraham Lincoln*, 2:677.

28. Ibid.; *New York Times*, August 18, 1864, 4.

29. Burlingame, *Abraham Lincoln*, 2:677, 689; Seward, *Works*, 491, 502, 503–4.

30. Proceedings of the National Convention of Colored Men. Seward's latest biographer, Walter Stahr, agrees that these words suggested "that the courts or Congress or perhaps even Lincoln would allow slavery to persist in some form after the end of the war." Stahr, *Seward*, 408.

31. Burlingame, *Abraham Lincoln,* 2:673. Lincoln had given passes to Gilmore and Jacquess but had not empowered them to negotiate for the government.

32. Nicolay, *With Lincoln in the White House,* 158; Burlingame, *Abraham Lincoln,* 2:683; Chesnut, *A Diary from Dixie,* 425.

33. Burlingame, *Abraham Lincoln,* 2:623.

34. Ibid., 2:657, 690.

35. Welles, *Diary,* 2:156; Burlingame, *Abraham Lincoln,* 2:692. According to W. E. Smith, *The Francis Preston Blair Family,* 2:268, 284–87, Montgomery Blair gave Lincoln his resignation in June, so that Lincoln could act on it when he felt he needed to do so.

36. Burlingame, *Abraham Lincoln,* 2:694–95; Donald, *Lincoln,* 236–38.

37. Burlingame, *Abraham Lincoln,* 2:396; Magness and Page, *Colonization after Emancipation,* esp. 37, 41–42, 74, 77, 78, 80–81, and 82–83. This important and ably researched book documents the several instances in which Lincoln tried to move possibilities of colonization forward.

18. They Can Have Peace

1. Booth, *"Right or Wrong, God Judge Me,"* 124–26. Booth was writing in November 1864. Booth's reference to "poor old" John Brown was intended to be ironic, but he also admired the zealot's courage and use of violence.

2. See Lincoln's Proclamation of Amnesty and Reconstruction and his accompanying address to Congress, both in Lincoln, *This Fiery Trial,* 185–92.

3. Sumner to Lincoln, November 20, 1864, Abraham Lincoln Papers; Sumner, "Slavery and the Rebellion, One and Inseparable," 22–26, 30.

4. Donald, *Charles Sumner and the Rights of Man,* 202, 194–95, 200, 180, 193.

5. Others who supported Montgomery Blair for chief justice included William Seward, Gideon Welles, the businessman John Murray Forbes, and the newspaper editors William Cullen Bryant and Joseph Medill. See Burlingame, *Abraham Lincoln,* 2:732.

6. Ibid., 2:732, 736; Nicolay, *With Lincoln in the White House,* 255n.

7. Letter from Montgomery Blair to Abraham Lincoln, December 6, 1864, Abraham Lincoln Papers.

8. Ibid.

9. Ibid.; Montgomery Blair, Speech at Cooper Institute, 11.

10. Lincoln, *This Fiery Trial,* 213–14.

11. Ibid., 215.

12. Ibid.

13. Ibid.

14. Burlingame, *Abraham Lincoln,* 2:746–50.

15. Donald, *Charles Sumner and the Rights of Man,* 182–83, 195–96.

16. Ibid., 196.

17. Nicolay, *With Lincoln in the White House,* 253–54; Burlingame, *Abraham Lincoln,* 2:774.

18. Donald, *Charles Sumner and the Rights of Man,* 196–97; Nicolay, *With Lincoln in the White House,* 171.

19. Winkle, *Abraham and Mary Lincoln,* 109; Baker, *Mary Todd Lincoln,* 231.

20. Burlingame, *Abraham Lincoln,* 2:578; Winkle, *Abraham and Mary Lincoln,* 86; Burlingame, *Abraham Lincoln,* 2:606–7; Cecelski, *The Fire of Freedom,* 115–17, 122, 124–26.

21. Leech, *Reveille in Washington,* 329, 355; Burlingame, *Abraham Lincoln,* 2:751.

22. Welles, *Diary,* 2:373–74; 1:219, 414–15, 502.

23. Burlingame, *Abraham Lincoln,* 2:672–73; Durden, *The Gray and the Black,* 68–71.

24. Burlingame, *Abraham Lincoln,* 2:754–55.

25. Francis Preston Blair Sr. to Abraham Lincoln, February 8, 1865, and Blair's "address" to Jefferson Davis, January 12, 1865, Abraham Lincoln Papers; Escott, *"What Shall We Do with the Negro?,"* 204.

26. Welles, *Diary,* 2:231–32, 234, 237.

27. There is continuing debate about the Hampton Roads Conference, in part because only the Confederate commissioners made notes about the conference, after their return to Richmond, and in part because Lincoln has become an iconic figure in American culture, one whose actions tend to be interpreted to suit contemporary attitudes. For an extended treatment of the conference, see Escott, *"What Shall We Do with the Negro?,"* 202–18, and the various studies cited therein.

The correct figure on the number of slaves who by this time had in practice become free was almost 500,000.

28. This point about delayed or "prospective" ratification has been much debated, with some historians rejecting Stephens's account as completely unreliable. But he reported this not only in a speech and book in 1870 but also in a conversation with the editor of an Augusta, Georgia, newspaper only a few months after the Hampton Roads Conference. There is little doubt that Stephens at least understood Lincoln to have made this suggestion.

29. Lincoln foresaw how difficult Reconstruction would be if the defeated Southerners refused to cooperate in rebuilding the Union. Knowing the extent of racism in both North and South, he did not expect sudden and dramatic improvements in the social status of the former slaves. The argument of David Donald also helps to explain Lincoln's actions. Donald speculates "that Lincoln's remarks stemmed from his realization that slavery was already dead," that is, that the events of war had fatally wounded slavery as an institution. Many Republicans in Washington and in the cabinet held that view.

30. Lincoln, *Collected Works,* 8:260–61. Interior Secretary John Usher felt that Lincoln was so committed to this proposal that he would have gone forward with it had only one member of the cabinet been in favor. Burlingame, *Abraham Lincoln,* 2:759.

31. Escott, *Military Necessity,* 137–39.

19. WITH MALICE TOWARD NONE; WITH CHARITY FOR ALL

1. Leech, *Reveille in Washington,* 366–68; Welles, *Diary,* 2:251–52; Burlingame, *Abraham Lincoln,* 2:766.

2. Booth, *"Right or Wrong, God Judge Me,"* 135–36, 130–31, 14. At this point Booth's plan was still to kidnap Lincoln. Lucy Hale's father was the newly appointed ambassador to Spain.

3. Lincoln, *This Fiery Trial*, 220–21.

4. Welles, *Diary,* 2:139, 242.

5. Donald, *Charles Sumner and the Rights of Man,* 205–6;

6. Baker, *Mary Todd Lincoln,* 237; Welles, *Diary,* 2:197.

7. Hay, *Inside Lincoln's White House,* 218.

8. Lincoln, *This Fiery Trial,* 217–18.

9. Burlingame, *Abraham Lincoln,* 2:779–82.

10. Ibid., 2:779, 797, 780.

11. Ibid., 2:788–91.

12. Ibid., 2:795–96, 799, 785.

13. Ibid., 2:793; Welles, *Diary,* 2:269, 264.

14. Welles, *Diary,* 2:269, 264, 279–80; Burlingame, *Abraham Lincoln,* 2:791–94

15. Burlingame, *Abraham Lincoln,* 2:800.

16. Welles, *Diary,* 2:279.

17. Lincoln, *This Fiery Trial,* 224–26. The Louisiana legislature did not give the ballot to African Americans.

18. Ibid., 225, 227. On one earlier occasion Lincoln had suggested, in a private letter to Louisiana's governor in the 10 percent regime, that the right to vote be given in this way to some black men.

19. Ibid., 227.

20. Ibid., 227, 223; Hay, *Inside Lincoln's White House,* 73; Stahr, *Seward,* 435. Hay quoted Seward making this statement about slavery being "dead" as early as August 1863, and similar comments can be found in Welles's diary.

Opposition by ten of the eleven states that actively supported the Confederacy would defeat the amendment. In addition, three Northern states had voted against Lincoln in 1864 and were unlikely to approve. Thus, if ratification of the Thirteenth Amendment depended on voluntary Southern cooperation, Lincoln probably would have needed five formerly rebel states to give their approval—a tall order.

20. Assassination

1. Booth, *"Right or Wrong, God Judge Me,"* 130, 14, 15; Clarke, *John Wilkes Booth,* 87, 116.

2. Booth, *"Right or Wrong, God Judge Me,"* 15; Burlingame, *Abraham Lincoln,* 2:811, 815.

3. Hay, *Inside Lincoln's White House,* 195; transcript of PBS, *Abraham and Mary Lincoln;* Burlingame, *Abraham Lincoln,* 2:812.

4. Burlingame, *Abraham Lincoln,* 2:807, 546, 702; Wyatt-Brown, "Psychology of Hatred and Ideology of Honor," 280.

5. Burlingame, *Abraham Lincoln,* 2:777–78; Berry, *House of Abraham,* 171–72.

6. Burlingame, *Abraham Lincoln,* 2:799; Baker, *Mary Todd Lincoln,* 241, 237.

7. Burlingame, *Abraham Lincoln,* 2:807–9.

8. Ibid., 2:807, 817. Both Sewards were injured but survived.

9. Ibid., 2:817; Booth, *"Right or Wrong, God Judge Me,"* 16–17.

10. Burlingame, *Abraham Lincoln,* 2:817.

11. Donald, *Charles Sumner and the Rights of Man,* 216.

12. Welles, *Diary,* 2:283–88.

13. Baker, *Mary Todd Lincoln,* 248–49; Nicolay, *With Lincoln in the White House,* 177

14. Welles, *Diary,* 2:290, 293; Nicolay, *With Lincoln in the White House,* 177.

15. The quotation, of course, comes from Alexander H. Stephens's "Cornerstone" speech, which can be found in Durden, *The Gray and the Black.*

21. Unfinished Business

1. Ben Butler later reported that near the end of the war Lincoln had spoken of his fear and expectation that Southern whites would oppress the freed people and had referred once again to the need for colonization. Since no third party witnessed this conversation, scholars are uncertain whether to credit Butler's report.

2. Hay, *Inside Lincoln's White House,* 218.

3. Lincoln, *This Fiery Trial,* 220–21; Alexander Stephens quoted in Durden, *The Gray and the Black,* 7–9; Welles, *Diary,* 1:502.

4. Frederick Douglass, Oration in Memory of Abraham Lincoln.

5. Ibid.

6. See, e.g., the *Toledo Blade,* September 21, 2012, "Lincoln's Lesser-Known Preliminary Emancipation Proclamation Receives Public Spotlight," accessed October 10, 2012, at http://www.toledoblade.com. When informed of this error, the author of the AP article refused to admit any inaccuracy.

Selected Bibliography

Act for the Release of certain Persons held to Service or Labor in the District of Columbia. http://www.archives.gov/exhibits/featured_documents/dc_emancipation_act /transcription.html.

Anti-Negro Riots in the North, 1863. No editor. New York: Arno Press, 1969.

Baker, Jean H. *Mary Todd Lincoln: A Biography.* New York: W. W. Norton, 1987, 2008.

Beck, Warren A. "Lincoln and Negro Colonization in Central America." *Abraham Lincoln Quarterly* 6, no. 3 (September 1950): 162–83.

Bernstein, Iver. *The New York City Draft Riots: Their Significance for American Society and Politics in the Age of the Civil War.* New York: Oxford University Press, 1990.

Berry, Stephen. *House of Abraham: Lincoln and the Todds, a Family Divided by War.* Boston: Houghton Mifflin, 2007.

Berwanger, Eugene H. *The Frontier against Slavery.* Urbana: University of Illinois Press, 1967.

Blair, Frank P. Address at the Mercantile Library Association of Boston, January 26, 1859. Washington, D.C.: Buell & Blanchard, Printers, 1859.

———. Speech at Cooper Institute, New York City, January 25, 1860. http://babel .hathitrust.org/cgi/pt?id=hvd.hx4q1z#view=1up;seq=5.

———. Speech in the House, April 11, 1862. *Congressional Globe,* 37th Congress, 2nd Session, 1631–34.

Blair, Montgomery. Argument of Montgomery Blair, of Counsel for the Plaintiff in Error in *Dred Scott, (A Colored Man), vs. John F. A. Sandford.* http://www.scribd.com /doc/58575200/Scott-v-Sandford-ARGUMENT-of-Montgomery-Blair.

———. Letter to Abraham Lincoln. December 6, 1864. Library website of The Lincoln Institute, an American History Project of The Lehrman Institute. http://www .mrlincolnandfreedom.org/inside.asp?ID=67&subjectID=4.

———. Letter to the Meeting held at the Cooper Institute, New York, March 6, 1862. Washington: Printed at the Congressional Globe Office, 1862. "From Slavery to Freedom: The African-American Pamphlet Collection, 1824–1909," American Memory website, Library of Congress. http://www.memory.loc.org.

———. "Slavery and the War." Speech delivered before the Members of the Legislature at Annapolis, Md., on Friday, January 22, 1864, printed in the *New York Times,* January 26, 1864.

———. Speech at Cooper Institute. September 27, 1864. Samuel J. May Anti-Slavery Collection, http://dlxs.library.cornell.edu/m/mayantislavery/browse_W.html.

———. "Speech of the Honorable Montgomery Blair on the revolutionary schemes of the ultra abolitionists and in defense of the policy of the President, at Rockville Maryland, October 3, 1863." http://archive.org/details/speechofhonmontgomooblai.

Blight, David W. *Frederick Douglass' Civil War: Keeping Faith in Jubilee.* Baton Rouge: Louisiana State University Press, 1989.

Booth, John Wilkes. *"Right or Wrong, God Judge Me": The Writings of John Wilkes Booth.* Edited by John Hodehamel and Louise Taper. Urbana: University of Illinois Press, 1997.

Burlingame, Michael. *Abraham Lincoln: A Life.* 2 vols. Baltimore: Johns Hopkins University Press, 2008.

Cain, William E., ed. *William Lloyd Garrison and the Fight against Slavery: Selections from* The Liberator. Boston: Bedford/St. Martin's, 1995.

Campbell, Stanley. *The Slave Catchers: Enforcement of the Fugitive Slave Law, 1850–1860.* New York: W. W. Norton, 1972.

Cecelski, David S. *The Fire of Freedom: Abraham Galloway and the Slaves' Civil War.* Chapel Hill: University of North Carolina Press, 2012.

Chase, Salmon P. *Inside Lincoln's Cabinet: The Civil War Diaries of Salmon P. Chase.* Edited by David Donald. New York: Longmans, Green, 1954.

Chesnut, Mary Boykin. *A Diary from Dixie.* Edited by Ben Ames Williams. Sentry edition. Boston: Houghton Mifflin, 1949.

Clarke, Asia Booth. *John Wilkes Booth: A Sister's Memoir.* Edited by Terry Alford. Jackson: University Press of Mississippi, 1996.

Cox, Samuel Sullivan. Speech in the House of Representatives, February 17, 1864. *Congressional Record,* 38th Congress, 1st Session, 708–13. American Memory website, Library of Congress. http://www.memory.loc.org.

Croly, David Goodman, and George Wakeman. *Miscegenation: The Theory of the Blending of the Races, Applied to the American White Man and Negro.* New York: H. Dexter, Hamilton & Company, 1864.

Current, Richard N. *The Lincoln Nobody Knows.* New York: Hill and Wang, 1958.

Declarations of Causes of Seceding States: Civil War South Carolina. http://www.AmericanCivilWar.com/documents/causes_south_carolina.html.

Donald, David. *Charles Sumner and the Coming of the Civil War.* Naperville, IL: Sourcebooks, 1960, 1989, 2009.

———. *Charles Sumner and the Rights of Man.* New York: Knopf, 1970.

———. *Lincoln.* New York: Simon & Schuster, 1995.

Douglass, Frederick. Oration in Memory of Abraham Lincoln. April 14, 1876. http://teachingamericanhistory.org/library/index.asp?documentprint=39.

Durden, Robert F. *The Gray and the Black: The Confederate Debate on Emancipation.* Baton Rouge: Louisiana State University Press, 1972.

Escott, Paul D. *The Confederacy: The Slaveholders' Failed Venture.* Santa Barbara, CA: Praeger/ABC-CLIO, 2010.

———. *Military Necessity: Civil-Military Relations in the Confederacy.* Westport, CT: Praeger Security International, 2006.

———. *"What Shall We Do with the Negro?": Lincoln, White Racism, and Civil War America.* Charlottesville: University of Virginia Press, 2009.

Fehrenbacher, Don E. *Slavery, Law, and Politics: The Dred Scott Case in Historical Perspective.* New York: Oxford University Press, 1981.

Finkelman, Paul, ed. *Defending Slavery: Proslavery Thought in the Old South: A Brief History with Documents.* Boston: Bedford/St. Martin's, 2003.

Foner, Eric. *Free Soil, Free Labor, Free Men: The Ideology of the Republican Party before the Civil War.* New York: Oxford University Press, 1995.

Freehling, William W. *The South vs. the South: How Anti-Confederate Southerners Shaped the Course of the Civil War.* New York: Oxford University Press, 2001.

Gage, Joan. "A White Slave Girl: 'Mulatto Raised by Charles Sumner.'" Mirror of Race Project, http://mirrorofrace.org/wp/essays/.

Gienapp, William E. *Abraham Lincoln and Civil War America: A Biography.* New York: Oxford University Press, 2002.

Goodwin, Doris Kearns. *Team of Rivals: The Political Genius of Abraham Lincoln.* New York: Simon and Schuster, 2005.

Gossett, Thomas F. *Uncle Tom's Cabin and American Culture.* Dallas: Southern Methodist University Press, 1985.

Greeley, Horace. "The Prayer of Twenty Millions." http://www.civilwarhome.com /lincolngreeley.htm.

Harris, William C. *With Charity for All: Lincoln and the Restoration of the Union.* Lexington: University Press of Kentucky, 1997.

Hay, John. *Inside Lincoln's White House: The Complete Civil War Diary of John Hay.* Edited by Michael Burlingame and John R. Turner Ettlinger. Carbondale: Southern Illinois University Press, 1997.

Headley, Joel Tyler. *The Great Riots of New York, 1712–1873.* Indianapolis: Bobbs Merrill, 1970.

Hoffer, Williamjames Hull. *The Caning of Charles Sumner: Honor, Idealism, and the Origins of the Civil War.* Baltimore: Johns Hopkins University Press, 2010.

Holt, Michael. *Political Parties and American Political Development: From the Age of Jackson to the Age of Lincoln.* Baton Rouge: Louisiana State University Press, 1992.

Hunter, David. General Orders No. 11. http://faculty.assumption.edu/aas/Manuscripts /generalorders.html.

Jefferson, Thomas. *The Works of Thomas Jefferson in Twelve Volumes.* Edited by Paul Leicester Ford. Federal edition. New York: G. P. Putnam's Sons, 1904–5.

Kaplan, Sidney. "The Miscegenation Issue in the Election of 1864." *Journal of Negro History* 34 (July 1949): 274–343.

Leech, Margaret. *Reveille in Washington, 1860–1865.* Garden City, NY: Garden City Publishing Co., 1945.

Lefler, Hugh Talmage, and Albert Ray Newsome. *North Carolina: The History of a Southern State*. 3rd ed. Chapel Hill: University of North Carolina Press, 1973.

Lincoln, Abraham. Abraham Lincoln Papers, Library of Congress. Available on American Memory website, http://memory.loc.gov.

———. *The Collected Works of Abraham Lincoln*. Edited by Roy Basler. 9 vols. New Brunswick, NJ: Rutgers University Press, 1953.

———. *This Fiery Trial: The Speeches and Writings of Abraham Lincoln*. Edited by William E. Gienapp. New York: Oxford University Press, 2002.

Litwack, Leon. *North of Slavery: The Negro in the Free States, 1790–1860*. Chicago: University of Chicago Press, 1960.

Lockard, Joe. "Ida May." Antislavery Literature website, http://antislavery.eserver.org /prose/idamay.

Lowell, James Russell. "The President's Message." *North American Review*, January 5, 1864, 234–60.

Magness, Phillip W., and Sebastian N. Page. *Colonization after Emancipation: Lincoln and the Movement for Black Resettlement*. Columbia: University of Missouri Press, 2011.

Martin, Waldo, ed. *Brown v. Board of Education: A Brief History with Documents*. Boston: Bedford/St. Martin's, 1998.

McCague, James. *The Second Rebellion: The Story of the New York City Draft Riots of 1863*. New York: Dial Press, 1968.

McClellan, George B. *The Civil War Papers of George B. McClellan: Selected Correspondence, 1860–1865*. Edited by Stephen W. Sears. New York: Ticknor and Fields, 1989.

McPherson, James M. *Battle Cry of Freedom*. New York: Oxford University Press, 1988.

———, ed. *The Negro's Civil War: How American Negroes Felt and Acted during the War for the Union*. New York: Pantheon Books, 1965.

Nicolay, John G. *With Lincoln in the White House: Letters, Memoranda, and Other Writings of John G. Nicolay, 1860–1865*. Edited by Michael Burlingame. Carbondale: Southern Illinois University Press, 2000.

Norton, Mary Beth, David M. Katzman, Paul D. Escott, Howard P. Chudacoff, Thomas G. Paterson, and William M. Tuttle Jr. *A People and a Nation: A History of the United States*. 4th ed. Boston: Houghton Mifflin, 1994; 5th ed., 1998.

Parrish, William E. *Frank Blair: Lincoln's Conservative*. Columbia: University of Missouri Press, 1998.

Pearson, Henry Greenleaf. *The Life of John A. Andrew, Governor of Massachusetts, 1861–1865*. 2 vols. Boston: Houghton, Mifflin, 1904.

Pfau, Michael William. *The Political Style of Conspiracy: Chase, Sumner, and Lincoln*. East Lansing: Michigan State University Press, 2005.

Pike, Mary Hayden Greene. *Ida May: A Story of Things Actual and Possible*. Leipzig: Bernhard Tauchnitz, 1855.

Potter, David M. *The Impending Crisis, 1848–1861*. New York: Harper & Row, 1976.

———. *Lincoln and His Party in the Secession Crisis*. New Haven: Yale University Press, 1962.

Proceedings of the National Convention of Colored Men ... October 4, 5, 6, and 7, 1864. http://people.hofstra.edu/alan_j_singer/Gateway%20Slavery%20Guide%20 PDF%20Files/5.%20Abolition_Complicity%201827-65/5.%20Documents%201827 -1865/1864a.%20(A)%20Syr.%20Convention.pdf.

Public Broadcasting Service (PBS). *Abraham and Mary Lincoln: A House Divided.* Produced and directed by David Grubin. Written by David Grubin and Geoffrey C. Ward. 2001. Transcript available on American Experience website, www.pbs.org.

Randall, James G., and David Donald. *The Civil War and Reconstruction.* 2nd ed. Boston: D. C. Heath, 1961.

Resolutions of the Illinois Legislature. *Illinois State Register.* January 7, 1863. http:// edale1.home.mindspring.com/Resolution%20of%20the%20Illinois%20Legislature% 20in%20Opposition%20to%20the%20Emancipation%20Proclamation.htm.

Rhodes, James Ford. *History of the United States from the Compromise of 1850.* 9 vols. New York: Harper and Brothers, 1913–22.

Rice, C. Duncan. *The Rise and Fall of Black Slavery.* Baton Rouge: Louisiana State University Press, 1975.

Richards, Leonard. *Gentlemen of Property and Standing: Anti-abolition Mobs in Jacksonian America.* New York: Oxford University Press, 1970.

Ripley, C. Peter, ed. *The Black Abolitionist Papers.* 5 vols. Chapel Hill: University of North Carolina Press, 1985–92.

Rose, Willie Lee, ed. *A Documentary History of Slavery in North America.* New York: Oxford University Press, 1976.

Schecter, Barnet. *The Devil's Own Work: The Civil War Draft Riots and the Fight to Reconstruct America.* New York: Walker, 2005.

Seaman, L., LL.D. *What Miscegenation Is! And What We Are to Expect Now That Mr. Lincoln Is Re-elected.* New York: Waller & Willets, 1865. Available in the Samuel J. May Anti-Slavery Collection, http://dlxs.library.cornell.edu/m/mayantislavery /browse_W.html.

Seward, William H. *The Works of William H. Seward.* Edited by George E. Baker. Boston: Houghton Mifflin, 1890.

Shakespeare, William. *Richard III.* Restored and Rearranged from the text of Shakespeare, As Performed at the Theatre Royal, Covent Garden. London: Printed for R. and M. Stodart, 81 Strand, 1821.

Shapiro, Samuel. "The Rendition of Anthony Burns." *Journal of Negro History* 44, no. 1 (January 1959): 34–51.

Silbey, Joel. *The Transformation of American Politics, 1840–1860.* Englewood Cliffs, NJ: Prentice-Hall, 1967.

Smith, Elbert B. *Francis Preston Blair.* New York: Free Press, 1980.

Smith, John David, ed. *Black Soldiers in Blue: African American Troops in the Civil War Era.* Chapel Hill: University of North Carolina Press, 2002.

Smith, William Earnest. *The Francis Preston Blair Family in Politics.* 2 vols. New York: Macmillan, 1933.

Stahr, Walter. *Seward: Lincoln's Indispensable Man.* New York: Simon and Schuster, 2012.

Stashower, Daniel. *The Hour of Peril: The Secret Plot to Murder Lincoln before the Civil War.* New York: Minotaur Books, 2013.

Steers, Edward Jr., and Harold Holzer. *The Lincoln Assassination Conspirators: Their Confinement and Execution, as Recorded in the Letterbook of John Frederick Hartranft.* Baton Rouge: Louisiana State University Press, 2009.

Stowe, Harriet Beecher. *Uncle Tom's Cabin.* 1852. New York: Pocket Books, 2004.

Sumner, Charles. "The Antislavery Enterprise: Its Necessity, Practicability, and Dignity," Literally Reported in the *New York Tribune,* May 18, 1855. W. M. Watts, Crown Court, Temple Bar, 1855. http://archive.org/details/cihm_53283.

———. "The Barbarism of Slavery." Speech in the Senate on the bill to admit Kansas as a free state, June 4, 1860. http://archive.org/details/barbarismofslaveoolcsumn.

———. "The Crime against Kansas: The Apologies for the Crime: The True Remedy." Speech in the Senate, May 19, 1856. *Congressional Globe,* 34th Congress, 1st Session, House Report 182, Appendix.

———. *Freedom National; Slavery Sectional. Speech of Hon. Charles Sumner, of Massachusetts, on His Motion to Repeal the Fugitive Slave Bill, in the Senate of the United States, August 26, 1862.* Boston: Ticknor, Reed, and Fields, 1852.

———. "Indemnity for the Past and Security for the Future." Speech in the Senate, May 19, 1862. In *The Works of Charles Sumner,* 7:11–77.

———. *Landmark of Freedom. Speech of Hon. Charles Sumner, Against the Repeal of the Missouri Prohibition of Slavery North of 36° 30′. In the Senate, February 21, 1854.* Boston: John P. Jewett and Co., 1854.

———. "Our Domestic Relations; or, How to Treat the Rebel States." *Atlantic Monthly* 12, no. 71 (September 1863).

———. "Slavery and the Rebellion, One and Inseparable." Speech at Cooper Institute, November 5, 1864. Samuel J. May Anti-Slavery Collection, http://dlxs.library.cornell.edu/m/mayantislavery/browse_W.htm.

———. Speech to Massachusetts Republicans, October 1, 1861. Library website of The Lincoln Institute, an American History Project of The Lehrman Institute. http://www.mrlincolnandfreedom.org/inside.asp?ID=74&subjectID=4.

———. *The Works of Charles Sumner.* 15 vols. Boston: Lee and Shepard, 1870–83.

Thoreau, Henry David. "A Plea for Captain John Brown." Speech delivered October 30, 1859. http://law2.umkc.edu/faculty/projects/ftrials/johnbrown/thoreauplea.html.

Tidwell, William A. *Come Retribution: The Confederate Secret Service and the Assassination of Lincoln.* Jackson: University Press of Mississippi, 1988.

Welles, Gideon. *Diary of Gideon Welles, Secretary of the Navy under Lincoln and Johnson.* Introduction by John T. Morse Jr. 3 vols. Boston: Houghton Mifflin, 1909, 1910, 1911.

White, Andrew Dickson. *Miscegenation Indorsed by the Republican Party,* Campaign Document, No. 11. Samuel J. May Anti-Slavery Collection, http://dlxs.library.cornell.edu/m/mayantislavery/browse_W.html.

Whiting, William. "Dangers in the Present Crisis of the War." Letter from Wm. Whiting Esq., Solicitor to the War Department, republished in the *New York Times,* August 12, 1863.

Winkle, Kenneth J. *Abraham and Mary Lincoln.* Carbondale: Southern Illinois University Press, 2011.

Wyatt-Brown, Bertram. "Psychology of Hatred and Ideology of Honor: Booth's Lincoln Conspiracies." In *The Battlefield and Beyond: Essays on the American Civil War,* ed. Clayton E. Jewett. Baton Rouge: Louisiana State University Press, 2012.

Index

Recent Books in the Series
A NATION DIVIDED: STUDIES IN THE CIVIL WAR ERA